THE PEAK DISTRICT

F. R. BANKS

LONDON
ROBERT HALE & COMPANY

© *F. R. Banks 1975*
First published in Great Britain 1975

ISBN 0 7091 4913 1

Robert Hale and Company
63 Old Brompton Road
London SW 7

To
DAVID and GILL
Lovers of the Peak

Composed by Specialised Offset Services Ltd, Liverpool
and printed in Great Britain by
Lowe and Brydone Ltd, Thetford

Contents

		Page
1	Introduction to the Peak District	11
2	The Limestone Country	19
3	The Gritstone Country	27
4	Ashbourne: Gateway to the Peak	34
5	From Ashbourne to Leek and Macclesfield	42
6	The Manifold Valley	50
7	The Valley of the Dove	56
8	The Western Moorlands	64
9	The Tissington Trail	71
10	From Ashbourne to Wirksworth	78
11	The Derwent Valley to Rowsley	86
12	The 'High Peak' Trail	94
13	From Wirksworth to Youlgreave	102
14	From Youlgreave to Buxton	111
15	Haddon Hall	120
16	Bakewell: Capital of the Peak	127
17	The Wye Valley: Bakewell to Buxton	135
18	Buxton: the Peakland Spa	143
19	From Buxton to Glossop	150
20	Lyme Park, and thence to Glossop	158
21	From Bakewell to Castleton via Eyam	165
22	Chatsworth	174
23	The Derwent Valley: Chatsworth to Hathersage	183
24	The Hope Valley and Castleton	191
25	Edale and Kinder Scout	201
26	From the Upper Derwent to the Little Don	208
27	From the Ashop Valley to Longdendale	214
	Index of Places	221

Illustrations

		facing page
1	Entrance to the Peak District National Park	18
2	Dovedale, the Stepping Stones	18
3	Hartington Hall	19
4	The Roaches	19
5	Jenkin Chapel	34
6	Fenny Bentley Old Hall	34
7	Tissington village	35
8	Rowsley, Peacock Hotel	50
9	Arbor Low stone circle	51
10	Lathkill Dale	51
11	Sheldon, Magpie Mine	66
12	Haddon Hall	67
13	Ashford, Sheepwash Bridge	82
14	Monsal Dale	83
15	Wormhill, Well Dressing	98
16	Buxton, The Crescent	99
17	Lyme Park	114
18	Eyam, Plague Cottages	115
19	Tideswell Church	130
20	Chatsworth House	131
21	Calver Mill	146
22	Froggatt Edge	147
23	Castleton, from Peveril Castle	162
24	Peveril Castle, the Keep	163
25	The Winnats	178
26	Mam Tor	179

27	Kinder Scout, the plateau	194
28	Ladybower Reservoir	195
	Map of the Peak District	*pages* 12-13

The Map has been drawn by David R. Banks. Illustrations Nos 1, 2, 3 and 6 are from photographs by the author; the remainding illustrations are from photographs by Frank Saunders, Peak Park Joint Planning Board.

1 Introduction to the Peak District

The Peak District is the southernmost link in the Pennine Chain, that 'backbone' of northern England which stretches for over 150 miles from the hills of the Scottish Border right down into the North Midlands.

One of the curiosities that must puzzle a newcomer to the Peak District is that there are no peaks, in the sense of sharply-pointed hills. Wild mountainous moorlands, rugged dark escarpments, lush green uplands — yes; beautiful valleys, deep narrow ravines, white limestone crags — but no peaks! Why, then, if this region has no peaks, is it called the Peak District?

Peakland, the old name for the district, would seem to be derived in the first place from the people or tribe who lived here in Saxon times, on the northern frontier of the Kingdom of Mercia. The first reference to these people, in a Saxon charter of the seventh century, calls them the 'Pecsaetna'. 'Saete' or 'saetan' is an Old English word for 'dwellers' and is found also in Dorset (the 'dwellers around Dorchester') and Somerset; 'Pec' or Peak may be from the Old English 'peac', meaning a hill in general, not necessarily a pointed one. So the Pecsaetan, it would seem, were the 'dwellers among the hills'. But 'peac', according to Eilert Ekwall (*The Concise Oxford Dictionary of English Place-Names*) may be related to a Dutch word meaning a dagger, a Swedish word meaning a cudgel and a Norwegian word meaning a stick. So is it too fanciful to suggest that the Pecsaetan could just as easily have been the people who carried daggers, cudgels or sticks?

In the *Anglo-Saxon Chronicle*, under the year 924, the district is referred to as 'Peaclond', which should be interpreted as the 'land of hill-dwellers' (if not 'of dagger-carriers') rather than the land of peaks. By the twelfth century, when the original meaning of the name had been

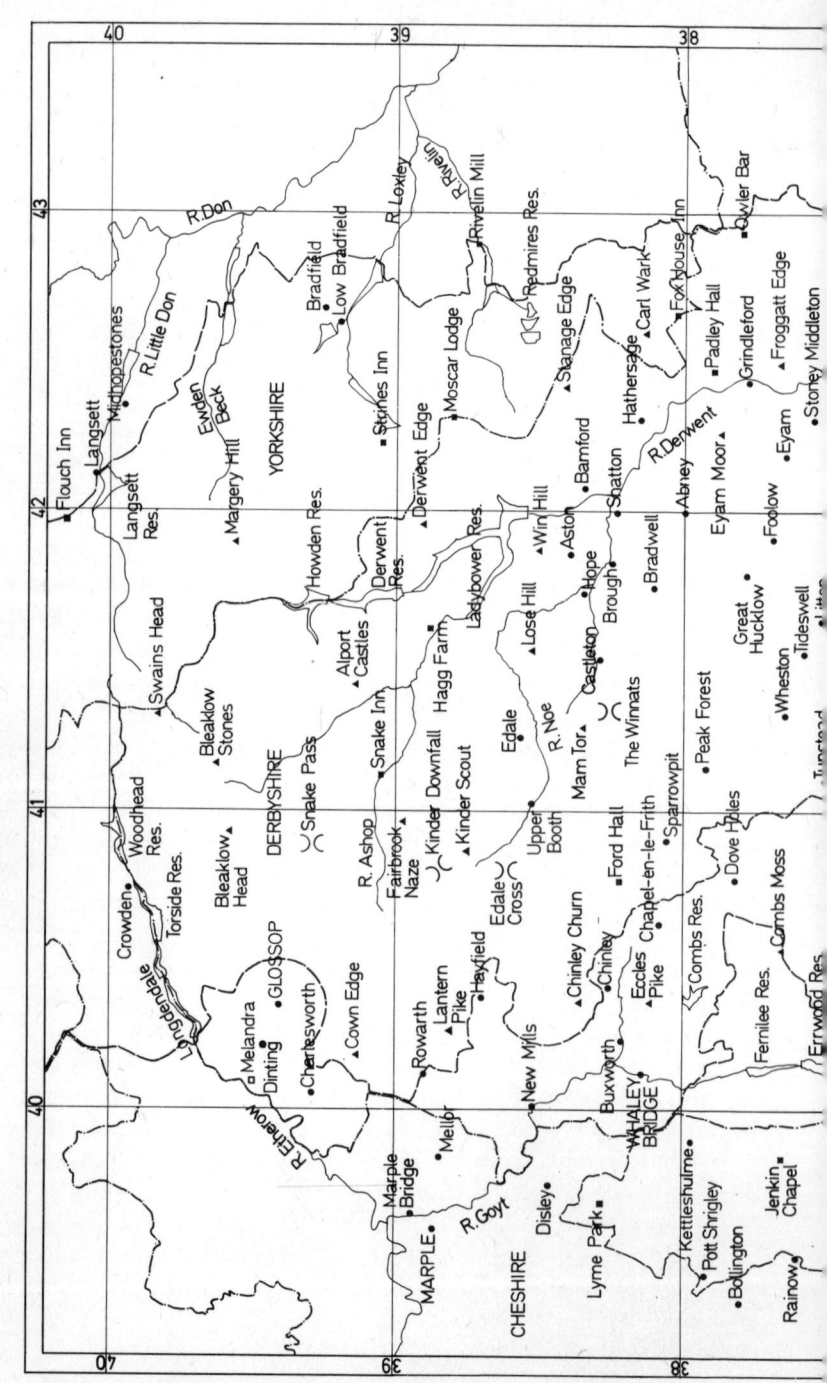

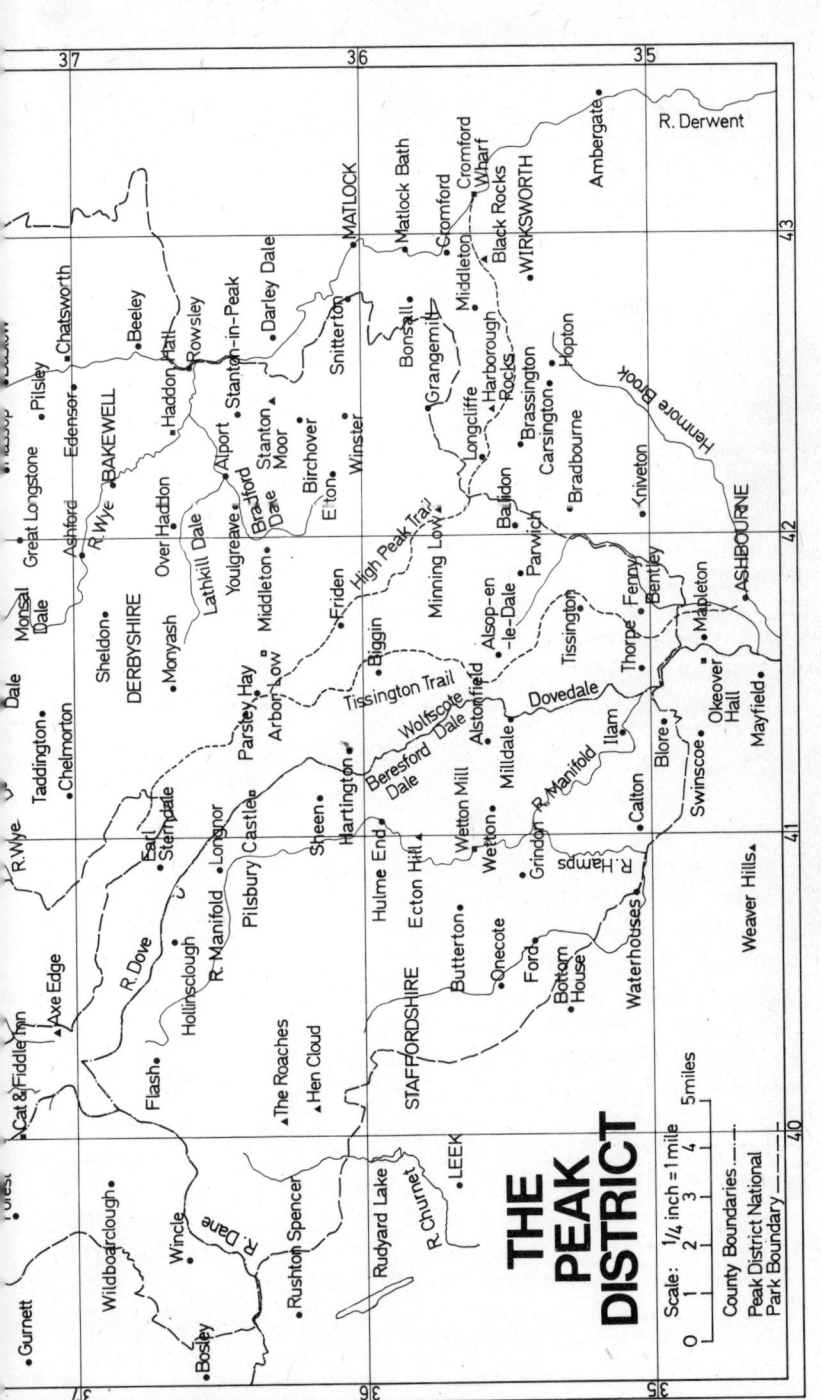

forgotten, the district had become 'Pec' or 'Pech', The Peak, and in the early nineteenth century Sir Walter Scott popularised this form in his novel *Peveril of the Peak*. District is a comparatively modern addition to the name and it is this, more than anything, that has created the false impression of a 'district of peaks'. Peakland is perhaps a better name for the district, but it has rather a literary flavour. Lovers of the Peak District usually refer to it merely as 'the Peak', so you will excuse me if I appear to use all three names indiscriminately.

The Peak District lies mainly in the north and west of Derbyshire, but extends into the Moorlands district of Staffordshire and also, to a lesser extent, into Cheshire and the West Riding of Yorkshire. It comprises two distinct and indeed contrasting types of landscape. Much of the northern half, usually called the High Peak, consists of a vast expanse of wild and lonely gritstone moorland, with great tracts of heather, bilberry and coarse grass, split up by numerous peat hags. These are at their most formidable on Kinder Scout, which rises to 2088 feet and is the highest part of the Peak, and on Bleaklow, farther north. Though within a short distance of Manchester and Sheffield, this is one of the most sparsely populated areas in England. But it is by no means all desolation, for into the recesses of the moors penetrate well-cultivated valleys, guarded by belts of dark crag known locally as 'edges'.

The southern half of the Peak District, less frequently called the Low Peak, is an undulating upland plateau of the carboniferous limestone, divided by dry-stone walls (i.e. built without mortar) into a chequerwork of rich green fields, and intersected in many places by deep ravines whose walls are white cliffs that gleam when the sun shines on them. These are seen at their best in Dovedale, in the Derwent valley at Matlock, in Lathkill Dale, and in the Wye valley in Millers Dale and Cheedale. The swift clear rivers of the limestone country are famous for their fishing, and the district abounds in caverns, particularly in the neighbourhood of Castleton.

The north and east parts of the Peak District are watered by the Derwent (whose upper valley is a miniature Lake District of attractive reservoirs) and by its tributary, the Wye, rising near Buxton. Through the south and west parts of the

Peak flow the Dove and its tributary the Manifold. Farther west is the valley of the Dane and to the north-west is that of the Goyt (one of the feeders of the Mersey), while the Peak District is usually regarded as being bounded on the north by the Etherow, flowing through Longdendale to join the Goyt.

In 1951 an area of 542 square miles was designated the Peak District National Park, the first in Britain. The reason for its selection as the first was not because it is the most beautiful part of England (a matter for argument, anyway) but because it is surrounded by a ring of industrial places – Manchester, Sheffield, Nottingham, Derby, Stoke-on-Trent and their satellites – with their mining and manufacturing activities. For these towns and cities the Peak serves as a convenient and effective 'lung', and for this reason perhaps the district was thought to be most in need of conservation. It is indeed this contrast between the open unspoiled country of the Peak and the congested streets and factory areas of the industrial towns around its perimeter that gives the region its particular quality and the national park its particular value.

The boundaries of the Peak District which I have observed in this book do not coincide with those of the national park. I have included such old towns as Ashbourne, Leek, Macclesfield, Wirksworth, Matlock and Buxton, all of which lie outside the boundary of the park and were purposely excluded, though all have played a vital part in the life and economy of the region. The national park boundary makes a big indentation to avoid taking in Buxton and the large limestone quarries in the neighbourhood, and this gives the outline of the park on the map rather the appearance of a wolf's head, with the mouth taking a big bite at Buxton.

I would have preferred Buxton to have been included in the National Park for its historical and architectural interest, but the authorities will no doubt tell me that this would have been impracticable. Not only would Buxton itself have been difficult to administer within the park, but the many limestone quarries in the district, it will be argued, do not contribute to what is expected of the landscape of a national park. Perhaps the inclusion of these quarries might have resulted in some control over their vast expansion (though I doubt it). The only town inside the boundary of the national park is Bakewell, which has become the headquarters of the Peak Park Planning Board and can be regarded as the capital of the Peak District.

While on this subject, I would like to pay a small tribute to the work of the Peak Park Planning Board. It is fashionable today to throw mud at local government officers for their remoteness from and lack of consideration for the needs and wishes of ordinary mortals (and some of the mud no doubt deserves to stick), but the Peak Park officers have earned themselves a justifiable reputation for their achievements in tackling a difficult job. The fact that the planning board is the only one that has operated free of the jurisdiction of any county council has perhaps made the administration easier, but nevertheless the board's officers deserve to be congratulated on everything they have tried to do to make the Peak District more accessible and more enjoyable for the thousands to whom it is a means of escape.

To return to the boundaries. Apart from the exclusion of the Buxton area and the other towns around the boundary of the national park, the decision where to draw the northern boundary must have created some discussion. It is difficult to agree on a definite line of demarcation between the Peak District and the moorlands of the southern Pennines. That preferred by the National Parks Commission, which takes in Black Hill and the country north of Longdendale, seems to me to be purely arbitrary. The Black Hill range belongs more naturally to the moors of the West Riding which enclose it than to the Bleaklow and Kinder Scout groups to the south. The main road from Manchester to Sheffield through the deep trench of Longdendale forms as natural a boundary as any, and it is the one I have adopted in this book.

The whole of the Peak District is contained on Sheet 11 (North Midlands and Yorkshire) of the Ordnance Survey 'Quarter-Inch' Map of Great Britain. This is satisfactory enough for general motoring, but walkers and others who want to explore the Peak in more detail will require a map on a larger scale. The Tourist Map of the Peak District, on a scale of 1 inch to 1 mile, covers all the area described in this book. By far the greater part of the district is covered also by Sheet

111 (Buxton and Matlock) of the One-Inch Series map, which extends over an area from Ashbourne in the south to Hayfield, Kinder Scout and the Ladybower Reservoir in the north and to Whaley Bridge and the Roaches in the west. A map called 'The Dark Peak', on a scale of 1 to 25,000 (about 2½ inches to 1 mile) covers the whole of the gritstone area north of Whaley Bridge, Chapel-en-le-Frith and Bradwell (but not the country east of the Ladybower Reservoir).

The region from Hayfield and the Ladybower northward is included on Sheet 102 (Huddersfield) of the One-Inch map, with an overlap of about three miles between this map and Sheet 111. That part of the district west of the Whaley Bridge line is covered by Sheet 110 (Stoke-on-Trent), which extends as far north as Macclesfield, and Sheet 101 (Manchester), which includes Lyme Park and its surroundings.

The new Ordnance Survey 1:50000 Series of maps which are now coming out are no real improvement on the existing series. As they are on a larger scale, they are easier to read, but the information is no more up to date, the heights and distances are 'metric', and each map covers a smaller area (at a greater cost!). Much of the Peak District is covered by Sheet 119 (Buxton, Matlock and Dovedale), which extends north to Dove Holes (near Buxton) and Grindleford, and west to the Goyt Valley. The area to the north is covered by Sheet 110, that to the west by Sheet 118, while Sheet 109 includes the country between these maps.

Not only are all these Ordnance Survey maps interesting productions in their own right, but the user of this book, whether in the home or in the field, will find such maps an invaluable companion. Indeed the theme of the book may be taken to some extent as the interpretation of the Ordnance Survey map of the Peak District, and I hope the reader will adopt the map as his guide through the chapters of the book. To make the finding of places easier, I have inserted the National Grid reference number after each place described (the method of reading these numbers is explained on the Ordnance Survey maps).

One little problem to be solved at the outset is just where to start our survey, where to come into the Peak District. No one approach is better than another, and it is not important where we start, as long as we keep going until we get to the other end. Visitors from Manchester will naturally approach the Peak from the north-west, those from Sheffield from the north-east, those from Nottingham and beyond from the south-east and those from Stoke from the south-west. As I myself live to the south of the Peak District (but not too far south), I will start from that direction, at Ashbourne.

But first I want to say something about the two kinds of landscape in the Peak District: the limestone country and the gritstone country.

Peak District National Park sign

Dovedale, the Stepping Stones

Hartington Hall

The Roaches

2 The Limestone Country

Geologically, the Peak District consists almost entirely of immensely thick beds of Carboniferous Limestone (sometimes called Mountain Limestone) with overlying beds of Millstone Grit and Shale which are usually referred to collectively as Gritstone. These rocks have all been uplifted along a central spine in what geologists call an 'anticlinal fold', that is, in the form of an arch, with its axis running north and south.

Over the southern part of the Peak District the gritstones have been worn through, revealing a vast expanse of the limestone that lay below. So the scenery of the Peak can be divided into its two distinctive and contrasting types; the dark gritstones in the northern section (the High Peak) and the lighter limestone in the southern section (the Low Peak). The terms 'Dark Peak' and 'White Peak' for these two areas seems to be an invention of the Peak Park Planning Board that has been adopted by the Ordnance Survey (I have never heard anyone else use them).

No older rocks than the Carboniferous Limestone are exposed in the Peak District. Unlike the chalk or the oolitic limestone of other parts of England, it shows no continuous outcrop extending across the country. The carboniferous limestone was laid down at a much earlier stage than these other rocks and consequently it appears only where the overlying deposits have been eroded or where subsequent folding of the strata has brought it to the surface.

The limestone country, extending from Dovedale and the Weaver Hills north to the Hope Valley, is easily recognisable from the pale grey or grey-white of the stone, which can be turned to a dazzling white when the sun brings out the colour, and by the smoothly undulating uplands, their higher parts almost devoid of trees (except those planted by man) and divided by dry-stone walls into a whitebound chequerwork of rich green fields. This upland plateau, great areas of which reach well over 1000 feet, is dissected by many deep and often narrow ravines, charmingly wooded, whose walls are bare gleaming crags of the limestone.

The Carboniferous Limestone is so named to differentiate it from other limestones (the oolitic, the magnesian, for instance) and also because it is part of a geological group that includes the Coal Measures (carbon is the chief constituent of coal). Small isolated patches of the Coal Measures lie on both sides of the Peak District, for example at Totley Moor and Big Moor on the east and at Goyt Moss on the west. They must once have covered part at least of the limestone, as coal was certainly worked from many small pits in this area until the last century.

The limestone is composed very largely of carbonate of lime, which originated by being laid in a sheltered sea, and was given its special substance by countless millions of tiny invertebrates that floated in the water. This wide carboniferous sea must have been for the most part quite shallow, as the creatures which abounded were mainly those that could not live at any great depth. That the limestone was formed in sea-water is shown by the fossil shells and corals in many beds of the stone; they can be found quite readily, for instance, in the Hoptonwood Quarry and in the field-walls in the neighbourhood of Dovedale. The sea must have remained relatively calm and clear, too, as very little inorganic material is present in most of the limestone. In places where sand or mud was carried into part of the sea, however, the stone often contains a quantity of darker, rather earthy material.

The waters of this shallow carboniferous sea were subject to some surface movements, resembling waves, and this caused the formation of reefs along its shores in places, like the ridges or dunes thrown up by the sea on a gently-sloping sandy beach, but on a gigantic scale. Such reef-formations can be distinguished as elongated but narrow hills with steep slopes ending at the top in long serrated ridges. These remarkable features can be seen in Thorpe Cloud and Bunster, the hills on either side of the entrance to Dovedale, and even better in Chrome Hill and Parkhouse Hill, over-looking the upper part of the Dove valley. The fine-grained reef limestones are rich in fossil remains, and in Treak Cliff, facing down the Hope Valley, the presence of sea plants, too, has been established.

When the sea eventually dried out, some 300 million years ago, whitened remains of the tiny creatures were left behind, to form a hardened deposit of the grey-white substance so familiar in the field walls and dale sides of the Peak District. The enormous deposits of limestone were laid down in beds or strata varying from an inch or two in thickness to ten feet or more, the resulting rock formation amounting to as much as 2500 feet in one place.

Where the beds of the limestone are thick, the exposed outcrops appear solid and compact. In this they differ from the outcrops of the oolitic limestone of the Cotswold escarpment or the magnesian limestone belt that extends from the Derbyshire-Nottinghamshire border north through Yorkshire. Though, as I said, the substance consists mainly of carbonate of lime, the existence of some non-calcareous material causes a considerable variation in texture and colour, a russet tinge being given to the limestone by the presence of iron and a dark grey shade being the result of a siliceous deposit known as chert.

The solid uniformity of the great expanse of the limestone is broken here and there by dark outcrops of a different character. The building up of the limestone beds was in fact interrupted from time to time by volcanic outbursts and this material was poured out over the sea floor. The result is a series of beds of an almost black basalt, made up of fine crystals of minerals such as olivine, felspar and augite, created by the rapid cooling of the molten material.

The basalt, then, was formed from a lava poured out on the floor of the carboniferous sea, spreading over a wide area before it solidified, after which further deposits of the limestone were laid down above it. In the Peak these dark formations are often known as 'toadstones'. As the beds of basalt are relatively thin compared with the limestone, and their effect on the landscape is slight, the dark lava is most in evidence on the faces of smooth limestone crags, as on High Tor, near Matlock, and in Millers Dale.

Other volcanic rocks, called dolerite, were intruded into

the limestone beds in a molten state at a much later period. They can be seen in Calton Hill, south of the Bakewell-Buxton road near Taddington, where the rock is quarried for road 'metal', and in Tideswell Dale, where a soft bed of the limestone, called limestone shale, has been recrystallised by the heat of the molten rock.

After the drying out of the carboniferous sea, earth movements or pressures from both an east and a west direction caused the bending of the strata into its anticlinal form. The limestones deposited on the floor of the sea (like those of the gritstones above them) were heaved up into a great mountain mass. But natural forces, among them the vast moving glaciers of the Ice Age, have planed down the highest and central portion of this great mass, wearing away the gritstone over the southern part until the limestone has been revealed below. Thus was exposed an irregularly-shaped dome, some 24 miles long from north to south and about 12 miles from east to west.

The earth movements which pushed up the limestone into a central dome also caused local folding of the rocks and some contortion of the strata. This is much more marked on the western side of the Peak District, for instance on the Staffordshire side of the Dove, than on the eastern side. It is particularly well seen in Apes Tor, at the north end of Ecton Hill, between the Dove and the Manifold, where the strata has not only been tilted so that it stands almost vertically on edge, but it has been folded back on itself to take the form of a letter 'V'.

As a result of the bending of the limestone strata, assisted by natural weathering agents, the horizontal beds are cut by cracks and fissures, almost invariably at right angles to the lines of bedding. The rocks tend to fracture cleanly into fairly regular blocks along well-developed 'joints'. Where one rock formation has slipped down or fallen away from another, it has left a precipitous, often vertical face or series of faces, as can be seen in the 'steps' of Harborough Rocks, near Brassington. The joint-faces also determine the steep sides of the dales and ravines which are the most striking feature of the limestone country.

The immense white crag of High Tor, the highest limestone

cliff in England, shows splendidly a joint-face forming the side of a dale. Dovedale, with its great buttress-like walls, is the best known example of this kind of scenery, but others can be seen in Wolfscote Dale, the northern extension of Dovedale, in Lathkill Dale, in Middleton Dale, near Eyam, and in the Wye valley (Millers Dale and Cheedale).

Under the action of weathering agents, such as acidulated water and frost, the limestone has been modelled here and there into strange and often beautiful forms. The action of such agents, too, can be seen in the great fans of limestone scree in some of the dales, fragments of rock which have been broken from the crags above and are known in the Peak as 'slitherbanks' or 'slithery banks'. There are most distinctive in Lathkill Dale and near Iron Tors in Wolfscote Dale.

A remarkable feature of the beds of limestone is that they are soluble in water containing carbon dioxide. Rain water usually takes up a quantity of this gas from the atmosphere and is thus capable of having a dissolving effect on the limestone on which it falls. As limestone is by its nature a porous rock, the water readily penetrates the surface and sinks underground. It will continue to seep through until it reaches a harder or less permeable band of rock, or a deposit of some other substance, such as basalt, when it will spread or run along the upper surface of this until it reaches the open air again in a series of springs. The line or succession of points at which the water emerges is known as the spring line, and this has determined the position of a great many of the villages in the limestone country. Because of the penetration of the limestone by water, too, the upland areas remain conspicuously dry, even after heavy rain.

The solubility of the limestone has assisted the enlargement of the many joints and fissures, thus helping in the creation of the dales. The porosity of the limestone also means that some of the rivers and streams sink through the surface and flow underground. The best known of such rivers is the Manifold, which after a spell of dry weather sinks out of sight below Wetton Mill and comes to light again in the grounds of Ilam Hall. Other rivers which disappear in dry spells include the Lathkill in its upper course, while some valleys which are now completely dry, like Cave Dale and

The Winnats, near Castleton, and Great Rocks Dale, north of the Wye, almost certainly once had streams running through them. Some streams have perhaps always flowed underground or have started to do so after the last retreat of the glaciers.

Underground exploration, a popular sport in the Peak District, has revealed many of these streams penetrating caves which they have cleared of the non-calcareous material that once filled them. Among the best known caves are Peak Cavern (one of 'Seven Wonders of the Peak'), near Castleton, the blue john caverns in Treak Cliff, and the Dove Holes, two wide but shallow caves in Dovedale. A recent geological theory is that the dales, instead of being eaten down from the surface by the action of streams, combined with the widening of the joints in the limestone, were once systems of caverns which were dissolved out and eroded by flood-waters until the roofs fell in. An example of this action on a relatively small scale would be Reynard's Arch, in Dovedale, once the entrance to a cave the roof of which has collapsed behind the arch, though the inner section of the cave survives intact. Adopting this theory, Poole's Cavern, near Buxton, is perhaps a dale in formation, but the assumption that the whole of Dovedale may once have been a long serious of caves requires a considerable feat of the imagination.

It has been suggested that the working of the numerous lead veins or rakes of the limestone country has opened up easier routes for the percolation of the surface water. During the late seventeenth and eighteenth centuries, too, many drainage tunnels or channels, locally called 'soughs' (pronounced 'sufs'), were driven through the limestone in the chief area of lead mining, west of the Derwent valley. More than 30 miles of such soughs have been explored or revealed. The construction of these has brought down the saturation level (the 'water table') towards the level of the Derwent itself. At the same time, the existence of these many rakes and soughs has accentuated the dryness of the higher parts of some of the limestone dales.

Earlier travellers through the Peak District thought "the whole glory of the country is in its dales". But seen from the air the limestone valleys mostly appear as no more than deep scratches in the green surface of the plateau. The dales are mostly so narrow, in fact, that the chief transport routes have always kept to the uplands. The Roman road from the neighbourhood of Wirksworth to Buxton, for instance, followed long ridges of the limestone for almost the whole of the way.

Between these deeply-cut dales, the limestone uplands reach a height in many places of well over 1000 feet, but they are not the bleak moorland that might be expected at such an altitude. The Peakland farms are often to be found high up on the plateau, invariably at some point where the spring water emerges. Because of the porosity of the limestone, combined with the freedom of the strata from inorganic material, only a relatively thin layer of soil covers the uplands in most places. This means that arable cultivation is unprofitable, as the soil is too thin and poor for ploughing, and the land is mainly given over to the raising of sheep or cattle. Better conditions for arable farming are created by the superficial covering of clay or gravel that sometimes occurs locally.

Though the soil is poor, especially in comparison with the lush pastures of the Midland Plain, the presence of the lime colours the grass a rich, light green hue. A varied growth of flowers, too, can be enjoyed in summer, including the wild thyme, the meadow crane's bill, the yellow mountain pansy, and several species of orchid. Another feature of the limestone plateau is the absence of trees, more particularly at heights of over 1000 feet. The uplands were once, most likely, much more thickly covered with trees than they are now, but the prevalance of sheep grazing, introduced on a large scale in the Middle Ages, restricted the natural growth of trees. The ash and other trees are native to the Peak District, but several of the more common trees, such as the beech and the sycamore, have been introduced by man, and belts of these have been planted to shelter the farms and farmlands. Many of the dales, by contrast, carry a thick growth of natural woods, not only on the valley floors but along the steeply-sloping sides as well.

Like the farms, many of the stone-built villages of the Low Peak are to be found on the high uplands. Indeed, some of the dales are much too restricted to hold a village of any size. As already stressed, the Carboniferous Limestone differs considerably in its texture and structure from the oolitic limestone of the Cotswolds, and the villages, understandably, differ too. The exposed rocks of the Peakland limestone in their thick, massive beds are harder and rougher than the Cotswold limestones, and the stone does not lend itself as readily to delicate ornament or to such elegance of building as we find in the Cotswolds.

The lead mining industry of the Peak District, the main source of its wealth for over a thousand years, is now defunct, and by far the most important industry is the quarrying of limestone. The huge quarries in the neighbourhood of Wirksworth, Buxton and Stoney Middleton are all too obvious. Other minerals found in association with the limestone, and thrown to one side as useless by the lead miner, are now being exploited commercially. Chief among these is fluorspar (calcium fluoride) and many old lead rakes are now being opened again for this. Fluorspar is the principal source of fluorine compounds in the chemical industry, of fluorine anaesthetics in medicine and of heat-resistant enamels, and it is used as a flux in the making of steel. More then 120,000 tons are extracted every year in the Peak, mainly from rakes extending along a strip of the limestone country from Wirksworth to Castleton. A special kind of fluorspar with blue and yellow bands, known as Blue John, is obtained from caverns in Treak Cliff, above Castleton, and has been used for making ornaments since the eighteenth century.

Another mineral found with the limestone is barytes (or baryte; barium sulphate), of which some 20,000 tons are being taken out each year. It is used in the manufacture of toothpaste, paint and glossy paper, as the source of barium in the chemical industry and in the drilling of oil wells (in the North Sea, for example). Calcite (calcium carbonate), less extensively quarried, is also used in the chemical industry, as well as for floor and wall surfacing and other kinds of decoration and for the white lines on roads. Stalactites are made of calcite. Amateur geologists will amuse themselves in looking for specimens of these minerals in the Peak.

3 The Gritstone Country

In the northern section of the Peak District, that is, north of the Hope Valley, the Carboniferous Limestone is completely covered by the overlying beds of the gritstone deposits. These consist of two quite distinctive kinds of outcrop: the hard, intractable rock known as Millstone Grit (sometimes as Moorstone Grit) and a much softer and more friable material, the Shales.

These gritstones which make up the High Peak and the barren moorlands stretching north along the Yorkshire Pennines are responsible for some of the highest and wildest country in England, reaching over 2000 feet in places. This is for the most part a desolate and lonely region, covered with great tracts of heather, bilberry and cotton grass, and split up by a waste of peat bogs. Its character is well seen in the heights of Kinder Scout, north of Edale, and Bleaklow, farther north.

Though surrounded by the highest density of population in England (such teeming cities as Manchester and Sheffield are within a few miles of its boundaries), the High Peak is one of the most sparsely inhabited regions in the country. Sheep are maintained on the moors, but for mile after mile the only signs of the handiwork of man are the dark gritstone walls. The gritstone cannot bring brightness to the landscape, as the limestone does, but these rather sombre moorlands have a fascinating quality of their own. The moorland plateaux, too, are intersected by long deep valleys invariably cultivated and mostly free of industry (unlike the similar valleys farther north in Yorkshire), and the tops of the valley sides are often lined by scarps of hard dark crag known locally as 'edges'.

The gritstones were formed in a precisely similar way to the limestones, by being laid down in a shallow sea. But here the invertebrates that gave the limestone its particular texture and colour are absent; they are replaced by a coarse and gritty sand. These gritstones form a series of deposits well over 2000 feet thick. While being laid down, they were apparently affected by strong currents, as in many places conglomerates or pebble beds are found among the smaller gritstones. Some of the pebbles measure several inches across and so could not have been transported by slowly moving streams.

It is the presence of these conglomerates that gives the Millstone Grit its distinctive character as a rough, tough, pebbly gritstone of a very coarse texture. It varies considerably in colour, from a rose-pink to light brown and even to grey in places, but exposure to the atmosphere tends to turn it a dark brown. The Millstone Grit has sometimes been confused with granite (a volcanic rock), and indeed the quartz and felspar that occur most abundantly in the Millstone Grit are among the principal constituents of granite. It has been suggested in fact that the conglomerates of Millstone Grit may have been produced by the denudation of some great granitic mass which was taking place, perhaps assisted by the action of rivers, at the same time as the gritstone strata were being laid down.

Along with the carboniferous limestone, the gritstones were shaped by primeval forces into an arch or anticline along a north-south axis, so that in the southern part of the Peak the surface limestone dips down to east and west and disappears under the outcrops of the Millstone Grit. In consequence, the gritstones extend down either side of the limestone country, forming the moorlands above the Derwent on the east side and Combs Moss, Axe Edge, the Roaches and the Moorlands district of Staffordshire on the west.

As with the limestone, the Millstone Grit has broken away along strong joint planes, and this, assisted by the pronounced weathering of the softer shales, has shaped the long, precipitous dark-brown escarpments or edges which are the most distinctive feature of the Millstone Grit. Such edges are particularly well seen in the Roaches (west of the Leek-Buxton road), on Stanage Edge (on the Derbyshire-Yorkshire border), on Millstone Edge above Hathersage (so called because millstones were manufactured there), on the edges that line the eastern side of the Derwent valley, and farther south at the Black Rocks above Cromford.

The scooping out of softer beds of the gritstone, especially along the weaker bedding planes, often assisted by the movements of the glaciers and the action of the elements (wind, rain and frost), has resulted in the creation of the hard blocks of Millstone Grit, called tors, many of them of curious shape, that stand out on the moors. These almost detached rocks, some of them supported on very narrow bases, can be seen on the Roaches, on Stanton Moor, at Robin Hood's Stride, on Kinder Scout and on the moors east of Hathersage and the Derwent reservoirs.

The gritstone slopes created by the anticlinal fold dip down at a gentle angle to east and west, so behind the edges we find broad, easily-shelving plateaux. Great areas of these reach over 1000 feet above sea-level and consist of open, breezy expanses of uncultivated moorland. The surface of these uplands is mostly sandy, due to the erosion of the gritstone, and is consequently well drained, and these dry areas are enjoyed by such plants as heather, bracken, bilberry and crowberry.

Where the rainfall is heavier, as it is on the central dome of the gritstone, where the drainage is poor, or where a deposit of boulder clay left by the retreating glaciers in the Ice Age conceals the gritstone, the moorlands are covered by wide tracts of peat, decaying and partly carbonised vegetable matter, best seen on Kinder Scout and Bleaklow. Such peaty tracts, frequently called 'mosses', are often thickly grown with sphagnum, or bog-moss, or with cotton-grass, the soft white tufts of which, a familiar sight on the moors in summer, have given the name of 'featherbed moss' to several areas.

The deposits of peat are not only widespread, extending over many square miles, but on Kinder Scout and Bleaklow, for instance, they are often 12 feet or more in thickness. The presence of boulder clay and other deposits left behind by the glaciers, so obstructing the drainage of the gritstone moors, has been suggested as a reason for the origin of these peaty formations. But tests have shown that the deepest parts of many peat bogs were established during the Stone Age, when a growth of birch woods on the gritstone contributed to their formation. Little peat has been formed in recent times, and the action of the many streams, combined with the erosion caused by the wind, is gradually wearing away much of the surface peat.

Few trees or shrubs are to be seen on the exposed moorlands. The growth of heather, too, has been affected during the last century or more by the smoke blown over from the industrial areas of south Lancashire, as the moors lie in the path of the prevailing west wind. Heather has been replaced to some extent by patches of the more adaptable crowberry. (Perhaps the cleaner air that our cities are enjoying will result in a resurgence of the heather.) To some visitors the gritstone moorlands present "a grey and austere aspect", but those who have got to know them find solace and even inspiration in the vast stretches of open, untouched country. While the limestone country needs the sun to bring out its colour and character, the gritstone regions can be enjoyed under almost any conditions.

Sheep graze on the heather and on the coarse grass that is encroaching on the moors in many places; and round the fringes of the moors some tracts have been brought under the plough, but the gritstone regions still support only a scanty population. The few remote grey farms are almost the only habitations and in many places, particularly on the higher parts, derelict farmsteads speak of failure under difficult conditions, though more and more abandoned farms and even barns are being taken over and renovated by commuters from Manchester, Sheffield and elsewhere.

Although some farmsteads will be found high up along the fringes of the moorlands, especially on the western side of the Peak (where farms tend to be smaller), the villages of the gritstone country all avoid the uplands and shelter down in the dales, or at least below the limits of cultivation at the edge of the moors, where their positions are established by the spring lines.

Though it is a hard, coarse stone, difficult to work, the Millstone Grit has been used extensively for building since early times, when its very imperviousness was no doubt in its favour. Castles, churches and bridges were built of the Grit, and it was transported into Lincolnshire and the East Riding for church building as early as the Saxon period. Timber seems never to have been used to any large extent in the gritstone areas of the Peak District, and after it became scarce, towards the end of the Tudor period, houses were almost all built of Millstone Grit. The stone was commonly used in the limestone areas, too, for the main structural parts, for doors and windows and for lintels and coping stones, the infilling of the walls being of the local limestone. Thinly bedded varieties of the gritstone, obtainable only from certain quarries, were used for flagstones and as roofing slabs. Such slabs are in fact no longer quarried, so if you want a gritstone roof for your new or renovated house, you will have to find a house or farm building which has recently been demolished.

Interspersed with the hard Millstone Grit are beds of the much softer deposits, the Shales, which lack the pebble formations that give the Grit its particular quality. The shales have perhaps been subjected to considerable pressure; they are certainly much more friable and they mostly occur in thinner beds. The best place to see the juxtaposition of the grits and the shales is on the face of Mam Tor, above the head of the Hope Valley, where the alternate bands of the hard and soft deposits are quite distinctive. Fragments of the soft shales frequently break away and fall down the precipitous face, a natural curiosity that has given Mam Tor its nickname of the 'Shivering Mountain' and made it one of the Wonders of the Peak.

Landslips, sometimes of considerable extent, have occurred where the Millstone Grit outcrops over steep slopes of the shale. They are especially noticeable on the north side of Mam Tor, facing the village of Edale, as well as below the 'shivering' face, where new landslips carry away the road from time to time.

Here the shales occur only in very thin beds, but much thicker beds can be encountered in the south side of Kinder Scout. In walking down the narrow valley of the Grindsbrook from the plateau of Kinder Scout to Edale, we cross the Kinderscout Grit, which shows as a very pronounced edge ringing the plateau, the Grindslow Shales (soft shales interbedded with thin sandstones), the Mam Tor Sandstones (a fine grained gritstone) and the Edale Shales, in that order. The various strata can be seen outcropping in the valley side, while the harder Grits form terraces across the sloping valley floor. The Mam Tor Sandstones also form the long, sharp ridge connecting that hill with Lose Hill, above Hope.

Because of their softness, the shale beds have been worn down, where they outcrop extensively, to form valleys and depressions. In the major valleys they are usually covered by alluvial deposits of sand and gravel brought down by the denudation or weathering of the Millstone Grit. The Noe, in Edale, and the upper Derwent are incised into such deposits, and series of terraces have been formed here by changes in the river levels, as they have cut down into the alluvial deposits.

The shale beds form two long belts or bands between the limestone dome and the gritstone edges down the east and west sides of the Peak. The rivers have sought out these softer areas and have carved themselves deep valleys. Along the east side, the shales have been eaten into to form the beautiful, well-wooded valley of the Derwent, overlooked on the east by the almost continuous escarpment of the Millstone Grit. Because of this long, unbroken rampart, the Derwent receives only minor tributaries on that side until it reaches as far south as the Amber. On its west side, however, it takes in several larger tributaries, such as the Ashop, the Noe and the Wye.

Southward from Rowsley, where it is joined by the Wye, the Derwent flows in a wide valley, but just below Matlock it enters the narrow gorge cut through the carboniferous limestone, between the sheer precipice of High Tor on the one hand and the wooded slopes of the great dome of Masson on the other. The course of the river has brought it against a projecting band of the hard limestone, thrown up into an unusual east-west ridge by local folding of the strata. A slight detour to the east would have enabled the river to continue along its shale bed, which forms a depression behind High Tor, but the river has chosen instead to penetrate the limestone, ignoring this easier passage, until it reaches Cromford on the farther side, where it returns to the shale bed.

The upper courses of the Dove and the Manifold, on the west side of the limestone country, are corresponding examples of valley formation using the shales. On the west side of the great anticlinal fold, the river Dove flows for some distance over a shale bed, but below Hartington it, too, forces a passage through the solid limestone, emerging at length from the famous gorge of Dovedale.

The gritstones also occur to the south of the limestone region, in a segment from Matlock round towards Macclesfield. Here they are not so much in evidence, though the Millstone Grit does outcrop in isolated patches over a wide area; around the Amber valley, at Alport Height (south-east of Wirksworth), in Wetley Rocks (south of Leek) and in The Cloud, near Congleton, for instance. They make their presence felt, too, in the field walls which can be seen in places, such as south of the road from Leek to Ashbourne.

4 Ashbourne: Gateway to the Peak

Ashbourne (418346), the 'Southern Gateway' to the Peak District, is an old market town on the Henmore Brook, a tributary of the Dove. With its many fine red-brick houses, it conveys the atmosphere of a Midland town, but the occasional stone buildings tell us that the limestone country of the Peak District is not far away to the north, and the town has always played an important part in the agricultural life of the Peak.

Though Ashbourne stands on the line of Hereward Street, the Roman road that ran across country from Rocester to Chesterfield, there is no evidence of a Roman settlement here. There must have been a settlement of some kind in Saxon times, for Ashbourne had one of at least five minster churches in Derbyshire (the others being at Bakewell and Repton, with two in Derby), but in the Domesday Survey of 1086, where it is called 'Esseburn' (the 'ash tree stream', now the Henmore Brook), it is described as "waste".

Ashbourne would appear to have been newly laid out as a planned or 'planted' market town about the middle of the thirteenth century, probably by one of the De Ferrers family, Earls of Derby, who were then lords of the manor. The market is first recorded in 1257 and it had been created a borough by 1281 (though later it lost this status). Ashbourne earned its prosperity as an agricultural centre not only from its position on a principal thoroughfare from Manchester to Derby and the south, but also because of its sheltered and strategic position, where the foothills of the Peak give way to the undulating country of the Midland Plain.

The sloping, triangular Market Place, where the distinctive products of these two contrasting areas could be exchanged (the sheep, wool and lead of the Peak for the corn, timber and horses of the Plain), was formerly much larger than it is

Jenkin Chapel

Fenny Bentley Old Hall

Tissington village

now and stretched down to meet the main street through the town. But later infilling has resulted in the Market Place being divorced from the main street. Apart from its weekly market, established by 1296 (and now held on a Saturday), Ashbourne had two fairs in medieval times (annual markets, in effect, but on a larger scale), but the town prospered so that these grew to seven in the seventeenth century and eleven by 1853.

Evidence for the planned pattern of Ashbourne is shown not only in the large Market Place but also in the long main street, St John Street and its continuation westward, Church Street. The Parish Church, which still stands at one end of the town, was rebuilt in the thirteenth century (in the south transept is a dedication brass of 1241) and is the finest example in the North Midlands of the Early English style of that time. The characteristic features of this style are best seen in the south doorway, with its ribbed moulding and so-called 'dog-tooth' ornamentation, and in the tall 'lancet' windows of the chancel. James Boswell described the church as "one of the largest and most luminous . that I have seen in any town of the same size" and George Eliot thought it "the finest mere parish church in the kingdom".

The tower and spire were raised their 215 feet and the south arcade and aisle were built about 1330-50, and I like to think they may be the work of Henry Yevele, called by his biographer, John Harvey, "the greatest English architect . who perfected the Perpendicular style and produced the noblest works of its early maturity". Yevele was born about 1320 at Yeaveley (4 miles south of Ashbourne) or possibly at Uttoxeter, farther south-west on the Dove, where the family was living by 1327. Henry was learning his craft as a mason (or builder) in the district at the time Ashbourne church was being enlarged and he would certainly see the work here, even if he didn't do it himself. Yevele was in London by 1353, when he was admitted as a Freeman to the City of London; he subsequently became architect to Edward III and was responsible for designing the magnificent naves of Westminster Abbey and Canterbury Cathedral.

The church is unusual (for a parish church) in having chapels to the transepts. In the north transept chapel are interesting fifteenth- and sixteenth-century tombs of the Cokaynes, who lived at Ashbourne Hall, and the Bradbournes of Hulland. The Cokaynes and the Bradbournes owed much of their prosperity to the offices they held under the Duchy of Lancaster. They were hereditary foresters in the royal forest of Duffield Frith, which lay to the east of Ashbourne and was used for the rearing of deer, horses, cattle and sheep. The transept contains an almost complete series of monuments of the Cokaynes, ranging from that of Sir John, who died in 1372, and his son Edmund, killed at the Battle of Shrewsbury in 1403, to that of Sir Thomas Cokayne, one of the founders of the Grammar School, who died in 1592. The only absentee is a Thomas Cokayne who died in 1488 and whose tomb we shall see at Youlgreave. The alabaster tomb of the Sir John Cokayne who died in 1447 is attributed to Thomas Prentys and Robert Sutton, the carvers who had their workshops near the famous alabaster quarries at Chellaston, south of Derby.

The Cokaynes were followed at the Hall by the Boothbys, and among the monuments in the transept is that of Sir Brooke Boothby, who died in 1789 and whose portrait by Joseph Wright of Derby hangs in the Tate Gallery in London. Wright has shown him in an unusual pose, stretched out on the ground in a woodland setting, and clutching in his hand a book inscribed on the spine with the word 'Rousseau'. The French philosopher lived for a year at Wootton Hall, farther down the Dove, and Boothby was one of his admirers.

Far more famous than Sir Brooke's monument is that to his granddaughter, Penelope, who had been painted by Sir Joshua Reynolds (when she was three years' old) but who died in 1791 before she reached the age of six. The figure of the little girl, in white Carrara marble, is the masterpiece of Thomas Banks and inspired the figures of the 'Sleeping Children' in Lichfield Cathedral by Sir Francis Chantrey. The inscriptions round the pedestal are in four languages: English, Latin, French and Italian; and that in English tells us that "She was in form and intellect most exquisite. The unfortunate parents ventured their all on this frail bark, and the wreck was total". Apparently they separated at the child's grave, never to speak again.

On the other side of Church Street is the old Grammar School, founded in 1585, ostensibly by Elizabeth I (whose name it bears), but actually paid for by Sir Thomas Cokayne and other wealthy townsfolk. The Elizabethan building, begun in 1586 and completed in 1610, has a long array of mullioned windows below steeply-roofed gables in the style of Peakland manor houses of the period. It is now used as the boys' boarding house; the newer school buildings are at the other end of the town.

Opposite the old Grammar School is a house named The Mansion (though often called Dr Taylor's House), built in stone about 1685, with a recessed front between two gabled wings towards the garden. In 1764 it was provided with an octagonal domed drawing room between the wings and a new façade, in brick, facing the street. This work was carried out by Joseph Pickford, the Derby architect, for Dr John Taylor, who was rector of Market Bosworth in Leicestershire and St Margaret's, Westminster, and a prebendary of Westminster Abbey. Taylor was a schoolfellow and friend of Dr Samuel Johnson, who often rode over from Lichfield (sometimes accompanied by Boswell) to stay with him, and he preached the sermon at Johnson's funeral in the Abbey. Boswell tells us that "Taylor's size and figure and countenance and manner were that of a hearty English squire, with the parson superinduced". The building is now the girls' boarding school of the Grammar School.

Next to the Grammar School is the Grey House, a stone house in almost exactly similar style to The Mansion, with the pedimented porch, Venetian windows and other features favoured by Joseph Pickford. It is not his work, however, but was designed in the 1760s for himself by Brian Hodson, a retired innkeeper and the proprietor of the baths at Buxton, who fairly copied the house opposite. A later resident, curiously enough, was Dr Alexander Boswell, a descendant of Johnson's biographer.

Next to The Mansion are two of the many almshouses that were established in Ashbourne in the seventeenth and eighteenth centuries. Those fronting the road were founded in 1630 by Roger Owfield, a London fishmonger of Ashbourne origin, and those at right angles were endowed in

1669 by Christopher Pegge. Both were originally low ranges of one-storey stone building, but an upper storey was added to Owfield's Almshouses in 1848. Behind the churchyard is another group of almshouses, in brick, founded in 1723 by Nicholas Spalden, who also endowed, in 1753, the Clergy Widows' Almshouses, to the east along Church Street, "for entertaining the widows of four clergymen of the Church of England". The street front of these, recently restored, is arranged round an open courtyard.

Church Street was in fact almost entirely rebuilt in the eighteenth century and is the finest street in Derbyshire (except for Friargate in Derby). Here we see Georgian brick buildings imposed on the medieval town plan. A pictorial map of Ashbourne of about 1547 which has survived shows the partial infilling of the market place and the long burgage plots, narrow strips of land held for a small yearly rent, with a building fronting the street and a croft or garden behind. Nos 24 and 28, on the south side next to the Clergy Widows' Almshouses, are probably the oldest Georgian houses in the street, though No 24, which has classical pilasters, has not been improved by a modern shop front. Other good brick houses are The Ivies (No 49), opposite Pegge's Almshouses, and Vine House (No 15), farther east. No 27, between these, has been occupied by Foster Brothers, fishing-tackle makers, since 1763, though the front was rebuilt about 1820 and has unfortunately been roughcast over.

Dig Street, on the south at the east end of Church Street, probably takes its name from a medieval ditch, perhaps a fortification of some kind. It crosses the Henmore Brook to Compton, which has a wide street, the beginning of the Derby road. It has been suggested that the head of the street was the site of a rival market, for Compton was once outside the borough boundary. This quarter began to be developed in the late thirteenth century and the inhabitants frequently disregarded the tolls and other dues that had to be paid for trading within the borough; in 1276 Edward I's officers complained that the king was being defrauded of much of his revenues. Compton, in fact, did not come under the jurisdiction of Ashbourne until 1873. Lloyd's Bank here, built in the late eighteenth century, probably by Joseph

Ashbourne: Gateway to the Peak

Pickford (it has the Venetian windows and arched recesses seen in many of his designs), was the town house of the Beresfords of Fenny Bentley, and the "beautiful Miss Beresfords" used to boat on the brook below the house.

Victoria Square, on the north side of St John Street, was part of the Market Place before the infilling began. The roughcasting over a butcher's shop here disguises the jettied timber-framed gable of a former inn, the Tiger, probably of the sixteenth century. Timber framing (among the few examples in the neighbourhood of the Peak District) can be seen in the yard behind, which still conveys a good impression of the yards which were once a common feature of Ashbourne.

Over St John Street stretches the wooden beam supporting the unusual sign of the Green Man and Black's Head, the principal inn of the town. There were formerly two inns, but the trade of the vanished Blackamoor's Head was taken over by the Green Man, which has a good mid-eighteenth-century front and an attractive yard reached through the entry. A luncheon takes place at the inn on Ashbourne's two most important days of the year: Shrove Tuesday and Ash Wednesday, when the traditional game of football is played in the streets and around the town.

The game starts each day on the Shaw Croft, an open space (now a car park) behind the inn. The ball, which is of leather filled with cork and decoratively painted, is thrown up (or 'turned up', as the phrase is) at two o'clock, usually by a sporting or other celebrity. The late Duke of Windsor 'turned up' the ball on one occasion, when he was Prince of Wales. The game is played between the 'Up'ards', who live on the north side of the Henmore Brook, and the 'Down'ards', who live on the south side, which formerly meant Compton and its neighbourhood, and this division into teams probably stems from Ashbourne and Compton once being separate places. Visitors can also take part in the game (if they are hardy enough). The ball can be kicked, carried or otherwise transported by human agency, into the Henmore Brook, through the streets (whose shop windows are boarded up for the occasion) or anywhere else. There are no boundaries, and a goal is scored by a member of the Up'ards touching the wall of Sturston Mill, a mile and a half upstream on the brook, or one of the Down'ards team touching a commemorative stone on the site of Clifton Mill, a mile and a half downstream. Play continues without a halt until a goal is scored (when the scorer keeps the ball and a second ball is turned up on the Shaw Croft) or until darkness falls, which in fact sometimes occurs without the ball being 'goaled'.

St John Street, with further good eighteenth-century houses, extends eastward from the Green Man towards Ashbourne Hall, of which only part remains, now used as a branch of the county library. The Hall was rebuilt about 1780 for Sir Brooke Boothby on the site of the house of the Cokaynes where Prince Charles Edward Stuart stayed in December, 1745, on his journey southward that was halted at Derby. His father, the 'Old Pretender', was proclaimed king as James III in the market place, but a few days later the prince was back again, on the march that ended on the fateful field of Culloden.

In the War Memorial Park opposite is a bust of Catherine Mumford, who was born in 1829 at a small terraced house (No 13) in Sturston Road (the Belper road, farther south). In 1855 she married William Booth, the founder of the Salvation Army, and with him carried on the army's social and religious work, particularly in the poverty-stricken areas of the East End of London, until her death in 1890. She became a public preacher in 1860, so initiating the first women's ministry.

In the fine town houses in St John Street and Church Street lived the clergymen, the attorneys and others, many of them the younger sons of the county gentry, as well as the wealthy lead merchants, ironmongers, maltsters, cheesefactors and other middlemen, all of whom helped Ashbourne to develop as a favoured social centre in the eighteenth century. The town became an important coaching stage on the route from London via Derby to Manchester. Industry began to make its mark at this period; in the yards behind the houses were built the workshops of the ironfounders, the lace embroiderers, the stocking knitters and other craftsmen, and as the population expanded in the nineteenth century, small rows of terraced houses were also built in many of the yards. By 1847 Ashbourne had thirty-three hotels, inns and taverns, twelve schools or academies, five attorneys, five surgeons and three booksellers.

But the decline of the coaching era in face of competition from the new railways arrested the prosperity of Ashbourne. Though a branch of the North Staffordshire Railway from Uttoxeter, opened in 1852, brought more tourists bound for Dovedale, the main lines avoided Ashbourne, and its progress was halted while that of Derby was rapidly advanced. This period of gestation during the most flourishing years of the Industrial Revolution, however, has helped to preserve the town centre. A corset manufactory was opened in the 1870s, and Ashbourne now also makes tapes and webbing and has a large condensery for processing milk (as well as being noted for its gingerbread), but it still conveys, as it did in 1833, "a pleasing idea of security and social happiness". It is fitting that in 1968 the centre of the town should have been made a conservation area.

5 From Ashbourne to Leek and Macclesfield

The Manchester road from Ashbourne keeps outside the south-western boundary of the Peak District National Park but it does serve as the jumping off point for many little-known places of great attraction, as well as taking us to the interesting old manufacturing towns of Leek and Macclesfield. The road runs west past the church to the Hanging Bridge, where it crosses the Dove from Derbyshire into Staffordshire. Originally a packhorse bridge, this was widened for carriage traffic in the eighteenth century and again for motor traffic in the present century, but the fifteenth-century arches can still be seen underneath. Downstream is a mill established in 1781 for cotton spinning by Sir Richard Arkwright (whom we shall meet at Cromford), and rebuilt in 1866, two years after it had been taken over by the company that still owns it, making tapes and narrow fabrics in many materials, including glass filament.

The road on the left of the Queen's Arms Inn conveys a good idea of what roads were like before the motoring age. It ascends to Mayfield (415346), a flower-decked village overlooking the valley of the Dove, with seventeenth- and eighteenth-century houses. At Mayfield Cottage, a farmhouse on the slope to the south-west, Thomas Moore, the Irish poet, lived for about four years (1813-17). Here he wrote *Lalla Rookh*, his fantasy of oriental splendour, as well as "Those Evening Bells", inspired by the chimes of Ashbourne which he could hear across the valley. The Leek road, by-passing Mayfield, makes a grinding ascent of over two miles to the limestone uplands at Swinscoe (413348). Behind we can enjoy the wide view over and down the Dove valley, and beyond the hamlet the road reaches the boundary of the National Park, which it follows as far as Waterhouses.

On the skyline, away to the left, we can see the Weaver Hills (409346), sometimes called the 'last of the Pennines' because they are the southernmost limit of the limestone country. From the grassy ridge of the hills (1217 feet) a charming view unfolds over the deep valley of the Churnet to the south.

Our road leaves on the left that which skirts the north side of the Weavers on its way towards Stoke, while roads on the other side lead to Calton (410350), a hamlet with seventeenth-century houses. The main road winds down at length to Waterhouses (408350), a limestone village on the Hamps, whose pleasant valley is descended by a path on the site of the Leek and Manifold Light Railway (see Chapter 6). The small church of Waterfall, a mile to the north, was rebuilt in the classical style in the nineteenth century, but retains its wide Norman chancel arch, curiously distorted.

To the south of the Leek road can be seen the huge limestone quarry cut into Cauldon Low, from which much of the stone for building the new motorways was taken. The road goes up the broadening valley of the Hamps, then crosses the river and ascends to reach its highest point (1076 feet) at the inappropriately-named Bottom House (404352). The Hamps winds away to the north to Ford (406353), a hamlet which has a fine seventeenth-century Old Hall in the Peakland style. Onecote (404355; pronounced 'On-e'), on the road from Bottom House to Hartington, has a charming little church rebuilt in 1753 with classical features but a Gothic tower. Commandment boards of 1755 show curious painted figures of Moses, Aaron and Joshua, the last in Roman costume.

From the Hartington road, north of Bottom House, a road runs along the high ridge of the Morridge ('moor edge'), with widespreading views over Leek in the Churnet valley and of the Roaches and other jagged gritstone outcrops to the west. It passes the oddly-named Mermaid Inn, isolated high up on the moors at a height of over 1450 feet, then leads out to the Leek-Buxton road below the Royal Cottage Inn (Chapter 8). Though much longer than the main road, this is the best way of reaching Leek.

Leek (398356) is an old market town and a centre of the silk weaving industry on a hill above the head reaches of the river Churnet. It is first mentioned in Domesday Book (1086) as 'Lec', a name meaning 'brook' that may have been derived from its position on the Churnet. The lords of the manor from Norman times were the powerful Earls of Chester, the sixth of whom, Ranulf de Blundeville, founded the abbey of Dieulacres, beyond the river. The vicar of Leek was thenceforth appointed by the abbot, an arrangement that continued until the dissolution of the abbey in 1539.

Leek has had a market since early medieval times, and this is still held on Wednesdays in the cobbled Market Place, though the Butter Cross of 1671 has been removed to the cemetery beside the road to Stone. But the town really began to develop from the end of the seventeenth century onwards with the introduction of the silk trade. This was given a considerable boost by the arrival of large numbers of Huguenot weavers from France after the revocation in 1685 by Louis XIV of the Edict of Nantes, which had given the Protestants a measure of religious freedom. The population of Leek at the beginning of the eighteenth century was less than 1000 but by the beginning of the nineteenth century it was over 3000 and by 1881 it had grown to 13,700. Leek is still a centre of the textile industry, specialising in silk weaving and dyeing.

In the Market Place and the streets around are several good eighteenth-century houses, one in stone dated 1724, but mostly in brick (which was becoming fashionable in the early eighteenth century) and with finely-carved doorcases. Thomas Parker, 1st Earl of Macclesfield, was born in about 1666 in a house (now partly a shop) on the west side of the Market Place. He became Lord Chief Justice and Lord Chancellor of England, but in 1725 (two years after founding the Grammar School at Leek) he was impeached for corruption and fined £30,000.

Prince Charles Edward Stuart passed through Leek in 1745 on his way to Derby. He arrived on 2nd December, "gay in silk tartan and blue-feathered bonnet", as pictured by W.M. Thackeray in *Henry Esmond*, and stayed at the Vicarage, a building mainly of 1714 next to the churchyard. Failing to gather many supporters, he left the next day for Ashbourne. Five days later he was back in the town, but this time he was not welcomed by the vicar, whose wife (it is said) ill at the time, expired at the prospect of being punished for harbouring the rebel prince.

In the churchyard are two Saxon cross-shafts, one of the tenth century, with interlace decoration, and the other, 12 feet high, with a band dividing it into a round section below and a square section above, a feature of Viking crosses of the eleventh century (these crosses will be discussed again at Bakewell). In the south aisle of the church are gathered fragments of other crosses, one of which is part of a wheel-head and another showing Christ carrying the Cross. Both of these are probably of the tenth century, and near by is a hog-backed Viking tombstone, also of the tenth century, of a type found mostly in the North-West of England.

The Church of St Edward the Confessor, once the centre of a large parish, was burned down (with much of the town) in 1297. Rebuilding was completed in 1320; the tower and nave, which has a fine timber roof with richly-carved bosses, date from this time. Two unusual wheel-windows in the aisles were introduced in the early fifteenth century, and in the north aisle is a brass to John Ashenhurst, who died in 1597, his four wives and ten children. The south porch was added in the classical style in 1670 and a considerable restoration took place between 1856 and 1867, when the chancel was rebuilt by G.E. Street. In the north aisle is a window with stained glass designed by Sir Edward Burne-Jones, the pre-Raphaelite painter, and made in the workshops of William Morris. Frames contain altar frontals worked at the Leek School of Embroidery, founded in the 1870s by Dame Elizabeth Wardle with the idea of using silk as a yarn for embroidering cloths. Their work included an exact copy of the Bayeux Tapestry which took thirty-four of the ladies twelve months to make in 1885-86.

At the summer solstice (20th-22nd June) a curious double sunset can be seen from the churchyard. The sun goes down behind the west flank of The Cloud (a hill west of the Macclesfield road), then reappears from behind the east flank before setting a second time. Sometimes the sun appears to double into two orbs, one above the other.

The growth of Leek in the nineteenth century led to the

building of more churches. Chief among these is All Saints', in Compton, south of the Market Place. Designed in 1887 in a late-Gothic style by R. Norman Shaw, it has an impressive interior.

Beside the Macclesfield road in the Churnet valley is the Brindley Mill, as it is now called. This corn mill, rebuilt in 1752, is thought to have been designed for himself by James Brindley, the engineer and canal builder, who was born at Tunstead in the Peak District and who operated the mill from 1742 to 1765. The waterwheel and grinding machinery are in good order and the mill is being restored by the Brindley Mill Preservation Trust, founded in 1970, who hope to open it to the public when the work is complete.

The road crossing the river near by leads to the fragmentary remains of Dieulacres Abbey (398357), formerly Dieulacrosse (or De la Croix), a Cistercian monastery founded in or before 1214 by Ranulf, sixth Earl of Chester, who was present at the coronations of Richard I, John and Henry III and comes into *Piers Plowman*, the fourteenth century allegorical poem that comments on the social conditions of the time. Carved stones can be seen in the walls of a farm and its outbuildings, and close by is a fine timber-framed house of 1612.

The Macclesfield road, crossing the Churnet, runs above Rudyard Lake (394360), actually a reservoir nearly two miles long, built by James Brindley in 1770 to feed the Trent and Mersey Canal (and perhaps the oldest reservoir in Britain), with steep wood-fringed shores giving it the appearance of a natural lake, and now a favourite boating resort. From it Rudyard Kipling received his name, though he was born in India; his parents, before their marriage, used to escape here from the smoke and grime of Stoke.

Beyond Rushton Spencer (393362) the road crosses the Dane (Chapter 8) and enters Cheshire, with a view to the left of the prominent gritstone hill of The Cloud, and on the right of the tall Post Office Tower, 225 feet high, on Sutton Common, one of a chain of such towers, for television and radio telephony, stretching across country and linked with that in London. Beyond Bosley, a hamlet which has a Gothic church of 1777 (with a seventeenth-century pulpit) and a contemporary Gothic school, we cross the Buxton-Congleton road.

Our road skirts the Macclesfield Canal, built by Thomas Telford and opened in 1831 to link the town with the Peak Forest Canal and the Trent and Mersey Canal. Roads on the right lead to the hamlet of Gurnett (392371), where Plough House of 1802 stands on the site of the house in which James Brindley was apprenticed for seven years (1733-40) to a wheelwright, Abraham Bennett. The outbuilding was perhaps the original blacksmith's shop and stables of Brindley's time, and the long, low whitewashed building opposite was his workshop. A mile to the east, near the infant Bollin, which descends from Macclesfield Forest (Chapter 8), is Langley Hall, a house of 1696 with a fine doorcase that has an early example of a shell hood.

Macclesfield (391373), mostly built on a hill above the Bollin, facing the western foothills of the Peak District, is an old market town whose charter was granted in 1261. It was included in the Earldom of Chester, given by William the Conqueror to Hugh Lupus (i.e. 'the Wolf') for his services in helping to subdue the English. In 1238, when the male line failed, the manor reverted to the Crown, but Henry III settled it on Eleanor of Castile as part of her dowry when she married his son, later Edward I.

The Parish Church, facing the market place, was probably begun in 1278 for Eleanor of Castile, but has often been altered and enlarged. The Legh Chapel was added on the south of the nave in 1422 (but was altered in 1620); the Savage Chapel was built in 1504-07 by Thomas Savage, Archbishop of York (who is buried in York Minster). The chancel was rebuilt in 1883, and a new nave and aisles were built in 1898-1901, by Sir Arthur Blomfield, who also refaced and heightened the fourteenth-century tower, under which is an old ringers' loft, an unusual survival.

The church is notable for its monuments. Between the south aisle (the site of the former nave) and the Savage Chapel is the alabaster effigy of Sir John Savage V, who married a Dorothy Vernon of Haddon Hall. A Lancastrian, he fought on the Tudor side at the Battle of Bosworth Field and was killed at the siege of Boulogne in 1492. Next to this is the similar monument of his son, John Savage VI, who died in 1527. The principal monument in the Savage Chapel is that of Sir John Savage VIII, who died in 1597, and his wife, Elizabeth Manners, who because of her superior birth is placed at a higher level. She was the daughter of the first Earl of Rutland and therefore sister-in-law of *the* Dorothy Vernon. The work is ascribed to Nicholas Janssen, a Dutch sculptor who came over to this country and settled in London. On the wall near by is a rare indulgence or pardon brass to Roger Legh, who died in 1506. The inscription says that "The pardon for saying of V Paternost and V Aves and a Cred is XXVI thousand yeres and XXVI dayes of pardon".

At the east end of the south aisle is the splendid baroque monument, by William Stanton, to Thomas, third Earl Rivers, who died in 1694. In the chancel are two more monuments with effigies, one of them to Sir John Savage IV, who died in 1495, and his wife Katherine Stanley, sister of the first Earl of Derby. They were the parents of Archbishop Savage.

Macclesfield has been the principal seat of the silk-weaving industry in England since 1743, when Charles Roe built the first silk mill, two years before Prince Charles Edward passed through the town. By 1767 the town had some thirty silk mills, as well as many cotton spinning factories and copper works (which had been started by Roe in 1758). Some fine examples of the early textile factories are still to be seen. In Park Green, on the Leek road, is a large mill, formerly of Frost and Sons, built in 1785, with Victorian additions. Behind this mill is its forerunner, where Brindley in 1735 enhanced his reputation by removing and restoring machinery which had been damaged in a fire. Another early textile mill survives in Wordle Street, west of Mill Street, the main street, and the Card Factory in Chester Road was formerly a textile mill.

Many good streets and terraces of workers' houses, well worth preserving, are to be found in the southern part of the town: in Mill Lane (near Park Green), in Park Street, to the west, in High Street, and around Nelson Street and Rodney Street near by (the names of these indicate that they were built in the late eighteenth or early nineteenth century).

Macclesfield Sunday School, a huge brick building of 1796 in Roe-Street, west of Mill Street, looks very much like a mill (especially from behind) and must be the largest sunday school in England.

The Town Hall, north of the Market Place, built in 1824 by Francis Goodwin, has two ponderous porticos. Farther north, in Jordangate, are two fine houses, the Macclesfield Arms Hotel of 1811 and Jordangate House, built in 1728, with a classical doorcase; and the Rural District Council offices in King Edward Street occupy another fine house, of 1758. West Park, north of Chester Road, has a small but interesting museum of local history and three Viking cross-shafts, all of the eleventh century, have been re-erected here.

6 The Manifold Valley

The best way of reaching the Manifold Valley from Ashbourne is to take, not the main Buxton road out of the market place, but a by-road to the left of this which crosses over to the valley of the Bentley Brook. On the way we pass the Mapleton Lane terminus of the Tissington Trail (Chapter 9).

The road rounds the end of a hill to the quiet village of Mapleton (416348) or Mappleton (there is no consistency locally about either the spelling or the pronunciation), in the wide valley of the Dove. Beyond the eighteenth-century church, whose tower has an unusual dome with a lantern, we cross the river into Staffordshire and enter the grounds of Okeover Hall (415348). An avenue of limes leads to the beautiful wrought-iron gates, made in the early eighteenth century by Robert Bakewell, the great Derby ironsmith. There have been Okeovers at Okeover since the twelfth century; the hall and the fourteenth- to fifteenth-century church close by were pillaged by Prince Charles Edward's Jacobites in 1745 while on their way to Ashbourne. The present house was rebuilt in brick about 1780 and a new wing was added, in the same style, in 1960.

The road north of the Hall climbs high out of the valley, entering the Peak National Park before reaching Blore (413349), which consists of little more than the over-restored Hall, once the home of the Basset family, and the ill-cared-for church. In the north chapel here is a large alabaster monument raised about 1640 by Elizabeth Basset to her father, William, who died in 1601. His much-worn inscription describes him as a courtier and soldier, "witty, handsome, good, valiant, unparalled, of pure blood from William's Conquest" (what more could you want!). One of the effigies in armour represents William himself, the other is of Henry

Rowsley, Peacock Hotel

Arbor Low

Lathkill Dale

Howard, who died in 1616, son of the Earl of Suffolk and the first husband of Elizabeth, of whom, oddly enough, there are two kneeling figures. She later married William Cavendish, first Duke of Newcastle, and shared in the glories of Welbeck Abbey and Bolsover Castle when they were visited by Charles I and his queen.

By keeping to the right at the cross-roads we can enjoy a delightful view of the approach to Dovedale (Chapter 7) with its twin guardians, the conical Thorpe Cloud on the east and the long ridge of Bunster on the west. In a field stretching up the side of Bunster, west of the Izaak Walton Hotel, the Dovedale Sheep Dog Trials, founded in 1892 and claimed to be the oldest in England, are held every year during the third week in August.

The road descends into the valley at Ilam (413350; pronounced 'Eye-'), crossing the Manifold three-quarters of a mile above its junction with the Dove. This estate village, with its tile-fronted houses, mostly built about 1840 for Jesse Watts-Russell, occupies a beautiful position at the foot of Bunster and just below a great looping bend where the Manifold emerges from a narrow, thickly-wooded ravine into a magnificent amphitheatre. The church, standing in the hall grounds, was mostly rebuilt in 1884, but it has a blocked Saxon doorway and a Saxon font, curiously carved with human figures and dragons. Above the entrance to the south chapel of 1618 are two maidens' garlands (we shall see more at Ashford-in-the-Water). In the chapel is the medieval shrine of St Bertram or Bertelin, who flourished about A.D. 700 and was perhaps a Mercian prince. The nineteenth-century mausoleum on the other side contains a sculptured group of 1826 by Sir Francis Chantrey commemorating David Pike-Watts. In the churchyard, overlooking the Manifold, are two Saxon cross-shafts, the tall one, with a fragment of its head, dating from about A.D. 900, the short one from about 1035.

Ilam Hall, on the hillside above the church, was rebuilt about 1830 in the Tudor Gothic style for Jesse Watts-Russell. With its beautiful grounds it was given in 1934 to the National Trust and is now a youth hostel. From the terrace there is a fine view over the village to Bunster and Thorpe Cloud. Across the Manifold below the hall is St Bertram's

Bridge, and some distance above this the river, after a spell of dry weather, rises from an underground course. Dr Johnson apparently doubted this phenomenon, though (according to Boswell) he "had the attestation of the gardener, who said he had put in corks where the Manifold sinks into the ground, and had caught them in a net placed before one of the openings where the water bursts out". Johnson often visited Ilam Hall and the grounds inspired the 'golden valley' (though he transports it to Abyssinia) described in his only novel, *Rasselas*, written in the evenings of a single week to pay for his mother's funeral.

A terraced path known as Paradise Walk leads through the hall grounds near the Manifold, passing the large but sadly-weathered shaft of another Saxon cross, of the eleventh century. The path joins the road from Ilam, which shortly afterwards divides: the right branch climbs steeply to the eighteenth-century farmhouse of Castern Hall; the left branch crosses the Manifold, whose bed is usually dry here (except after heavy rain), and ascends above the river, with good views across and down the valley on the way to Throwley Hall (411352), where the ruined seventeenth-century house was built by the Meverell family and passed by marriage to the Cromwells, descendants of Thomas Cromwell, Henry VIII's minister.

Roadusers can reach the next section of the Manifold Valley only by making a long detour through Calton and Waterhouses (Chapter 5), but from Throwley Hall a path goes down into the valley just below its junction with that of the Hamps. Opposite, near this point, is the upstanding limestone crag of Beeston Tor (410354), with a cave in its foot where a hoard of ninth-century Saxon coins was found in 1924 by the Rev. G.H. Wilson.

The cart-road crossing the Hamps runs alongside the course of the Leek & Manifold Valley Light Railway. This interesting line, begun in 1896 and opened in 1904, was built mainly to carry away milk and other products from the farms around the valley. It had a gauge of only 2 feet 6 inches, and ran from Waterhouses (which was connected to Leek by a branch of the North Staffordshire Railway) down the Hamps Valley to the Manifold, then up that valley to Hulme End, on the road from Hartington to Bottom House. Though passengers were carried at holiday times, the railway was never a financial success; the farms were too inaccessible, and it arrived too late to combat the growing road traffic. It was closed in 1934, after which the Staffordshire County Council laid out two sections as a route for walkers and cyclists: from Waterhouses to a road below Wetton and from Swainsley to Hulme End (the intermediate section is accessible to cars).

At Weag's Bridge, above its junction with the Hamps, the Manifold is crossed by an excessively steep road connecting Grindon, above the west side of the valley, with Wetton, above the east side. Grindon (408354), an isolated village over 1000 feet up on the limestone uplands, is built round a wide, irregular green and has a church of 1831 with a prominent spire. In the south aisle is a memorial to eight men who lost their lives in 1947 when an aircraft crashed on the uplands while bringing food to the village, then cut off by a heavy fall of snow.

Wetton (410355) is another high-lying village, with some good sixteenth- and seventeenth-century houses and a Gothic church of 1820 attached to a fourteenth-century tower. The lane leading south-east is continued by a cart-road towards Long Low, a prehistoric monument that consists of two burial mounds, over 500 feet apart, joined by a straight, flat-topped bank, an arrangement not recorded elsewhere in England. This earthen bank, now standing some 4 to 6 feet high (and supporting a modern field wall), encloses a dry-stone wall against which large flat stones have been rested on either side. When the northern mound was excavated, an intact burial chamber was found containing the remains of 13 human skeletons, as well as the bones of oxen, pigs, deer and dogs. In the southern mound were traces of cremation, dating this monument to late in the New Stone Age, at the beginning of the next period, the Bronze Age (say about 1600 B.C.).

Another road descending from Wetton into the Manifold Valley affords a good view of Thor's Cave (409354), a gaping opening in a great limestone crag towering precipitously above the valley. Here in the mid-nineteenth century, Samuel Carrington, the schoolmaster of Wetton, found flint arrowheads, bone combs, bronze brooches and bracelets, iron adzes and Roman pottery ware (now mostly in the Sheffield City Museum). The road, reaching the valley floor, turns upstream to the beautifully situated eighteenth-century farm of Wetton Mill (409356). A mill was established here before 1577 by William Cavendish, second son of Bess of Hardwick, and it belonged to the Earls of Devonshire until at least 1617, but it was finally abandoned in 1857. In the hills around the Mill are many small limestone caves, some of which have only recently been excavated, and below the farm the Manifold begins the subterranean course which takes it down to Ilam Hall.

A steep road climbs out of the valley on its western side to Butterton (407356), another village over 1000 feet up on the limestone uplands, with a church of 1871 which has a distinctive spire. Motorists continuing up the Manifold Valley may choose either the old railway track on the west side of the river or the twisting farm-road on the other side. The railway track provides the easier route, though in my opinion it ought to be reserved for walkers and cyclists. The track passes through a tunnel to the farm of Swainsley, at the foot of another road from Butterton, and beyond this point motorists are excluded from the final section of the track to Hulme End.

On the east side of the valley rises Ecton Hill (409357; 1212 feet), long famous for its copper mines. These were probably first worked in the mid-seventeenth century, but the introduction of gunpowder, first used in the Mendips in 1684, led to a great increase in mining activity. By 1764 most of the rights belonged to the Duke of Devonshire and it is popularly believed that the Crescent at Buxton was built for the fifth Duke out of the profits of the mines. The ore is said to have contained about 15 per cent copper, and pure copper in 1785 made £86 per ton. Between 1776 and 1817, some 53,857 tons of copper ore, worth £677,112, were produced from the Duke of Devonshire's mines, with a profit of £244,734, or about £6000 a year.

About fifty miners were employed at Ecton, working six-hour shifts at 2d. an hour; the ore was broken with 'buckers' or flat-headed hammers by about fifty women, who were paid between 4d. and 8d. a day for piece-work. Girls between eight and twelve years old sorted the ore, and they were paid 2d. to 4d. a day.

Of the several copper mines sunk into the hill, the northermost was called Deep Ecton or Old Ecton. By the 1850s this was being worked in three vast hollows to a depth of 1380 feet from the top of the hill, one of the deepest mines in Europe. But between 1880 and 1900 most of the mines ceased working, and there are now over 1000 feet of disused levels below water, so that they are extremely dangerous to enter. One arched entrance opens into a large cavern, but what looks at first like the floor is in fact a great still pool of copper-green water covering a submerged shaft at least 960 feet deep.

Ecton Hill is a long ridge of the carboniferous limestone which has been thrown up in the shape of an arch, with its axis running north and south. Subsequent earth movements have caused folding of the rocks in many places, the most interesting being Apes Tor Quarry, at the north end, where the strata has the form of a letter 'V'. This is well seen from the road between the farm of Ecton and the hamlet of Hulme End (410359), near the place where the Manifold begins its long penetration of the limestone hills. At Hulme End the river is crossed by the road from Hartington to Bottom House, and a little to the west is the northern terminus of the Leek & Manifold Valley Railway. The engine shed and the ticket office and waiting room still survive here, and the railway is recalled also by the name of the inn beside the river.

Beyond Hulme End the Manifold flows through a more open, pastoral valley. The small village of Sheen (411361), to the east towards the Dove, has a church of 1852 by William Butterfield, a Victorian lover of medieval Gothic, who also designed the school and vicarage near by. Below Longnor (Chapter 8), the Manifold is less than a mile away from the Dove (though separated from it by a steep ridge), and from here onward the two rivers follow almost parallel courses, the Manifold rising below the Buxton-Leek road only half a mile from the source of the Dove.

7 The Valley of the Dove

The usual route from Ashbourne to Dovedale is to take the main Buxton road north out of the market place and to turn left on a by-road in a mile, crossing the Bentley Brook. This road ascends under the Tissington Trail (Chapter 9) and soon reaches the boundary of the Peak District National Park, the entrance to which is indicated (as it is on most main roads) by a symbol resembling a millstone (not a real millstone, as it has no hole in the middle). From beside the stone we can look over the charmingly wooded valley of the Dove and see the twin summits of Thorpe Cloud and Bunster straight ahead, standing guard over the entrance to Dovedale.

We turn left, leaving the old road towards Buxton beside the Dog & Partridge Inn, and drop down to Thorpe (415350), a characteristic limestone village perched high above the Dove. The lane passing the church, which has a Norman tower, is continued by a cart-track down to Coldwall Bridge. Though crossed by no more than the track, the bridge is broad and spacious, and in fact it dates from the time when the turnpike road from Leek to Wirksworth came this way, climbing up the hill to Thorpe.

Beyond the village rises the distinctive cone of Thorpe Cloud (942 feet), a limestone reef-formation which rises steeply on the east side of the Dove (Cloud comes from the Old English 'clud', meaning a rock or hill). From the craggy top we have a splendid view westward up the lower reach of the Manifold Valley to the village of Ilam, beyond which the Gothic turrets of Ilam Hall can be seen jutting out of the trees, in its superb amphitheatre of hills. Beyond the Dove, deep set in its valley, extends the long limestone ridge of Bunster, rising to just over 1000 feet, and to the right of this is an enticing view of the thickly wooded slopes above Dovedale. Farther to the right we can see, on a clear day, as far as the moorland dome of Axe Edge, where the Dove rises.

The stepping stones at the head of the lowest section of Dovedale can be reached by descending the steep north-west ridge of Thorpe Cloud. Most visitors, however, will take the road from Thorpe which crosses the Dove on its way to Ilam (Chapter 6), just above its junction with the Manifold. The Dove forms the boundary between Derbyshire and Staffordshire for the whole of its length from Axe Edge to the point where it flows into the Trent. From the bridge below Thorpe a short road (very busy in summer) runs up the west or Staffordshire bank of the river to the car park and the stepping stones.

Dovedale (414351) is the beautiful wooded ravine by which the river forces its way through the southern limestone of the Peak District, emerging at length between the hills of Bunster and Thorpe Cloud. "Was you ever in Dovedale?" Lord Byron wrote to his fellow-poet, Thomas Moore, "I assure you there are things in Derbyshire as noble as in Greece or Switzerland". (Byron was perhaps a little biased, as his home was at Newstead Abbey in neighbouring Nottinghamshire.)

Dovedale is by far the best known of the Peakland dales and it is fortunate that some 820 acres are now preserved by the National Trust. Being the most popular dale, it could become the most easily desecrated. Dovedale in fact is much too popular in summer for my taste; a better time to see it is in the fresh green of spring or in the autumn when the leaves are changing their tints and there is nowhere lovelier in the Peak District. But the best time of all, perhaps, is in the winter after a fall of snow, when there is hardly anyone about.

The Dove as a fishing stream needs no praise from me. It was first made famous by Charles Cotton, who lived near the river and who in 1676 added a second part to Izaak Walton's *The Compleat Angler*, published in 1653. The surface of the river is broken up by numerous little man-made weirs; these make cool, clear pools where the fish gather and also serve to aereate the water, which I am told helps the fishing.

Beyond the car park a footbridge crosses the river to a path which goes along the east bank of the Dove to the famous Stepping Stones, one of the most photographed places in the Peak District. The hills containing this lowest reach rise steeply on either hand, their green slopes breaking here and there into outcrops of the grey-white rock. The distance from the car park to Mill Dale, where the next road comes down, is nearly 3 miles, and the path ascends the Derbyshire bank all the way. From the stepping stones Thorpe can be regained round the north side of Thorpe Cloud by way of Lindale, which is rich with the yellow-flowered water-musk in summer.

At the stepping stones the dale makes a sharp right-angle bend round Dovedale Castle, the end of a long spur sent down by Bunster. As we walk up the dale we see curious spires and tors of the limestone which have been given fanciful names, such as the Twelve Apostles. In less than half a mile from the stepping stones the path climbs away from the river, up to the end of a long ridge known as Sharplow Point, sometimes called Lover's Leap, though I doubt whether anyone, however lovelorn, was so foolhardy as to attempt to leap across the valley from here. Upstream is a delightful view through the restricted dale, with the jagged rocks of Tissington Spires extending into it. Those who do not wish to explore the whole of the dale should proceed at least as far as Sharplow Point.

Beyond the Point the path descends to the river bank again, below the foot of the Spires, and a little farther on it passes below a great arch in the limestone rock of the dale side. This was once the mouth of Reynard's Cave, but the roof of the cave behind fell in some countless eons ago, so the mouth of the cave is now farther back in the hillside. Higher up on the Staffordshire side of the Dove is the beautifully shaped rock of Dovedale Church, with limestone spires springing from among the trees. The dale narrows to the Straits and, as the river contracts between rocks rising almost straight from the water, the path is little more than a rocky foothold, in flood time covered with water. We pass a rock which, when we look back, bears a marked resemblance to a lion's head. Beyond this we approach the handsomest group of rocks in the dale, known as Pickering Tor, a great rounded bastion of limestone with five distinct projecting points. Facing these is Ilam Rock, a tall, detached needle-shaped rock, standing up out of a deep pool in the Dove. It looks inaccessible, but it has been climbed.

Beyond the rock, on the Staffordshire side, the woods give way and the tributary Hall Dale comes in on that side. The Dove now bends sharply to the right and the narrow ravine we have been following is transformed. In front of us rises a noble hill with a fine serrated edge, called The Nabs, and farther on we come to the Dove Holes, two great arched recesses in the rocky hillside, the larger having a span of 55 feet and a height of about 30 feet. The holes are shallow and have obviously been hollowed out with the assistance of the rushing Dove.

From the Dove Holes a steep track climbs up Nabs Dale on the east towards the Ashbourne-Buxton high road. The track winds between wooded crags, affording half way up a pretty view across to Alstonfield church, on the Staffordshire uplands. It leads to Hanson Grange, an old farmstead with a recorded history of over six centuries. In 1240, Roger de Huncedone gave all his property here to the Benedictine monks of Burton Abbey (on the Trent), who were also owners of the neighbouring Bostern Grange.

After its short, sharp twist by the Dove Holes, the river turns north again, rounding Raven's Tor, one of the finest and broadest of the limestone crags, and runs through a more open valley for Milldale (413354), where the path crosses the river by Viator's Bridge, a seventeenth-century packhorse bridge. "What's here?" says that character in *The Compleat Angler*, "the sign of a bridge? Do you use to travel with wheel-barrows in this county? . . . This bridge was certainly made for nothing else. Why! a mouse can hardly go over it; it is but two fingers broad." Certainly one cannot attempt to drive a car over it, which is perhaps just as well.

Mill Dale is, strictly speaking, the name of this section of the Dove valley, but Milldale is the name given to the hamlet beyond the bridge, where Hopedale comes down on the left from the direction of Alstonfield. Here we meet the first road since leaving that between Thorpe and Ilam; it turns up the dale and in fact is the only road traversing the dale between Thorpe and Hartington. About half a mile on is Lode Mill, where the Dove is crossed by the road leading down from the direction of Alsop-en-le-Dale (Chapter 9) and climbing out on the other side for Alstonfield.

Alstonfield (413355) is sometimes spelt (as on the Ordnance Survey map) Alstonefield, but the name was formerly 'AElfstan's Feld' (or tract of open country) and had nothing to do with 'stone', though there is plenty of that around. The village has attractive limestone houses, scattered round a green, and a church which has a Norman chancel arch but is mainly in the Perpendicular style of the fifteenth century. The walls show a curious chequerboard pattern made up of blocks of the local limestone interspersed with a red or yellow sandstone that must have come from some distance away to the south. The church has a wealth of seventeenth-century box-pews, with their original brasswork, and a fine two-tier pulpit of 1637, but the main object of interest is the seventeenth-century carved and panelled pew of Charles Cotton, the poet-angler. This stands at the east end of the north aisle, presumably not in its original position, unless Cotton had it placed here so that he could take a nap during a boring sermon.

In the churchyard is a fragment of a tenth-century cross-shaft, with interlace decoration, and across the way can be seen the Manor House, with the date of 1587 on the two-storey porch. The nineteenth-century school, beyond the green, has a modern extension showing the use of small pieces of broken limestone cemented together into blocks (they are made near Bakewell). These are now permitted by the Peak Park Planning Board in lieu of solid limestone blocks, which are indeed now unobtainable.

From Lode Mill we resume the turfy path beside the Dove, still on the Derbyshire bank. The valley bottom is wider than in the lower part of Dovedale and the dale is less thickly wooded, but the sides are just as steep, the limestone crags lining the dale are just as fine, and the open views are perhaps finer. Here and there are falls of small pieces of rock, broken off from the crags above; these are called 'screes' in the Lake District but 'slitherbanks' locally.

Below Iron Tors a track ascends a short but steep dale on the east to Coldeaton (414356), a farm on the site of a 'deserted village', one from which the unfortunate inhabitants were cleared out in the Middle Ages, probably because the surrounding lands were taken over by monastic overlords as sheep runs. Near Drabber Tor, farther on in the dale, another steep valley comes in on the same side, Biggin Dale, where the screes are coloured with herb-robert in summer. The main dale, too, is rich in wild flowers; meadow sweet, meadow crane's bill and many others. Wolfscote Hill (1272 feet), a National Trust property between Biggin Dale and the main dale, commands a splendid view into and down the Dove.

Beyond Drabber Tor the Dove penetrates the delightful Wolfscote Dale (413357), with steep rocky sides and a narrow valley floor. In the crag on the east near the north end of the dale is a small cave where Charles Cotton is said to have hid when he was being pursued by his creditors, which happened pretty often. Then the path, leaving the limestone gorge, crosses a broad meadow to reach the end of a lane at the foot of Beresford Dale (412358), about 3 miles above Lode Mill.

The next section of the path runs through a densely-wooded little ravine, with a succession of tiny weirs set close together across the river. In the depths of the trees is Pike Pool, made famous by Walton and Cotton, named not from its fish, however, but from a tapering spire of limestone which stands up out of the pool on the Derbyshire side. Near the north end of this dale, but completely hidden among the trees and quite inaccessible, is the famous Fishing House, built by Charles Cotton, who no doubt entertained Izaak Walton here with fishing stories. Over the doorway is the inscription 'Piscatoribus Sacrum 1674', with the initials 'I.W.C.C.', entwined in a monogram.

Charles Cotton was born in 1630 at Beresford Hall, on the west side of the dale, and spent most of his life here. He is best known for his addition to *The Compleat Angler* of his friend Walton, but he also made a fine translation of Montaigne's Essays and he was a sensitive poet revelling in the beauties of the dale: "O my beloved nymph, fair Dove, Princess of rivers, how I love, Upon they flowery banks to lie, And view thy silver stream, When gilded by a summer's beam;..." He also wrote a long and rather tedious poem called 'The Wonders of the Peake', describing Poole's Cavern, St Anne's Well at Buxton, the Tides-well, Eldon Hole, Mam Tor, Peak Cavern and Chatsworth. Cotton planted the woods around Beresford Dale, but he was forced to sell the Hall in 1681 and he died in London in 1687. The house was pulled down in 1856 and only fragments now remain, on private ground.

The path, emerging from the woods of Beresford Dale, where there is just a glimpse of the Fishing House, crosses the fields to Hartington (412360), a pleasant village mainly built round a large open space, once the market place, in a rich agricultural district. The Earl Ferrers was granted a charter as long ago as 1203 and Hartington is one of the oldest market centres in the Peak District. The Market Hall was rebuilt in a modified classical style in 1836, but Hartington has now lost its market. It has some good houses of the eighteenth and early nineteenth centuries, built in the local limestone, and towards the river is a large factory making Stilton cheese.

Hartington was once the centre of an enormous parish stretching beyond Buxton on to the moors. The church, above the village, is mostly of the late thirteenth century, but it has a fifteenth century tower and an unusual porch, and in the south transept is a remarkable thirteenth-century effigy of a lady, shown as though she were in her coffin, with only her head and feet appearing. A lane climbs up from the village to Hartington Hall, built in 1611 by the Bateman family (well known in Derbyshire archaeological circles) and now a youth hostel. Though considerably restored, it is an excellent example of the seventeenth century vernacular architecture of the Peak District, built of limestone but with a gritstone slab roof.

Beyond Hartington the valley of the Dove opens out to a wider strath for a distance. One gets the impression that the valley may once have been blocked near the head of Beresford Dale and if so, this section would have been covered by a broad lake. A narrow lane ascends the Derbyshire side to the farm of Pilsbury (411363), beyond which are the mounds of a Norman-type 'motte-and-bailey' castle of which absolutely nothing seems to be known. The

The Valley of the Dove

castle would appear to have had two baileys or courtyards but no motte, the place of this being taken by a curious upstanding knob of the limestone. The valley is ascended by footpath as far as Crowdecote (410365), or Crowdicote, a hamlet whose old inn, the Packhorse, still preserves a pack saddle inside.

The road crossing to the Staffordshire side of the Dove ascends to Longnor (Chapter 8), that on the Derbyshire side climbs up between the hills of Aldery Cliff and High Wheeldon (1383 feet). This distinctively conical hill was given to the nation as a memorial to the men of Derbyshire and Staffordshire who fell in the Second World War, and then made over to the National Trust. Aldery Cliff is the first of a line of reef-formations that extends westward to Parkhouse Hill and Chrome Hill.

Hidden away in a little valley behind these is the quarrying village of Earl Sterndale (409367), with a curious inn name, the Quiet Woman (why is she 'quiet'? Well, she has lost her head!). The nineteenth-century church, incredibly bombed during the War, has since been restored; it retains its crudely-shaped font, which is possibly Saxon. From the road above the village an enticing view opens towards the upper Dove, with the sharp ridges of Parkhouse Hill and Chrome Hill seen in profile, and the long swelling moorland of Axe Edge beyond. The road crosses the course of the Cromford and High Peak Railway (Chapter 12) before leading out to the main Ashbourne-Buxton road.

8 The Western Moorlands

Longnor (408365), on a steep ridge between the Dove and the Manifold at the point where the rivers come closest together, is an upland village many of whose houses are built of gritstone and retain their stone-slab roofs. This indicates that we are about to leave the rich green fields of the limestone country for the darker moorlands of the gritstone. On the market hall of 1873 is a board giving the tolls that were in force in 1903, but Longnor (like Hartington) has now lost its market. In the churchyard behind can be found the gravestone of William Billinge, who took part in the capture of Gibraltar in 1704, served in the campaigns of the Duke of Marlborough and died in 1791 (it is said) at the age of 112. "Billeted by Death, I quartered here remain, When the trumpet sounds I'll rise and march again."

The Buxton road, running north from Longnor, crosses the upper Dove valley to Glutton Grange, a fine three-storeyed farmhouse of 1675. It ascends a short steep dale between Hitter Hill and Parkhouse Hill (408367), a striking example of a reef-formation with a jagged edge, to join the road from Earl Sterndale (Chapter 7). In Dowel Dale, farther west between Parkhouse Hill and Chrome Hill, is a cave where finds of the New Stone Age have been made.

Roads on the south side of the upper Dove valley provide us with views of Parkhouse Hill and the long serrated edge of Chrome Hill (407367; pronounced 'Croom'), reaching over 1200 feet, the last of the long series of reef-formations on the Derbyshire side of the valley. Chrome Hill is obviously limestone, from its distinctive outcrops, but Hollins Hill, the next hill westward, is of gritstone, so here we are on the boundary between the two formations. This is evident, too, from the field walls in this neighbourhood, which change quite suddenly from limestone to gritstone. Because the stone for these walls is taken out of the ground in the immediate vicinity, they are always a sure indication, when no outcrops are visible, of what kind of rock is below the surface.

The roads south of the Dove converge on Hollinsclough (406366; pronounced '-cluf'), a secluded hamlet charmingly placed at the head of the valley, where the hills begin to close in again. The small church (unfortunately now derelict) and the attached school were built in 1840 under a single sandstone roof. Behind, by way of contrast, is the modern pre-fabricated school.

The road climbs steeply west of Hollinsclough, above the head waters of the Dove, which push through a deep ravine (the 'clough' from which the village takes its name). The river then skirts the hillside above the head reaches of the Manifold, which rises just below the Buxton-Leek road near the white Traveller's Rest, which at about 1500 feet is the third highest inn in England. (The highest is the Tan Hill Inn, on the lonely moorlands between Swaledale and Teesdale, in the North Riding; the second is the Cat and Fiddle Inn, which we shall pass later on.)

The source of the river Dove is less than half a mile to the north of the inn, just below the whitewashed farm of Dove Head (403368), on the Buxton road near the point where it crosses the county boundary. The road skirts the long, exposed moorland ridge of Axe Edge (403370), whose highest point (1810 feet) affords a wide view over Buxton and the upper valley of the Wye. This moorland country is the nursing mother of five rivers, for not only do the Dove, the Manifold and the Wye rise here (and flow towards the North Sea), but also the Dane and the Goyt (which empty their waters into the Irish Sea). The north flank of the moor is crossed by another road from Buxton, one branch of which runs south-west for the Dane Valley and Congleton, while the other turns away westward for the Cat and Fiddle Inn and Macclesfield.

To the south of the Traveller's Rest a by-road turns off for Flash (402367), sometimes still given its older name of Quarnford, which is 1525 feet up on the edge of the moors and the highest village in England, or at least the village with the highest parish church (founded in 1744, but rebuilt in

1901). The village has given its name to the term 'flash', meaning counterfeit money. Over a mile across the hills to the north-west, and reached by devious farm-tracks, are the Three Shire Heads (401368), a delightful spot where a bridge crosses the Dane just below a pool where Staffordshire, Derbyshire and Cheshire meet. This was a haunt of coiners and other malefactors in the last century, and as the police could then only act within their own county, the lawbreakers could easily escape capture by crossing into the next county.

The Leek road goes on southward, passing the uninviting Royal Cottage Inn (402364), the fourth in altitude in England, at just below 1500 feet. (The Traveller's Rest, on the Kirkstone Pass in the Lake District, often claimed to be the highest inn, comes fifth at about 1450 feet.) On the right farther south are the Ramshaw Rocks (401362), the first and most accessible of a long series of gritstone edges, where the outcrops or tors have been weathered into fantastic shapes. From the hamlet of Upper Hulme, a by-road on the right skirts the foot of Hen Cloud (400361), a solid mass of the gritstone rising to about 1250 feet and the most impressive of the series of outcrops. Farther on are The Roaches (400363) or Roches (a name perhaps derived from the French for rocks), with a tumbled escarpment over a mile and a half long whose skyline resembles the battlements of a huge fortress. From the summit ridge (1658 feet), which has more weathered rocks of curious shapes, there is a wide view over the moorland country to the north. The marshy ground to the east of the ridge is whitened in summer with cotton-grass.

The Black Brook, to the north of The Roaches, flows down a rugged moorland glen to join the Dane below the farm of Gradbach. In the hillside to the south just below the junction of the streams is a remarkable chasm known as Ludchurch (398365) or Lud's Church, shut in by towering rock walls, hung with moss and fern, and hardly 20 feet apart at the top. The name is thought once to have been Lollard, and the followers of the reformer John Wycliffe are supposed to have gathered secretly here. Tracks and lanes to the west of The Roaches take us down towards Swythamley Park (pronounced 'Swith-'), where the late eighteenth-century

Sheldon, Magpie Mine

Haddon Hall

house is hidden away in a well-timbered deer park. Wallabies introduced on the estate by Sir Philip Brocklehurst began to escape in 1938 and these graceful but very timid animals can occasionally be seen running wild on the moorlands as far east as Hen Cloud.

At Danebridge our road crosses the narrow valley of the Dane into Cheshire before ascending towards Wincle Grange (395365), a farmhouse part of which at least seems by its windows to date back to the fourteenth century and is therefore one of the few medieval secular buildings in the Peak District. Beyond the hamlet of Wincle our road meets the main road from Congleton to Buxton. Hidden in a clump of trees to the left here is Cleulow Cross (395367), the tall round shaft of a Saxon cross of the eleventh century.

The Buxton road descends steeply across the Clough Brook for Allgreave (397367), from which a road and foot-track go on into the beautiful upper reaches of the Dane Valley to reach Three Shire Heads, among the gritstone moorlands. The valley is believed to be the setting of the medieval romance of *Sir Gawain and the Green Knight*.

In the deep-set valley of the Clough Brook, north of the Buxton road, is the secluded hamlet of Wildboarclough (398368), which has a red sandstone 'Edwardian Gothic' church of 1904. The post office below this occupies part of the three-storeyed Crag Mill, a cotton mill built about 1770 and therefore one of the earliest in the Peak, while the early nineteenth-century Crag Hall, higher up, was the home of the mill manager. Beside the bridge over the brook are the foundations of a textile mill (demolished in 1957), where James Brindley installed the machinery, and near by is a row of early mill-workers' houses with Gothic windows.

The road passing these ascends the valley below the distinctive conical hill of Shutlingslow (1659 feet), the top of which (not easy of access) commands a fine moorland view. The road climbs to the east of Macclesfield Forest, a tract of moorland now partly afforested and with some pleasant little reservoirs in the upper valley of the Bollin. The forest, created by the Norman Earls of Chester, became a royal possession in 1237 and the kings of England came here to hunt in the fourteenth century.

The hamlet of Macclesfield Forest (397372), near the head of the Clough Brook, has the second highest parish church in England, at a height of 1300 feet. It was built in 1673, but was much restored in 1834. A colourful Rushbearing Festival (the only one, I think, outside Westmorland) is held here on the second Sunday in August. This is a reminder of the time when the earthen floor of the church was strewn with rushes, to be replaced by new ones every summer.

The road from Wildboarclough comes out on the Macclesfield-Buxton road, which winds steeply up to the east to reach the highest part of the somewhat bleak moorland at the Cat and Fiddle Inn (400371), which at 1690 feet is the second highest licensed house in England. The uninterrupted view westward over Cheshire extends in clear weather to the Mersey estuary, to the Welsh mountains as far away as Snowdon (most easily distinguished when it is snow capped) and even to the hills of Shropshire and the Welsh border in the south-west. Shining Tor (1834 feet), not a tor in the geological sense, but a long ridge stretching to the north, is the highest part of Cheshire, which is usually regarded as being a 'flat' county, a myth fostered by the use of the term 'Cheshire Plain' in the geography books.

The Buxton road, going on east from the Cat and Fiddle, enters Derbyshire just beyond the source of the Dane. On the other side, the old road to Buxton (which farther on becomes a fine moorland track) descends towards the head waters of the river Goyt. Starting above Derbyshire Bridge (401371), another road follows the river, which has cut a deep trench into the gritstone and the overlying coal measures here. It is difficult to realise that coal was once worked (though on a small scale) in this beautiful moorland area. Under a scheme successfully adopted in 1970 by the Peak Park Planning Board, no cars are allowed at weekends or on bank holidays in summer on the stretch of road down to the dam of the Errwood Reservoir. Minibus services operate from the car park above Derbyshire Bridge as far as Goytsclough Quarry and along the shore of the reservoir, but the intervening section of the road is closed to traffic, so that walkers can enjoy this part of the upper Goyt valley free of the stench of petrol fumes.

The Errwood Reservoir (401374), constructed in the valley by the Stockport Corporation and now a popular sailing venue, takes it name from Errwood Hall, built in 1830 for the Grimshawe family but allowed to fall into ruin when the estate was taken over for the reservoir. Its beautiful grounds, rising west of the valley, contain some fine trees, but are best seen in May, when the rhododendrons are a blaze of colour. Below the dam of the Errwood Reservoir is the attractive Fernilee Reservoir (401377), with steep wood-fringed shores. It is significant of the times that the Fernilee, opened in 1938, cost £480,000, but the slightly smaller Errwood, completed in 1967, cost £1½ million, or over three times as much.

The road ascending steeply from the east side of the Errwood dam follows the course of the Cromford and High Peak Railway (Chapter 12). The equally steep road on the other side, known as The Street (I wonder why?), crosses the moorland ridge north of Cats Tor (1703 feet) and goes down to Jenkin Chapel (398376), an isolated and unspoiled little church of 1733 with square secular-looking windows (and a chimney) and its original fittings (box-pews, pulpit and reading-desk), and a saddleback tower added in 1755. Saltersford Hall, to the south, is a rambling farmhouse of 1593, much altered later.

From the Windgather Rocks (appropriately named) near the north end of the Cats Tor ridge, a lane goes down to Kettleshulme (398379), a village of gritstone houses on the road from Whaley Bridge (Chapter 19). We can turn along this towards Macclesfield, then bear off by a quiet road crossing the moors south of Lyme Park. We descend to Pott Shrigley (394379), an attractive little village on the western flanks of the Peak, with a fine church of the fourteenth and fifteenth centuries.

Roads go on south-west to Bollington (393377), a long straggling town in the upper valley of the Dean, a tributary of the Bollin. It has cotton and paper mills, textile printing and dye works, and is bisected by the Macclesfield Canal, still used by pleasure craft. To the south, skirted by a narrow road leading to the Whaley Bridge-Macclesfield road, is the long hill of Kerridge (394376), which has large gritstone quarries long noted for their roofing slabs. The white stone pyramid at the north end, known as White Nancy, was put up about 1820 to commemorate the victory of Waterloo; it affords a view towards the moors on one hand, over the Cheshire Plain on the other, and north to Manchester and the moors beyond. Rainow (395376), a village on the Macclesfield-Whaley Bridge road to the south-east, has old gritstone houses nearly all of which have roofs of gritstone slabs from Kerridge.

9 The Tissington Trail

The Tissington Trail is a route for walkers and horse-riders on the course of part of the former Ashbourne-Buxton railway. Ashbourne was the terminal station from 1852 of a branch of the North Staffordshire Railway, familiarly known as 'The Knotty' (the knot is part of the Staffordshire crest). After this line was taken over by the London and North Western Railway Company, it was extended northward for Buxton. The engineer was Francis Stephenson and the railway was opened in 1899. The very attractive route climbed up on to the limestone uplands, with stations at Thorpe, Tissington, Alsop-en-le-Dale and Hartington, beyond which it went on to join the Cromford and High Peak Railway (Chapter 12) near Parsley Hay.

The railway was built mainly to carry away limestone and milk from the uplands, but passenger services were also operated and in fact the line became part of a through route from London to Manchester. These services ceased in 1954, though excursions for tourists continued until 1963, when the railway was closed as far as Hartington; the section from there to Parsley Hay remained open until 1967, after which the rails were removed.

The track was bought by the Peak Park Planning Board in 1968 from British Rail, and the Trail was opened in 1971 between Mapleton Lane and Hartington Station, a distance of 11½ miles; the further section of a mile and a half to Parsley Hay was opened in the following year. The track has been grassed over to make walking and riding easier, except north of Hartington station where the original ash bed has been retained. All the derelict station buildings have been pulled down, except for the signal box at Hartington, and their sites are now mostly car parks and picnic places. In 1973 a motor-bus service was inaugurated on Sunday afternoons in summer linking up the car parks (except that at Parsley Hay).

The Tissington Trail starts at the Mapleton Lane car park, less than half a mile from Ashbourne by the road to Mapleton (Chapter 6). To the south of this point the railway penetrated a hill by a tunnel which is now blocked. We shall follow the trail northward to its junction with the Cromford and High Peak Railway (now the 'High Peak' Trail), but will make divergences to visit interesting places near the route. Motorists can reach these just as easily (if less pleasantly) from the main Ashbourne-Buxton road, which follows a more or less parallel course to the trail.

The road runs north from Ashbourne, reaching the boundary of the Peak District National Park beyond Sandybrook Hall, then crosses the Bentley Brook to Fenny Bentley (417350), a cluster of attractive cottages in the valley. The Old Hall (now called Cherry Orchard Farm) is an early seventeenth-century manor house of the Beresford family, joined on to a late medieval tower house resembling the pele-towers of the English-Scottish border, but the only one of its kind in the Peak District. The church, much renewed and enlarged, has an elegant (if restored) early sixteenth-century chancel screen, with a coved beam, and the unique alabaster tomb of Thomas Beresford, who died in 1473. He and his wife lie in effigy in their shrouds, tied up at head and feet, and their sixteen sons and five daughters, all of whom predeceased them, are incised in similar fashion on the sides of the tomb.

The Tissington Trail from Mapleton Lane crosses the Bentley Brook by a seven-arched viaduct, 200 feet long, and, passing through some attractive pastoral scenery, enters the National Park in a mile and a quarter. The site of Thorpe Station (which has no car park) is a mile farther on, below the Dog & Partridge Inn and about halfway between Thorpe (Chapter 7) and Fenny Bentley, which can be reached by field path. The route crosses the Ashbourne-Buxton road as it climbs to the limestone plateau from Fenny Bentley and goes on to the next station, just east of Tissington.

Tissington (417352). approached from the main road by an avenue of pollarded limes, stakes a high claim to be the prettiest village in the Peak District and is famous for its well-dressing festival. The Fitzherbert family, long one of the most powerful in Derbyshire, have been here since the fifteenth century, and Tissington is very much the 'estate' village. A wide green stretches up from the much-photographed pond, with the old village school facing the lower end, the Hall on the one side of the green and the church standing on a rise looking over to it.

The limestone houses, mainly arranged in small groups around the green and the pond, were mostly built between 1830 and 1860 by the Fitzherberts. The Vicarage, on the west side at the foot of the green, is a good eighteenth-century house, while Old Church House opposite is characteristic of the seventeenth century. It has a roof of 'blue tiles' from Staffordshire which began to replace the stone slabs by the early nineteenth century.

The church, basically Norman, has a squat tower, a south doorway with a sculptured tympanum and a chancel arch of the twelfth century, and the tub-shaped font, carved with animals and human figures is also Norman (Dr Pevsner thinks it 'very barbaric'). The north aisle with its arcade were added in 1854 in what the Victorians thought was a good imitation of the Norman style. The church has an unusual two-decker pulpit and altar rails of the late sixteenth century and a wall monument, partly blocking the chancel arch, to Francis Fitzherbert, builder of the Hall, and his son Sir John (who died in 1642), facing their wives across prayer desks in typical Jacobean fashion. Other Fitzherberts are commemorated in the chancel but not the most famous of them, Maria, the wife (though not the queen) of George IV, who is buried at Brighton, where her monument shows her with three wedding rings on her finger.

Tissington Hall, set back behind a walled garden (best seen when the daffodils are out), was built in 1609 and is unusual in Peakland manor houses in having no gables; it has instead a battlemented parapet, as well as a two-storeyed porch with the arms of the Fitzherberts. The principal room downstairs runs right though the house from front to back, an unusual arrangement, but paralleled by the slightly earlier entrance hall at Hardwick Hall, built in 1591-97, though one would hesitate to ascribe the Hall at Tissington to Robert Smythson, the architect of Hardwick, on these grounds alone. The stable block to the south of the hall is contemporary, but considerable additions were made to the house itself between 1896 and about 1910.

Tissington is celebrated for its old custom of well-dressing, the first of the season in the Peak District. The custom is thought by some to have originated in the mid-fourteenth century, when the purity of the water from the limestone saved the village from the ravages of the plague known as the Black Death. Others say that it started in the early seventeenth century, as a thanksgiving for the never failing supply of water from the wells during a great drought.

Five wells are dressed at Tissington: the Hall Well, opposite the Hall, the Hands Well at the top of the street, the Yew Tree Well near the school, the Town Well to the east of the pond, and the Coffin Well (so called from its shape) in the back road east of the green. The ceremony starts on Ascension Day, but visitors going along to Tissington from the previous Monday onwards can usually see the wooden boards being prepared for their natural mosaics. Several boards are used for each well, a back-board for the main subject and head and side boards for subsidiary designs. The subject is decided on beforehand by the well dressers (usually several working on each board) and the design is marked out on white paper. Then, on the Monday at Tissington, the boards are covered with a thick layer of soft clay, smoothed over the boards and pressed firmly down, while being kept moist with water. The boards are then set up on trestles, the paper with the design is stretched face up over the clay, and the design is pricked through on to the clay surface.

Meanwhile the materials for making the mosaic are being collected. Any natural materials are allowed and these consist usually of the petals of wild flowers (or garden flowers, which last longer), leaves, reeds, moss and lichen, pieces of bark, alder cones (called 'black knobs' locally), rhubarb and other seeds, sheep's wool and even human hair; but materials that are not natural are frowned on. These being collected, the papers are lifted from the clay, the design is marked out clearly using alder cones, rhubarb seeds, other hard seeds, or lichen, and the lengthy work begins of filling in the pattern with the petals, etc., using the thumb or a small tool to press them into position, and working from the bottom upwards, so that the petals overlap like the slates on a roof (and for the same reason, to shed the rain).

All this work naturally takes some time; at Tissington, three days, but at Eyam (the last place in the Peak to hold its festival) one well-dressing group works all night preparing the boards before the ceremony. Scriptural scenes are preferred for the main designs, especially those referring to the gift of water, and the head-board usually carries a text from the Bible. But no hard and fast rules are laid down about what subjects should be portrayed: the designer of the Hands Well frequently introduces some modern theme; at Tideswell the principal well-dressing always portrays an English cathedral (a different one each year); and at Eyam in 1966 the chief dressing commemorated the great plague. Youlgreave often introduces a topical theme, and at Wirksworth one year a 'Ban the Bomb' scene was portrayed. The only golden rule is that nothing but natural materials should be used in the dressing.

The boards with their completed dressings are manoeuvred into position over or behind the requisite well on the morning of the ceremony. At Tissington on Ascension Day the wells may truthfully be said to be flowering. A service is held in the church (invariably crowded for the occasion) and this is followed by a visit to each well in turn, where a hymn or psalm is sung, a prayer is offered and the never-failing water is blessed by the clergy. The dressings usually stay in position for a week and they are viewed by a great concourse of people, some of whom come by car or coach from places well over a hundred miles away. If you want to see Tissington (but not the well-dressing), this is assuredly *not* the time to come.

Newton Grange (416353), in the angle between the Buxton road and the Tissington Trail, north of the village, is one of no less than fifty farmsteads in the Peak District to bear the suffix 'grange'. This dates from the Middle Ages, when great areas of the Peak were vast 'ranches' for sheep (and later, cattle) mostly owned by monastic overlords, many of them living some distance away. Newton Grange was owned by Combermere Abbey (in Cheshire), Hanson Grange and Bostern Grange near by belonged to Burton Abbey (in Staffordshire) and One Ash Grange near Lathkill Dale to Roche Abbey (in Yorkshire), while Dunstable Priory (in Bedfordshire) had a grange at Bradbourne.

With the dissolution of the monasteries in the 1530s, the lands all passed into private hands (Newton Grange came to the Beresfords), and this may explain to some extent the large number of manor houses and farmhouses in the Peak built from 1540 onwards. Other lands belonged in the Middle Ages to the Crown (especially in the Royal Forest of the Peak) or to the Duchy of Lancaster, which maintained over 5000 sheep in the Hartington area in the fourteenth century.

The Tissington Trail runs parallel with the road to the site of Alsop Station, with a good view to the east over the charmingly-wooded limestone uplands and into the valley which contains Alsop-en-le-Dale (416355). This consists only of a few farms, a restored church whose Norman doorway has unusual moulding in the form of a double chevron or zigzag, and a Hall of the seventeenth century which is remarkable in having a pair of tall gables, facing the sheltered garden.

The lane from Alsop goes on down the valley to Parwich (418354; pronounced 'Par-wij'), a village embowered in orchards and with good eighteenth-century houses round the green and along the main street. The church by the green, rebuilt in 1873, retains from the Norman period a carved tympanum, now over the west doorway, and the chancel arch, now under the tower. The medieval-looking font, also possibly Norman, has the date 1662 carved on it. Parwich Hall, dominating the village from the upper end, was built in 1747 and is remarkable in having a brick façade, stone being used only for the structural features. It must have cost more to make and cart the bricks here than to dig out the local limestone, and I can only assume this was done because brick had become fashionable by this time.

The section of the Tissington Trail from Alsop to Hartington is perhaps the finest from the walker's point of view. Passing under the Buxton road, it runs within half a

The Tissington Trail

mile of Dovedale and of the farmstead of Coldeaton (Chapter 7); it then traverses the Coldeaton Cutting, three-quarters-of-a-mile long and some 60 feet deep. Biggin (415359), a small village on the left farther on, has some seventeenth- and eighteenth-century houses. It lies in the parish of Hartington Nether Quarter, a relic of the days when a great tract of country extending from here to beyond Buxton belonged to the Duchy of Lancaster.

The Buxton road, running more or less parallel to the east, is joined by the old turnpike road from Nottingham, via Matlock, beyond the Newhaven House Inn (416360), a large colour-washed inn built about 1800 for the Duke of Devonshire. A road on the left farther on descends through Hand Dale to Hartington (Chapter 7), passing under a fine bridge which carries the Tissington Trail north of Hartington Station (414361), where the signal box is now the only survival. The Trail goes on to Parsley Hay (414363; not named on the Ordnance Survey map), short of which it joins the course of the Cromford and High Peak Railway (the 'High Peak' Trail; Chapter 12).

10   From Ashbourne to Wirksworth

The road from Ashbourne north-east to Wirksworth lies outside the boundary of the Peak District National Park, but it follows the interesting course of the Roman road of Hereward Street and it provides access to several places on the limestone country which I think ought to have been included in the national park. Hereward Street (not indicated on the Ordnance Survey map of Roman Britain) ran from Rocester up the west or Staffordshire bank of the Dove, crossed the river below Ashbourne, then struck across country to join Rykneld Street at Chesterfield, where the Roman settlement has recently been discovered.

Hereward Street did for the Peak District and its neighbourhood what the Fosse Way did for Britain as a whole; it linked up a number of other roads, all striking out from the local commercial centre of *Derventio* at Little Chester (Derby). 'Ward', according to R.W.P. Cockerton, the authority on Roman roads in Derbyshire, means 'watch', and 'Here' means 'army' (as in Hereford, the 'ford of the army'). So Hereward Street means 'army watch' street, and what would the army be watching over in this part of the Peak if not the lead mining industry, already important in Roman times. It seems very likely, therefore, that the Street would also take in the lead mining centre of *Lutudarum*.

The road ascends from Ashbourne to The Green (418347), the common land of the town before the Enclosure Act. Green Hall, on the north side, has a delightful brick façade of the early eighteenth century that apparently conceals an earlier timber-framed structure. The road goes on through Kniveton (421350), which has a characteristic limestone inn, the Red Lion, with a roof of blue tiles. The small church, much restored, has a Norman south doorway and an Early English tower.

A road on the left farther on descends into a valley at Netherton (422352), which has a Hall of 1684 with Peakland vernacular features (string courses around the walls and so on), then climbs out to Bradbourne (420352), a small village on a hill above the Ashbourne-Bakewell road as it ascends the valley of the Bradbourne Brook. The church has a fine Norman tower, with much-weathered carvings, and a nave arcade of about 1300, with unusual keeled piers. On the south wall inside is a painted inscription of the seventeenth century. In the churchyard is the shaft of a Saxon (or Mercian) cross of about A.D. 800. This was once in three separate pieces and has unfortunately been ill-used, so that much of the carving is badly worn, but the spiral decoration which can be seen on all crosses of this period stands clear.

The late sixteenth-century Bradbourne Hall, close by, has an array of gables in the Peakland manner and a good Jacobean staircase. It stands on the site of a grange of Dunstable Priory and was later the home of the Buckston family, one of whom fought at the Battle of Culloden in 1746. One of the houses of the Bradbourne family, who held the manor from the thirteenth century onward, was Lea Hall, now a farmstead, on the other side of the valley, near a lane crossing to Tissington. Beside the road near the ford here is an old corn mill whose machinery is still in good working order.

The Bakewell road, following the boundary of the national park, ascends on to the limestone plateau, and passes between the huge quarry near Ballidon (420354), which has a small (and over-restored) Norman church, and the jagged Rainster Rocks (422354), where prehistoric finds have been made.

Farther east is Brassington (323354), an old lead-mining centre (as we are reminded by the inn, the Miners' Arms) and now a quarrying village. The church, in a steeply sloping graveyard, has a tower and nave and chancel arcades all of the twelfth century. The porch is probably of the thirteenth century, as indicated by the Early English moulding of the arch, though this still has the round form associated with Norman work. The village, stretched out on the slope of the limestone hills, has some good houses of the seventeenth and eighteenth centuries. One whose gable end faces the inn still has a stone slab roof, but most of the others have roofs of blue tiles, sometimes called 'Staffordshire blues', introduced from the Potteries by the beginning of the nineteenth century, as recorded by John Farey in his great work on the agriculture, minerals and industries of Derbyshire, which he compiled in 1808-11. In colour and texture these tiles fit in well with the limestone walls, but they are now, unfortunately, beginning to be ousted (especially on modern houses) by cement tiles. Two contrasting examples of modern bungalows with cement tiles can be seen above the Bradbourne road. Tudor House, at the foot of the main street, is dated 1615 and is a fair example of a Peakland manor house, though not improved by its red-tiled roof.

The 'High Peak' Trail (Chapter 12) runs to the north of Brassington, skirting the foot of Harborough Rocks (424355; 1244 feet), which rises in terraces of weathered limestone commanding a wide view. Near the west end, behind the refractory brick works, is a cave which was occupied during the Early Iron Age and again during Roman times. The prefix 'Har' has apparently the same meaning as 'Here', and 'borough' originally meant a 'fortified place', so Harborough means the 'fortified place of the army'. Why did an army want a fortified place, if not to keep control over the lead workings? No 'fortified place', incidentally, has yet come to light, though I keep looking for one!

The road following the route of Hereward Street descends to Carsington (425353), a village with eighteenth-century limestone houses, tucked away in a sheltered fold of the hills. The church, 're-edified' (as an inscription says) in 1648, is a curious survival of the late-Gothic style. Carsington Pastures, the limestone hills to the north-west towards Brassington, are honeycombed with old shafts and rakes, and other relics of the lead-mining era.

Hopton (425353) is stretched out, like Carsington, along the spring line above the valley of the Scow Brook, the upper course of the Henmore Brook which flows down to Ashbourne. (The whole of the valley floor for over two miles from Hopton downstream is likely to be lost under a new reservoir.) Hopton Hall, hidden behind a brick 'crinkle-crankle' wall, is an Elizabethan house much altered in the eighteenth century and still the home of the Gells, whose monuments are in Wirksworth church. Farther along the street is a house with curious carving on the front, possibly representing the George and Dragon, as it was once an inn of that name, and just beyond are the almshouses founded in 1719 by Sir Philip Gell.

At Sycamore Farm, an eighteenth-century brick house with an unusual bowed front, Hereward Street is crossed by the line of the Portway, a road whose name may indicate that it was in use before the Roman settlement. Mr Cockerton has traced the route of the Portway right across Derbyshire from Sandiacre, where it crosses the Erewash from Nottinghamshire, to the fort of *Navio*, near Brough. The name 'Port', he says, means a 'road' or 'way', so Portway is in fact a duplication of terms; but it was in common use and indeed is to be found also along Hereward Street, while the name of Porter Lane is still in use for the road west of the Black Rocks towards Middleton (Chapter 12).

The Portway crossed the Derwent between Belper and Ambergate, ascended to join a road from *Derventio* at Sandyford, passed near Alport Height (where a Romano-British settlement has been excavated), then crossed the Ecclesbourne Valley south of Wirksworth to reach Hereward Street. To the north of Harborough Rocks (perhaps significantly) the Portway left the other road (which went on to Buxton), itself making northward to Grangemill on its way towards Robin Hood's Stride and Ashford-in-the-Water. Hereward Street, instead of descending to Wirksworth, as one might expect, avoided it by working round the head of the Ecclesbourne Valley towards the Black Rocks.

Wirksworth (428354) is an old-fashioned market and quarrying town at the upper end of the Ecclesbourne Valley (whose river flows down to join the Derwent), surrounded by hills scarred with huge limestone quarries that get bigger year by year. Formerly the lead-mining capital of the Low Peak, it has many buildings of the eighteenth century, when the industry was in its heyday. Lead mining first developed in this region during Roman times and Wirksworth is one of the claimants (Matlock and Chesterfield are others) to be the mining centre of *Lutudarum*, but the possible site of this will be discussed in Chapter 13.

Wirksworth, the 'enclosure' or 'homestead' of Weorc, no doubt a Saxon overlord, is first recorded in 835. In the ninth and tenth centuries the mines belonged to the abbey of Repton and were evidently of considerable importance, as lead worth 300 shillings had to be paid as an annual rent to the monastery of Christ Church, Canterbury. Wirksworth received grants of a fair, in 1307, and of a market, which has been held on Tuesdays since 1397. From its position (like Ashbourne) on the edge of the Peak District and neighbouring the rich pastoral country of the North Midlands, it had a mixed trade; lead, of course, from the hills, but also corn, sheep, cattle and dairy produce. Its prosperity depended principally on lead mining; the first court for settling disputes was established in 1288, when the surrounding mining area, known as the 'King's Field', belonged to the sovereign, who was entitled to a set proportion of all the lead that was mined.

The mining industry began to flourish with the introduction of ideas from Germany in the late sixteenth century. When Daniel Defoe visited Wirksworth in 1725 he found it "a large, well frequented town . . . the people generally coming twelve or fifteen miles to the market and sometimes much more; though there is no great trade . but what relates to the lead works, and to the subterranean wretches, who they call Peakrills, who work in the mines, and who live all round this town every way." The industry reached its apogee in the eighteenth century, and Wirksworth was at this time the largest town in Derbyshire, after Derby and Chesterfield. The industry began to decline after about 1760, though even in 1806 the town is described as being "eternally overhung with smoke from the lead and calamine works, the principal covering being here and there broken into pillars of white smoke from the smelting mills." This pall of smoke dispersed after 1827, when the last of the lead works were closed and the industry had been replaced by that of textile manufacturing.

The centre of Wirksworth is the precipitously sloping Market Place, many of the houses around which have fronts

Ashford, Sheepwash Bridge

Monsal Dale

of the late-eighteenth and early-nineteenth centuries concealing older structures. The Red Lion Inn, to the north, is an old coaching house with a façade of about 1750, and a fine mid-eighteenth-century house opposite has a brick wing with Venetian windows. Babington House, up the hill from this point, was built in 1588 for the Babingtons of Dethick, the most famous of whom was the Anthony Babington who in 1586 attempted to rescue Mary, Queen of Scots, from Wingfield Manor and lost his head as the result.

In the Moot Hall, built in 1814, north of the church, is kept the brass dish given to the lead miners of Wirksworth in 1513 by Henry VIII, the standard for all other measuring dishes; it holds 14 Winchester pints, or about 60 pounds of lead ore. The Great Barmote Court, established under the law of Edward I for settling lead mining disputes, is still held here twice a year, in April and October. No lead mining is now carried on in the Peak District, so the court now has a purely traditional function. Any member failing to attend, however, can be fined.

The church has carved Norman stones in its walls (including an Adam and serpent in the north aisle), but was rebuilt after 1272, when it came into the hands of the Dean of Lincoln, and was enlarged and altered in the fourteenth and fifteenth centuries. In the north wall is set a unique coped coffin-stone found upside down in front of the altar during a nineteenth-century restoration. It measures about 3 feet wide and about 5 feet long, but was originally longer, as two scenes are missing from the left-hand end. The stone is richly carved with about forty figures depicting scenes from the Life of Christ, and the iconography has enabled it to be dated between 653 and 693, so it is probably the oldest as it is certainly the finest Saxon carved stone in Britain.

In the south transept wall is a tiny carving of a twelfth-century lead miner (brought from Bonsall) with his pick and his 'kibble' (or bucket) for carrying the lead ore. The most interesting monument is that in the chancel to Anthony Lowe, who died in 1555, an early (if rather crude) example of Renaissance work, recently recoloured. He was a servant to Henry VIII (as the inscription tells us), as well as to three other monarchs. The figure in effigy on the monument, however, is not that of Lowe; he doesn't fit on the top of the tomb and he is wearing fourteenth-century armour.

In the chapel opposite are tombs of the Gells of Hopton Hall, among them that of Ralph Gell, who died in 1564 and is represented on an incised alabaster slab, a type of monument found only in Derbyshire and Staffordshire. Anthony Gell, Ralph's son, who died in 1583 and has a splendid Renaissance monument showing him richly robed, was the founder of the Grammar School that bears his name. An obscure wall monument commemorates Sir John Gell, the Parliamentary general who was the scourge of the Royalists in Derbyshire. The church has two fonts; one Norman and one dated 1662 which was installed when the rite of baptism was thought suitable again (after the fall of the Commonwealth) and the older one, thrown out at the Reformation, had been lost. The old custom of 'clipping' or walking round the church in procession takes place every year in September. On the east side of the churchyard are the Gell Almshouses of 1584 and a Gothic building of 1828 which formerly housed the Grammar School, founded in 1576.

Wirksworth is generally agreed to be the 'Snowfield' of George Eliot's novel *Adam Bede*. Samuel Evans, the original of 'Seth Bede', was buried in 1858 in the churchyard, and in the Ebenezer Chapel of 1810 (near the Moot Hall) is a tablet to Elizabeth Evans, who died in 1849. The novelist's aunt, she was the model for 'Dinah Morris' in the novel and her pulpit is preserved in the Bede Memorial Chapel of 1886 (now the Reformed Methodist Church), in the main street.

Further interesting houses can be seen in the main street descending south from the Market Place. The Hope and Anchor Inn at the corner has a fine Jacobean fireplace; Lloyd's Bank, farther down, succeeds a bank founded in 1780 by John Toplis in which Richard Arkwright II became a partner. Near an alley leading to the church is a cruck-frame, recently discovered by the demolition of the building in front; it is claimed to be of the fifteenth century, but has now been rather too well restored. The Registry Office (formerly the Wirksworth Savings Bank) and the Maternity Hospital (previously Waltham House), on the other side of the main street, are two good early nineteenth-century houses.

At the Spring Bank Holiday week-end Wirksworth still keeps up the old custom of well-dressing (as at Tissington), though there are no longer any wells and all the water is piped into the town. The mosaics are set up in and around the main street, between the Maternity Hospital and the Red Lion; and prizes are awarded for the best.

To the south of the town, near the Derby road, is Haarlem Mill, the older part of which was built in 1777-80 by Sir Richard Arkwright as a cotton spinning mill on land leased from Philip Gell of Hopton Hall. In 1792 Arkwright sub-leased the premises, but spinning ceased between 1813 and 1815, during the cotton depression, and the mill was converted to tape weaving, which is still carried on. The large four-storey brick and stone building is Arkwright's original mill; the long brick range at right angles was added at different stages between 1832 and 1885. The Speedwell Mill, on the right farther south, was originally the manorial corn mill, but was rebuilt as a cotton mill about 1790 by John Dalley. It was converted to tape manufacture in 1844, but now makes textile machinery.

Wirksworth is in fact the largest manufacturer of tape, both red and white, in the country (civil servants please note); it also makes webbing and other 'narrow fabrics', as they are now called. On the other side of the Derby road are two more tape mills: the Willow Bath Mill, founded in 1816 by John Prior, and the Gorsey Bank Mill farther up, built about 1881 by George Gamble. The eighteenth-century house above this mill has an upper storey that was perhaps used for framework knitting (see Chapter 13).

11 The Derwent Valley to Rowsley

The boundary of the Peak District National Park has been arranged so as to exclude all towns, as far as possible; in fact, only Bakewell is included in the Park. This is natural enough, given the terms of reference of national parks, but it means that the boundary has had to be drawn north of Ashbourne, Wirksworth and Matlock, and places in the neighbourhood of these towns which perhaps should have been included have in fact been left out.

Coming up the Derwent valley by the A6 from the direction of Derby, one senses the approach to the Peak District long before the National Park boundary is reached. Only a few miles north of the town, we can see, rising ahead, the long ridge of the Chevin, sometimes called the 'last of the Pennines', as it is the southernmost of the gritstone outcrops that line the valley. Between Milford and the textile-manufacturing town of Belper the valley sides begin to encroach, and we feel that we are beginning to get among real hill country.

Beyond Ambergate (434351), where the Derwent is joined by the Amber, the valley sides close in more steeply, and this can be regarded as the real 'gateway' to the Peak from the south-east. This stretch of the valley to Cromford is one of the most beautiful in England, but few motorists take much notice of it; they are all in too much hurry to get to Matlock or Manchester or whereever. On the east side are the wooded slopes of Crich Chase, rising towards the lighthouse war-memorial tower of Crich Stand, and on the other side are Shining Cliff Woods, the property of the National Trust and best seen when the rhododendrons are in bloom. In the restricted valley we find the river, the road, the railway and the Cromford Canal running parallel within a very short distance of each other.

At Whatstandwell we bridge the Derwent, then run through an avenue of trees (very lovely in autumn) and cross the track of the Cromford and High Peak Railway (Chapter 12). Castle Top, the highest of the farms above the valley to the east, was the girlhood home of Alison Uttley, who has described the neighbourhood in her children's stories. Then Rock House, the eighteenth-century home of Sir Richard Arkwright, comes into view below as the valley opens out and we approach Cromford.

Though Cromford (429356) has a Saxon origin (like most places in the Peak District), the present village is mainly the creation of Sir Richard Arkwright, who came here in 1771 and set up his first textile mill, the first cotton-spinning mill in the Peak District. Arkwright was born in 1732 in Preston, the youngest of thirteen children. He became a barber and wig-maker at Bolton and invented a preparation for dyeing hair (no doubt a useful source of income then, as now). Going about the country seeking hair to make wigs, Arkwright would hear the new inventions in the cotton industry being discussed (James Hargreaves had perfected his 'spinning jenny' in 1764), and in 1767 he began the experiments that led to the invention of the spinning frame (sometimes called the 'water frame' because it was finally powered by water), which he patented two years later. In 1768 he moved to Nottingham to avoid the machine breakers who were active in Lancashire, and built a mill whose looms were operated by a horse-gin, that is by a wheel which was turned by a horse walking round in a circle. Three years later Arkwright entered into partnership with Jedediah Strutt (afterwards to build his own mills in Belper, Milford and Derby), leased a plot of land at Cromford from Peter Nightingale of Lea (the great-uncle of Florence Nightingale) and built his first cotton-spinning mill here, the first cotton mill in England to be powered by water.

Arkwright's first mill of 1771 is thought to be the building facing the main road, though this was damaged by fire in 1930 and is now two storeys lower in height. A second stone-built mill erected in 1776-77 was almost completely demolished by fire in 1890 and only a few walls remain. The looms in this mill complex were operated from two sources, the Bonsall Brook, which descends the valley threaded by the Via Gellia (Chapter 13), and the Cromford Sough (pronounced 'suf'), a channel cut in 1673-82 to drain the lead mines between Cromford and Wirksworth. The 'tail' or adit of the sough, restored for the Arkwright two hundredth-anniversary celebrations in 1971, can be found behind the houses opposite the entrance to the Via Gellia. Other mills were built between about 1782 and 1791, but the fortress-like building facing the road leading down to the bridge is a warehouse of about 1785. Cotton spinning ceased in 1891 and the buildings have been used as colour works since 1921.

Arkwright also built an entirely separate mill, the Masson Mill (named from the hill above Matlock Bath), beside the Matlock road and powered from the Derwent. Across the river upstream is a remarkable convex weir designed to direct the water into a goit or channel beneath the mill. This mill was built in 1783-84, and extensions were made in 1898 (when it was taken over by the English Sewing Cotton Company) and again in 1911, but the original building can easily be distinguished by the plum-coloured bricks and the classical design of the windows.

Arkwright was involved in endless lawsuits over his patents, but nevertheless managed to make a great deal of money, and when he died he left a fortune of some half-a-million pounds. He established an 'empire' of cotton mills, extending from Derbyshire into Staffordshire, Lancashire and Scotland. He was knighted in 1786, not for his pioneer work in the textile industry (such a thing was unheard of in the eighteenth century), but for sending an address to George III on that monarch's escape from assassination. He bought the estate at Cromford in 1789, but died four years later of an asthmatic complaint and was succeeded in his business enterprises by his eldest son, usually called Richard Arkwright II. Wright of Derby, in his portraits, shows Sir Richard as a self-made man, though rather pompous and complaisant, but Wright depicts the son as very much the country gentleman.

Sir Richard Arkwright not only built the mills at Cromford, he also, as I said, created the village; indeed, this was the first 'industrial village' of its kind in the country. The old village, named from the ford over the Derwent, had moved some distance up the hill, east of the Wirksworth road, by the late eighteenth century, so Arkwright built a new village down towards the valley for the workers in his mills. Among the first houses were those known as Staffordshire Row, beside the Via Gellia, dating from shortly after 1771 and so called because they were inhabited by miners imported from Staffordshire. Those in North Street, off the Wirksworth road, were completed in 1776 and consist of two excellent rows of three-storey houses so designed that the topmost storey could be occupied by the framework-knitting machines of stocking workers (see Chapter 13). It was the practice for the women and children to go out to work in the mills, while the men stayed at home and made the stockings and other kinds of hosiery. The houses of two and three storeys climbing the Wirksworth road were also built by Arkwright (after 1777) and some still have their original cast-iron casement windows, with small panes. The school and schoolhouse at the farther end of North Street were built by Richard Arkwright II in 1832.

In the square west of the Derby-Matlock road, Arkwright built the Greyhound Inn (in 1778), looking very much like a town hall, and in 1790 he obtained a charter for a Saturday market in his new industrial village (it closed in 1880). He dammed up the Greyhound Pond, behind the inn, to provide a head of water for the first mills, and he also constructed the Bonsall Brook Reservoir farther up to supply power to a new corn mill, of about 1778, which has now been taken over by the Arkwright Society and is being restored as a museum.

On the right-hand side of the road passing the first mill complex is the well built Mill Manager's House, and above this we have a glimpse of Arkwright's eighteenth-century residence, Rock House (since enlarged). Part of the water from the Cromford Sough is taken over the road in an iron aqueduct of 1821 (the original aqueduct, of 1785, was of wood). The sough also served as the head source of the Cromford Canal (Chapter 12), of which Arkwright was one of the instigators. Farther down is the church, begun by Joseph Pickford for Sir Richard (who is buried here) and completed for his son in 1797, but much altered and

Gothicized in 1859. Arkwright also began Willersley Castle, on the farther side of the river (and discreetly hidden from the village, in the tradition of the time). Begun in 1788, it is the only known design of William Thomas, a London architect. A fire broke out before the house was completed and Arkwright died in 1792 before repairs could be effected. The house was first occupied by Richard Arkwright II, but the family sold the estate in 1926 and it is now a Methodist guest house.

The fifteenth-century bridge over the Derwent presumably occupies the site of the Saxon 'ford' of Cromford and before that of the Roman road of Hereward Street (Chapter 10), which came down the hill from the Black Rocks and went over by Starkholmes towards Matlock. Adjoining the bridge are the ruins of a contemporary bridge chapel, a not uncommon feature in medieval times, though only five such chapels now survive intact. Close by is a well-restored eighteenth-century Fishing House, recalling that in Beresford Dale. Bridge House, once a home of the Nightingales, facing the river on the other side, is an interesting building, partly Tudor, with an extension of about 1700.

Beyond the Masson Mill, the A6 enters the magnificent ravine by which the Derwent forces its way through the solid limestone, with some fine outcrops rising from the eastern bank. Matlock Bath (429358) is a small town and a weekend resort, over-popular on Sundays in summer, but beautifully situated in the depths of the gorge, with pleasant boating on a placid reach of the river. The thermal springs for which it became noted were first used in 1698 and fed the Old Bath, thought to have been situated close to the footbridge over the Derwent. The New Bath, to the south, was opened in 1735, Hodgkinson's Hotel, once a noted posting house, was built in 1768, and by the end of the century Matlock Bath was beginning to emerge as a spa.

The road between the town and Cromford was cut in 1817-22, but the real development of the spa came with the building of the Manchester, Buxton, Matlock and Midland Junction Railway (what romantic names these early railways had), the section of which between Ambergate and Rowsley was opened in 1849. This successfully turned the ravine of the Derwent into the 'Switzerland of England' (as it was called by the Victorians). The station at Matlock Bath was designed to be in keeping (probably by Sir Joseph Paxton, who was a shareholder in the railway company), though the station at Cromford, thought to have been designed by G.H. Stokes (the son-in-law of Paxton) is even more 'Swiss-like' in its architecture.

The thermal springs, which have a constant temperature of 68° F, now feed a fishpond near the Pavilion (built as the town hall in 1885), as well as swimming pools at the New Bath Hotel, farther south. Near the Pavilion is a petrifying well, where objects hung in the lime-impregnated water give the appearance of being turned to stone.

Above the town to the north the wooded slopes climb steeply to the Heights of Abraham, said to have been named by a soldier who was with Wolfe at Quebec. The Victoria Prospect Tower, high on the ridge, far above the noise and stench of motor traffic, affords charming views both up and down the ravine. It was built in 1844 to attract visitors to the show caves farther up: the Rutland Cavern, 560 feet long, and the Great Masson Cavern, over 2000 feet, both partly abandoned lead mines claimed (without any evidence) to have been first worked by the Romans. Beyond the caverns we can climb up to the top of the great dome of Masson (1110 feet), for an even wider view, over the Derwent Valley to High Tor and Riber Castle. The surrounding slopes are pitted with the remains of the lead mining industry which flourished in this neighbourhood.

High Tor (429359) is a broad limestone crag about 380 feet high, rising sheer above the river and the road between Matlock Bath and Matlock. Near the summit are two connected caves or fissures which are in fact worked out lead rakes. Dale Cottage, beside the road to Matlock, is a delightful small Regency house of 1820.

Matlock (429360), at the north end of the ravine, is a market town with textile mills and large quarries. Its former reputation as a spa (as distinct from that of Matlock Bath) was owed principally to the fashionable 'hydropathic establishment' opened in 1853 by John Smedley, who had textile mills at Lea, near the Derwent below Cromford. His huge building, capped by a prominent 'crown', halfway up a steep hill east of the bridge, was converted into the Derbyshire County Council offices in 1958, when the council was moved here from Derby. A tramway that climbed the hill from Crown Square between 1893 and 1927 has disappeared, but the shelter which stood at the foot has been re-erected in the Hall Leys gardens, south of the sixteenth-century bridge (widened in 1903) which crosses the river to Matlock Bridge. From the gardens we have a fine view up to Riber Castle, a pseudo-medieval folly built by Smedley in 1862-68 and now the centre of a fauna reserve, with British animals and birds. A pleasant walk leads from the gardens on the east bank of the Derwent below High Tor.

The parish church of Matlock, in the old village (called Matlock Town) above the gardens, was rebuilt in 1859-71, except for the Perpendicular tower. It has a strangely carved Norman font and six 'maidens' garlands' (like those at Ashford-in-the-Water), in a case near the door. Wheatsheaf Farm, south of the church, and the King's Head Inn, opposite, are characteristic late seventeenth-century buildings.

Beyond Matlock Bridge the valley of the Derwent opens out. The quietest and, by nature, the best road is on the west side, starting from the bridge and passing behind a large limestone quarry. A view opens out up the valley to Darley Dale before we reach the hamlet of Snitterton (428360). The Hall, built about 1590, up a side lane to the left, is the most excellent example of the Peakland vernacular architecture of the period between 1540 and 1700. Built of gritstone on the 'hall and double-cross wing' plan, it still has its gritstone slab roof, as well as the characteristic steep gables, large casement windows, mullioned and transomed, and a splendid Renaissance doorway, an early example of this style of decoration. The doorway is not in the middle of the central range, but slightly to the left, indicating that the hall, the principal apartment of the house, extends to the right of the doorway. The road from Snitterton, which comes out on the Winster-Darley Dale road, runs behind Oaker Hill (427361), which has a solitary tree on the top, the only survival of two that play a part in Wordworth's poem, 'The Brothers'.

The A6 goes up the east side of the Derwent to Darley Dale (427362), where the Whitworth Institute, built in 1890, and other buildings in the locality commemorate Sir Joseph Whitworth, the engineer, inventor of the Whitworth screw-thread, who lived for fifteen years until his death in 1887 at Stancliffe Hall (now a school), among the trees to the north of the village. The church, west of the main road, is mainly of the thirteenth to fifteenth centuries and has a fifteenth-century parclose screen and a window of 1860 by Burne-Jones. In the churchyard is perhaps the oldest yew in England, estimated to be at least seven hundred years old and with a girth of over 33 feet.

Beyond Darley Dale the gritstone heights of Stanton Moor (Chapter 13) rise to the west of the valley. In this direction, too, are buildings that incorporate what little remains of the Mill Close Mine (425362), on a site where mining had apparently taken place for centuries. The rights were bought by the London Lead Company in 1720, after which the mine became one of the most prosperous in the Peak, nearly half-a-million tons of ore being produced. The fall in the price of lead, combined with the prohibitive cost of pumping out the mine when it became flooded, led to its closure in 1939. The site was then taken over by a company that extracted barytes, but these works were closed in 1974 and the buildings are to be demolished.

A road bears to the right to continue up the Derwent valley through Chatsworth Park (Chapter 22), while the A6 crosses the river to Rowsley (425365; pronounced 'Ro-'), a village of warm-brown gritstone houses, among them the charming Peacock Inn, built in 1652 and taking its name from the crest of the Manners family of Haddon Hall (Chapter 15). In the rebuilt church, up the hill slope to the north, is part of a Saxon cross-head attributed to the mid-ninth century. Rowsley was for fourteen years (1849-63) the terminus of the railway that was intended to connect Derby with Manchester, and the original station (probably by Paxton) can still be seen, north of the road junction.

12 The 'High Peak' Trail

The 'High Peak' Trail is a route for walkers, cyclists and horse riders over some seventeen-and-a-half miles of the course of the Cromford and High Peak Railway. The name is misleading (hence my inverted commas), as the trail doesn't go anywhere near the High Peak, which is the gritstone moorland area around Kinder Scout. But of course it was adapted from the name of the railway, which incidentally didn't start from Cromford, but farther down the valley of the Derwent.

The Cromford and High Peak Railway was designed primarily to take away limestone and lime from the uplands down to the Cromford Canal in the Derwent valley on the east side of the Peak District or to the Peak Forest Canal in the valley of the Goyt on the west side. The Cromford Canal was engineered by William Jessop, with the assistance of Benjamin Outram, and built in 1789-94. It ran from Cromford (Chapter 11) to Langley Mill, in the Erewash Valley on the Derbyshire-Nottinghamshire boundary, and was in effect an extension of the Erewash Canal, completed in 1783. The canal was designed principally to carry cotton from Arkwright's mills at Cromford and iron products from the foundries of the Butterley Company (near Ripley), of which Jessop and Outram were founders.

The Cromford Canal ran through the Derwent valley to Ambergate (where it turned up the Amber Valley), crossing the river below Lea Bridge by an aqueduct (431355) 30 feet high and 200 yards long, with a central span of 80 feet. The Leawood Pumping House, whose distinctive chimney can be seen just north of this, was built in 1845 to pump water up from the Derwent to the canal. The canal had been fed from the Cromford Sough, but with the cutting of a new sough, the Meerbrook, which came out into the valley lower down, the water supply was considerably diminished. The engine house still contains its original beam engine, capable of raising up to 6 tons of water per minute.

The Peak Forest Canal (Chapter 19) was completed in 1800, and it was first intended to link the Cromford and the Peak Forest Canals with another canal, but the idea was given up, partly because of the number of locks that would have been required to take the canal out of the steep-sided valleys at either end, and also because of the lack of water on the limestone uplands necessary to keep the canal topped up.

So the idea was discarded in favour of a railway, from Cromford Wharf (431355; miscalled Highpeak Junction on the Ordnance Survey map), on the Cromford Canal, to Whaley Bridge in the Goyt Valley. The engineer was Josias Jessop, son of William Jessop; the line, 33 miles long and built to the now standard gauge of 4 feet 8½ inches, was begun in 1825 from the Cromford Wharf end, opened as far as Hindlow in 1830 and completed to Whaley Bridge in the following year.

The railway was designed for steam locomotives from the outset, and it would have been one of the earliest railways to use this form of power (the Stockton and Darlington Railway, the first to carry passengers, was opened in 1825), but courage failed and horses were used as the locomotive power at first. Steam locomotives were introduced on the easier sections in 1834, though horses continued to be used as well until 1841.

The railway was employed not only to take down limestone and lime (used mainly as a fertiliser, as it had been since the Middle Ages), but also to carry up goods, especially coal and water to the farms and villages on the uplands; indeed for many of these it was the only reasonable contact with the outside world. The goods were loaded on to or unloaded from the boats on the Cromford Canal and the same thing happened at Whaley Bridge, where a dock-house was built in 1832 over the terminus of the railway at the end of the Peak Forest Canal.

The building of the Manchester, Buxton, Matlock and Midland Junction Railway up the Derwent valley from Ambergate in 1849 had a disastrous effect on the canal trade and hence to some extent on that of the Cromford and High Peak Railway. The canal was bought by the railway company in 1852, and from this time its traffic continued to fall away steadily. In 1900 the tunnel under the Butterley ironworks collapsed, but the upper part of the canal remained in use, carrying coal to Cromford and lead from Lea Bridge, until 1938, when it was closed. This stretch of the canal has been purchased by the Derbyshire County Council and is to be preserved as an 'amenity waterway'; the tow path is open to walkers from Ambergate to Cromford.

In 1853 the Cromford and High Peak Railway was extended down the Derwent valley for three quarters of a mile to join the main line at High Peak Junction (432355) and this led to a revival of traffic, resulting in the opening of many new limestone quarries. The London and North Western Railway Company leased the railway in 1862 and bought it in 1887. Passengers were carried from 1844, but this service was discontinued in 1877, after a fatal accident. The financial difficulties of maintaining and operating the railway (as will become evident when we walk along it), combined with the growth of road transport, led to a decline in its traffic, though the section between High Peak Junction and Middleton Top continued to be worked until 1967, after which the rails were taken up and sold to Mexico.

At Cromford Wharf the railway ran alongside the canal, and here we can see a transit shed with an awning over the original terminus, and a workshop where the earlier locomotives were assembled and serviced. Inside this are some of the fish-bellied rails (so called from their shape) which were later replaced by the more orthodox edge-rails; and adjoining is a shed used for shunting. At the outset the railway had to face the problem of getting out of the Derwent valley. This it did by means of the Sheep Pasture Incline, 1320 yards long, ascending under the A6 and with a gradient of 1 in 8. This was much too steep for any locomotive and the waggons were pulled up by a stationary engine at the top of the incline, assisted by the gravity of waggons going down. Chains were used to haul up the waggons until 1856, when they were replaced by ropes, at first of hemp, then of steel. Some remains of these steel wire ropes can still be seen, as well as of those used for signalling to and from the engine house at the top. The line was single track, except in the middle section, where it was doubled to allow the down-going waggons to pass those going up. In 1888 two descending waggons broke away, shot down the incline and went straight over the canal and the railway, ending up in the field beyond, after which a system of signals was provided, with a catch pit above the road bridge (it still contains a truck that got away).

Though the winding-engine house at the top of the incline still stands, the engine itself (replaced in 1883) has gone and the huge pulley wheel, 14-feet diameter, over which the ropes from the waggons passed, was apparently stolen by vandals, who had to cut the wheel up to get it out. The water tank for topping up the engines has likewise gone (all the water had to be brought up on the railway) and an inspection pit near by has, unfortunately, been filled in.

A level stretch of the railway follows, with beautiful views over the Derwent valley around Cromford and Matlock Bath (such views are a feature of the Trail). The locomotives first used on the railway were Bury 2-2-0, but after the railway was taken over by the L & N W R, these were replaced by that company's own engines, some of which had been used on their other railway lines, such as the North London line from Broad Street to Richmond.

The course of the railway takes us past the foot of the Black Rocks (439355; the Ordnance Survey uses the singular for some unknown reason), a striking gritstone escarpment at the northern end of Cromford Moor (Chapter 13) and a favourite rock-climbing ground. Near by are a picnic site and the remains of a lead-smelter. The railway crossed the Wirksworth-Cromford road, beyond which branches went off to several of the large quarries which are a feature in this neighbourhood. At the end of this level stretch we tackle the Middleton Incline, 708 yards long with a gradient of 1 in 8¼. Passengers on the railway had to walk up these inclines, but here again the waggons were transported by a stationary engine at the top, though no catch pit was provided (presumably runaway waggons were not thought dangerous on this section).

The engine house at Middleton Top (427355) still contains the original steam winding engine, built in 1830 by the Butterley Company; it continued to work until 1963 and has recently been well restored by the Derbyshire Archaeological Society. The pulley wheel is 14 feet in diameter and the two-cylinder engine can develop 20 horse-power; the intricate signalling mechanism is also preserved. The boiler house adjoining contains the original boilers, though the doors have been ripped off (let us hope this vandalism will subside now that the remains of the railway have been taken over by the Derbyshire County Council). Near by can be seen some of the stone blocks that preceded wooden sleepers (as they did on many early railways) for supporting the rails.

Beyond the engine house and another picnic site, we traverse another relatively level section, passing through a tunnel, 113 yards long, one of only four on the railway. On the right beyond are large dolomite works, exploiting the magnesium found in the limestone strata here. Then comes the Hopton Incline (425354), which could be negotiated by locomotives; it was a mere 1 in 14, but even so was the steepest incline in Britain on which there were moving engines. The original length of 457 yards was reduced by an embankment to 200 yards to make the pull up easier; nevertheless, a train came off the rails in 1937, causing loss of life.

The railway, right up on the limestone plateau, runs below Harborough Rocks (424355; Chapter 10) and passes large refractory brick works (now disused). Several large quarries are seen, many of them first opened after the building of the railway, which had to manoeuvre round some awkward bends to avoid dropping into valley heads. As a result only waggons with no more than four wheels could be used. At Longcliffe (422355) the railway bridges two roads; the first bridge is of well-tooled stonework (like many on this line), but the second is partly of iron supplied by the Butterley Company. The 'High Peak' Trail enters the national park and takes a circuitous course round Minning Low (420357), a hill marked with a distinctive clump of decaying trees that can be seen over a wide area of Derbyshire.

On the top of Minning Low is a circular mound measuring

Wormhill, Well Dressing

Buxton, The Crescent

about 120 feet across and still standing 10 feet high, despite the natural denudation due to the elements. This has revealed two large and almost complete chambered tombs, as they are now usually called (sometimes indicated as 'long barrows' or 'tumuli' on Ordnance Survey maps). They date from the Neolithic or New Stone Age, which lasted from about 2000 to about 1600 B.C., during which period man settled down and became a farmer, living in communities and tilling the soil. Each chambered tomb consists of a large inner chamber reached by a passage, the whole covered by a massive capstone. The tombs were dug into in 1843 and 1849 by Thomas Bateman, who did much to reveal (and something to destroy) prehistoric Peakland, but no intact burials were found by him. The tombs had apparently been robbed as long ago as Roman times.

The Roman road from Buxton to Derby (or *Lutudarum*; see Chapter 13) passes the mound of Minning Low on its east side. From here towards Buxton the course of the road is clear; it is followed by parish boundaries and near Pikehall (419359) by a walled track which was once part of the post road from London via Derby to Manchester. The railway traverses a high embankment west of Minning Low, then, after negotiating some more sharp curves, crosses the Matlock-Newhaven turnpike road west of Pikehall. It passes the refractory brick works at Friden (417360); these heat-resistant bricks are made from sands containing silica which are dug out from large pits in the neighbourhood. A long line of trees to the right marks the course of the Roman road to Buxton.

The railway track passes under the Ashbourne-Buxton road by a fine bridge which bears a medallion commemorating Josias Jessop, the engineer, and depicting one of the original waggons. It is joined by the course of the railway from Ashbourne (the Tissington Trail; Chapter 9) just before reaching the site of the station at Parsley Hay (414363). From here the railway runs more or less parallel to the Buxton road, skirting several enormous (and still expanding) quarries. The stretch of line from Hurdlow to Hindlow was straightened out by the building of new embankments in 1894, but after the construction of the Hindlow to Buxton line by the L & N W R in 1892 the section of the Cromford and High Peak Railway almost to Whaley Bridge fell into disuse and all traffic henceforth passed through Buxton (except for local traffic to the quarries). The trail finishes at Dowlow (410367), west of the Buxton road, beyond the Duke of York Inn.

The old line, passing some large lime kilns (long since disused) and skirting round the huge quarries at Harpur Hill, reaches its summit level, of 1264 feet, at Ladmanlow (404371), beside the road from Buxton to Leek. This point is 987 feet above the terminus on the Cromford Canal and 747 feet above that on the Peak Forest Canal; and these heights alone indicate some of the engineering difficulties. The railway crossed the road from Buxton to Congleton and Macclesfield (where its embankment can be seen), then ran below Burbage Edge to reach the entrance to a tunnel, 580 yards long, closed like the rest of this section in 1892. Walkers following the course of the railway must make their own way over the ridge, which separates the upper reach of the Wye from that of the Goyt. The railway track emerges high above the Goyt valley and after traversing a tract of open, breezy moorland, descends sharply into the valley by the Bunsall Incline, which is 1115 yards long and has a maximum gradient of 1 in 7, the steepest on the railway. At the top was a stationary engine house (it has long since disappeared) and the incline itself has been converted into a road to serve the Errwood Reservoir (Chapter 8) in the valley below. (Driving a car up this incline, however, conveys a good idea of what it was like to be carried up in a waggon.)

The railway, avoiding the valley bottom, which now contains the Fernilee Reservoir (401377), ran along the eastern side and crossed the Buxton-Whaley Bridge road south of Shallcross (401379), where it can still be traced on an embankment through the fields. Beside the parallel lane to the right is part of an unusual Saxon cross-shaft of the eleventh century. The railway goes down again, by the Shallcross Incline (of 1 in 10¼), then passes through Whaley Bridge (410381; Chapter 19), finally descending to the dock-house at the end of the Peak Forest Canal by an incline, 180 yards long, with a gradient of 1 in 13½. The waggons on this incline were pulled up by a horse-gin, stationed at the top, from the completion of this section in 1831 until it was closed in 1952.

13 From Wirksworth to Youlgreave

The Cromford road, running north from Wirksworth (Chapter 10), ascends out of the head of the Ecclesbourne Valley and passes under the course of the Cromford and High Peak Railway to the west of the Black Rocks, which are the northern escarpment of Cromford Moor (429356). In 1777 a 'pig' or bar of lead was found on the moor bearing the inscription "Imp. Caes. Hadriani Aug. Met. Lvt". In 1783 a second pig was found near Matlock with the inscription "L. Arvconi Verecvnd. Metal. Lvtvd.", and since that time no less than twenty pigs of lead have been found, some of them spelling out the name of 'Lvtvdarum'. Two of them have been found in Sussex (near a Roman road), but eleven have been found in the neighbourhood of Brough, on the Humber, where the Romans had a port. It is evident that the pigs were lost (or stolen) while being taken to one port or another for shipment to the Continent. But where or what was *Lutudarum*?

It has been suggested that this may have been the name of the man in charge of the lead workings (though it doesn't sound like a personal name) or alternatively that it was the name given by the Romans to the lead mining district; but it seems much more likely to have been the name of the actual centre of lead mining activity. If this is so, where exactly was *Lutudarum*? Nothing has yet been discovered to locate the mining settlement, though there are some pointers to its whereabouts in the roads in the neighbourhood of Wirksworth.

Several Roman roads converge in the vicinity of the town. Two of these, Hereward Street, passing north of Wirksworth, and the Portway, passing to the west, have already been mentioned (Chapter 10). Another road, crossing the Portway near Alport Height, a prominent hill to the south-east of

Wirksworth, ran along the ridge east of the town and west of the Black Rocks to join Hereward Street before it descended to Cromford. The whole problem of these roads is much too complex to discuss here (especially as none of them is shown on the Ordnance Survey map), but it is significant that all the roads avoid Wirksworth and the site of *Lutudarum*, I feel sure, is not to be found here. The Ordnance Survey map of Roman Britain shows a road going straight from Buxton to Little Chester (Derby). This can indeed be traced as far as Minning Low (as we have already seen), but the course of the road southward from there is entirely conjectural, no finds have been made to justify it, and I suggest that the road turned away from Minning Low to reach the lead mining settlement at *Lutudarum*. When the site of this settlement is discovered (as it assuredly will be), I am convinced that it will be on the limestone uplands somewhere to the west of Wirksworth.

Porter Lane runs west from the Black Rocks to reach another road which climbs steeply from Wirksworth, passing the Middle Peak Quarry, one of the largest of the many limestone quarries in this neighbourhood. This road goes on through the rather nondescript quarrying village of Middleton-by-Wirksworth (427355), so called to distinguish it from two other Middletons in the Peak District, but inappropriately named, as it is 400 feet above Wirksworth. In the quarry to the west the limestone is actually being mined underground. Lorries drive for about a quarter of a mile to the working face, and excavation is carried out by means of 'roads' about 35 feet wide and 20 feet high, with pillars about 40 feet square supporting the roof. A large stone crushing plant has been installed underground and some 5000 tons are extracted each week for the chemical and sugar-beet refining industries.

From the brow of the hill beyond Middleton we have a wonderful view deep into a beautiful wooded ravine. Just below the road is the small Mountain Cottage, where D.H. Lawrence lived for a year in 1918-19, "in the darkish Midlands", as he says in his Letters, "on the rim of a steep valley, looking over the darkish, folded hills – exactly the navel of England, and feels exactly that". I wonder why

Lawrence thought the outlook 'darkish', an expression better applied to the gritstone country (but perhaps he never saw this). The limestone country strikes me as being particularly light, especially when it enjoys the sunshine.

The ravine below is popularly called the Via Gellia (pronounced 'Jell-'), though this is correctly the name of the road built by the Gells of Hopton in 1792 to connect their house with the new market established by Arkwright at Cromford. The major part of the ravine is correctly named the Griffe Grange Valley. We descend to this, reaching it at the point where the road comes in from Hopton, passing the Hoptonwood Quarries (426355), famous for their grey and pink limestones, which are extremely rich in fossils and have been much used for decorative effect in Westminster Roman Catholic Cathedral and other modern buildings.

The Via Gellia is extended up the valley to Grangemill (424357), at the valley head and the junction of roads from Ashbourne, Newhaven House and Bakewell. The derelict building of 1875 opposite the Hollybush Inn here was once a cheese factory. At Green Low, on a limestone ridge south of the Newhaven House road, can be seen a chambered tomb of the New Stone Age (about 2000 to 1600 B.C.), revealed by the erosion of the earthen mound that once covered it. The tomb, which consists of a single compartment, has lost its capstone (such as can be seen at Minning Low) and no burials were found during a recent excavation. But the lines of stones that revetted the mound on either side of the passage entrance can be seen, with a platform outside that was probably used for some ritual purpose.

We descend through the Griffe Grange Valley in the other direction, towards Cromford. The charmingly wooded ravine is rich in wild flowers, but is perhaps best seen in the autumn, when the leaves are changing their tints. Beside the road is a remarkable cottage made of 'tufa', carboniferous limestone from which the carbon has been extracted, and farther down is a mill spanning the stream. Rebuilt as a cotton mill in 1867 by Thomas Else of Matlock, this was taken over in 1890 by William Hollins, who here first made (in 1894) the woollen fabric known as 'Viyella' (a corruption of 'Via Gellia'). The fabric is now made in large mills at Nottingham and Pleasley, and the mill here is used for garnetting, the processing of textile waste.

At the Pig of Lead Inn, a reminder of the former industry of this district, we turn steeply up for Bonsall (428358), a secluded village at the head of a side valley separated from the Derwent valley by the great hill of Masson, with old stone houses arranged in no sort of order. In the seventeenth and eighteenth centuries many of the inhabitants combined the activities of lead mining and agriculture. James Bland, for instance, though described as a miner, left at his death in 1616 "one cow and two heifers". But in the 1770s Arkwright's mills at Cromford began to draw away labour from Bonsall and neighbouring villages.

Another industry carried on in the district was framework knitting, the making of stockings and other forms of hosiery on machines mounted on sturdy wooden frames (hence the name of the industry). The manufacture of hosiery by mechanical means began as early as 1589, when the Rev. William Lee of Calverton (near Nottingham), invented the 'stocking frame'. The Derby Rib Machine, a modification to Lee's machine which enabled ribbed stockings and gloves to be made, was patented in 1759 by Jedediah Strutt, but apart from this the original design remained practically untouched until well into the nineteenth century.

Framework knitting was mainly carried out in cottages and small workshops, the machinery usually being rented from a hosier, who also supplied the raw material (mostly cotton, but occasionally silk) and who purchased the finished products. By 1844 some 143 frames are recorded at Bonsall, making it one of the largest centres of the industry; the knitters worked mainly for hosiers at Belper, in the Derwent valley, and the oldest inhabitants tell how the women used to walk to Belper, nearly ten miles away, carrying the finished work.

Workshops where framework knitting was carried on can still be found in Bonsall and other villages in the Peak. They are to be distinguished by the long windows, usually on the upper floor, behind which stood the machines. One such, on the slope above the cross in Bonsall, housed six knitting frames and was still in use in the present century. The market cross has a shaft dated 1671, but the steps (no less than thirteen of them) are probably medieval and indicate an important market here at one time, though there seems to be no record of it. The King's Head Inn near by is a characteristic Peakland building of 1677, and farther up the street is the Manor House, built about 1670. The thirteenth to fifteenth-century church, on a shelf above the village, has a fourteenth-century tower and spire with unusual bands of quatrefoils, shields and flowers. Bonsall holds a well-dressing festival every year, early in August.

A by-road crosses Bonsall Moor, which is honeycombed with old lead mining shafts, to reach Winster (424360), a village of exceptional interest, stretched out along a shelf above a valley that descends to the Derwent. Winster became a market centre shortly after 1640, but its most prosperous period was the eighteenth century, the great age of lead-mining, and it has many fine houses of that time. These show the use of both limestone and gritstone in building, not surprisingly, as the village is almost on the boundary between these two deposits.

Among the most interesting buildings are the three-storey houses at the east end of the street, one of them dated 1754 and the next pair making a single composition with two classical porches and Venetian windows between these. In the centre of the village is the Market Hall, built in the late seventeenth or early eighteenth century (though its open arches on the ground floor have been filled in) and the first property in the Peak District to be acquired by the National Trust. The upper part is curiously built in brick, with stone dressings, but it has been suggested that this was originally timber framed. On the north side of the road is a framework knitter's house and workshop, with blocked upper windows, and just west of this is Winster Hall, the largest house in the village, probably built about the middle of the eighteenth century, with balustrading, rusticated quoins or corner stones, a round window, a pillared doorway and other classical features. Beyond the Hall is another interesting group of houses, one with a shell hood, and facing down the street from the west end is the seventeenth-century Dower House, one of the few buildings of before the eighteenth century in Winster. A Pancake Race takes place along the street every year on Shrove Tuesday.

A feature of the limestone uplands south of Winster is the number of field barns, small two-storey buildings with space for three or four cows at ground level and a hay loft over. Why there should be so many dotted about the fields so far from the farms and villages has not been satisfactorily explained. One suggestion is that they were used by independent small holders who lived in cottages rather than farmsteads, but another idea is that they belonged to lead miners who also engaged in a little agriculture. They would certainly be suitable for James Bland of Bonsall, his one cow and two heifers.

To the west of Winster, beyond the Grangemill-Bakewell road, is Elton (422360), whose village street runs at the junction of the limestone and the gritstone, making it possible to grow azaleas and other acid-loving plants in the gritstone on the north side, but not in the limestone on the south side. Elton has several good eighteenth-century houses, the outcome of lead mining prosperity, including Greengates Farm, a building of 1747 in which gritstone and limestone have been combined effectively, the gritstone being used for the dressings (quoins, doorway, window surrounds, coping stones, etc.) and the well-cut limestone for the infilling, an arrangement which can be seen here as effectively as in any house in the Peak. Elton Hall, now a youth hostel, has a date of 1688 on the wing projecting towards the road and of 1715 on the part at right angles to it.

High up on the side of Stanton Moor, north of Elton, is Birchover (423362), many of whose houses are set back behind pleasant gardens. Here we are on the gritstone, and near the foot of the village street are the outcrops of Rowtor Rocks. Thomas Eyre, an eccentric local parson who died in 1717, built himself a study in the rocks and had seats hewn out so that his friends could enjoy the prospect over the valley. He also rebuilt the small church below (much altered since). The rocks have no associations with the Druids, despite the name of the inn close by. On the way up to Stanton Moor we pass a large quarry where the gritstone is now made into fireplaces. The stone here is noticeably lighter in colour (almost pinky in fact) and less gritty than that farther north in the Peak.

Stanton Moor (424363), rising to over 1050 feet, is an outlying mass of the gritstone, mainly covered with heather, in the angle between the Derwent and the Wye, from which it stands up as a prominent feature. Near the western boundary is the Cork Stone, a weathered outcrop of millstone grit, named from its shape, and other weathered rocks stand out round the edge (it belongs to the National Trust), overlooking the Derwent valley, up which we can enjoy a splendid view towards Chatsworth. The prominent tower near the edge commemorates the passing of the Reform Bill under Earl Grey in 1832.

The moor is in effect a vast Bronze Age burial cemetery which has been extensively excavated over their two lifetimes by J.C. Heathcote and his son, J.P. Heathcote, who keeps a private museum of finds (urns, bronzes, flints and the like) at his home in the old post office in Birchover. At least seventy burial mounds (or round barrows) have been located on the moor, and it may well have been used as a place of worship within the period of about 1400 to 1000 B.C. by Bronze Age peoples or tribes who came from a wide area. Though most of the mounds are small, they are impressive by their number. One of the largest, in which twelve separate deposits of cremated human bones were found, accompanied by collared urns, a food vessel and flint tools, was left open after excavation to show the internal arrangements, but unfortunately it has deteriorated.

On the moor to the north of the barrow cemetery are the Nine Ladies, consisting of a circle of standing stones no more than 3 feet high but about 33 feet in diameter. In the centre was formerly a small mound that may have contained a burial. It seems quite likely that such circles may have been used as sacred enclosures where some religious or mystical rite was observed. Outside the circle, at a short distance, is a single upright stone known as the King's Stone. This is a feature frequently found in conjunction with such circles; other examples are the Rollright Stones in Oxfordshire and Long Meg and her daughters in Cumberland. (Why, incidentally, are stone circles usually feminine?)

Just below Stanton Moor on the west, but hidden at the edge of a wood, is another circle, Doll Tor, which consists of six small stones (two have now fallen). It is unimpressive, but of some historical significance. Burials with collared urns and incence cups were found in the centre of the circle, and in a mound-like extension on one side were four cremations, one with a star-shaped bead of blue faience, while in the centre of the mound were the cremated remains of a woman with a faience bead. Both beads came from Egypt and have been dated to about 1300 B.C.

Stanton-in-Peak (424364), at the north end of the moor, is an estate village, mainly of the nineteenth century, on a precipitous hill which descends to a tributary valley of the Bradford. Stanton Hall, in a park with a rare breed of black fallow deer, but hidden behind a wall, was built in the seventeenth and eighteenth centuries by the Thornhills, who also built the church (as a private chapel) in 1838. The locality commands a wide view westward to the church tower of Youlgreave, the spire of Bakewell and of the Wye valley descending past Haddon Hall.

To the west of the valley, which carries the Grangemill-Bakewell road, is the abrupt gritstone crag of the Cratcliffe Rocks (422362), sometimes called Cratcliffe Tor. About halfway up the crag, hidden behind a yew tree, is a small cave where a hermit lived in the fourteenth century, carving a remarkable crucifix on the wall. To the south-west (not marked on the Ordnance Map) are the upstanding rocks of Robin Hood's Stride, with two tors showing the curious effect of natural weathering on the Millstone Grit, and so called because the outlaw is supposed to have jumped from one tor to the other (about the length of a cricket pitch!). Needless to say, the rocks have no connection with Robin Hood; they are sometimes called Mockbeggars' Hall, from their resemblance to a tumbled ruin, but their previous name was Dollwood Tor. To the south of the rocks, between two field walls and about 100 yards from the corner of one of them, can be found a fine example of a hut site, one of several among the bracken, probably dating from the Roman period. The doorstep, the hearth stone and the surrounding wall of a large beehive hut are well defined. The hollow of the Portway, perhaps contemporary, can be traced running east of Robin Hood's Stride on its way from Grangemill to Ashford-in-the-Water and Brough.

To the north of the rocks, on the reclaimed Harthill Moor (422362), can be seen four upright stones (another serves as a gatepost), the only survivors of a circle known as the Nine Stones. One of these has been found by excavation to be 11½ feet long, though only 7 feet of the stone extends above the ground. If nine was the original number, the stones would have fitted into a circle roughly 45 feet in diameter. Beyond Harthill Hall, a seventeenth-century farmhouse of the Cokaynes, to the west, is Castle Ring, a small Iron Age hill-fort, probably of the first century B.C. It has a double rampart with a ditch between, but the earthworks have been interrupted on one side by the farm buildings.

The lane east of Harthill Hall descends into the valley of the Bradford, passing, at Upper Greenfield Farm, a good example of a longhouse, a type of building whose origins go back at least to the thirteenth century. A longhouse has the living quarters for the farmer and his family at one end and the byre for the cows at the other end, all under the same long roof.

Alport (422364; pronounced 'Ol-') is an attractive hamlet with an old corn mill and interesting houses, among them the seventeenth-century Monks' Hall, which has a large gabled front, and a fine eighteenth-century house on the other side of the road from the Wye valley (Chapter 15). Alport is just below the point where the Lathkill joins the Bradford, and we enjoy a fine view towards the entrance to Lathkill Dale as the road ascends to Youlgreave (Chapter 14).

14   From Youlgreave to Buxton

Youlgreave (421364), often spelt (as it is pronounced) Youlgrave, stands high up on a ridge north of the river Bradford. The main part of the village stretches beside one long street running west from the church, which closes the vista at the end, but on the south the houses also seem to tumble down the hill towards Bradford Dale.

The church, of absorbing interest, has the finest tower in Derbyshire (except for that of Derby Cathedral). It is built in the Perpendicular style of the fifteenth century, and from the outside the church itself seems to belong wholly to the later Middle Ages. But inside, on the south of the wide nave, we find a late Norman arcade with round arches and round piers with scalloped capitals. The north arcade, in contrast, shows the change to the slightly-pointed arches and voluted or 'stiff-leaf' capitals that identify the Transitional Norman period of about 1150-80, indicating that the church was being constructed about the beginning of this period. The south arcade was built while round arches were still the fashion, but by the time the north arcade came to be built, slightly later, the trend was beginning to change to the pointed arches of the Gothic style.

The aisles and chancel of the church were rebuilt in the fourteenth century, but when the tower came to be built, about a century later, it was placed some distance west of the end of the arcades, and the two were then joined by an aisleless section of the nave, to provide a bigger church, no doubt, but with rather a curious effect. Set into the blank north wall is the tiny figure, only 17 inches high, of a man in a long costume, probably of the twelfth century and perhaps a priest.

The font of about 1200 has a large tub-shaped bowl supported by a rounded stem and four shafts. On the side of the bowl is carved a dragon-like creature (said to be a salamander), upside down, and projecting from the bowl (but part of the same block of gritstone) is a rounded stoup, the only one of its kind in England and probably intended as a receptacle for the consecrating oil used in baptism. The font was previously at Elton, but it was thrown out of that church in the last century and found its way into the vicarage garden at Youlgreave.

In the north aisle is an interesting alabaster panel to Robert Gylbert, who died in 1492 and who is shown with his wife and seventeen children, kneeling on either side of a much-larger figure of the Virgin, the sons behind the father and the daughters behind their mother. In the chancel are a cross-legged and bearded knight of about 1325, holding his heart in his hands (a curiously medieval conceit), and the exquisite alabaster tomb of Thomas Cokayne (the missing member of the Ashbourne Cokaynes), who died in 1488. On the sides of the tomb are angels holding painted shields, and on the top is the effigy of a knight in plate armour. Round his neck is a collar with the Yorkist emblems of suns and roses, his head rests on a helmet with a cock's head (the family crest) and his feet on a jolly lion with a long swishy tail; but he is only 3 feet 6 inches long. The idea that he died young can be discounted (his moustache would seem to be original and not carved later by some vandal) and the fact that he is shown in armour is not significant (boys too young to fight were often depicted in armour). Such monuments in the Middle Ages were often carved by itinerant masons, and the simple answer may be that no larger block of alabaster was available at the time. The east window of the chancel contains glowing stained glass of the pre-Raphaelite school, designed by Sir Edward Burne-Jones and made in 1870 in the workshops of William Morris.

Youlgreave has two interesting buildings in the Peakland vernacular style. The Old Hall, in the main street, is a characteristic manor house of 1656 (much restored internally) of the 'hall and double-cross wing' type, while the larger and finer Old Hall Farm, up the lane behind, is a 'hall and single-cross wing' house of 1630. This has the hall (the living room; sometimes called the house-place) and the kitchen in the principal range of the building, and the parlour (the old name for a dining room) in the rather square cross-wing, with a storeroom over the kitchen, a bedroom over the hall and the great chamber (or solar, as it was still sometimes called at this time) over the parlour. Both houses are built of the local limestone, but with gritstone dressings.

Youlgreave (like Tissington) maintains the old custom of well-dressing, and five wells are decorated in a festival which takes place every year in June. It is perhaps invidious to compare the well-dressings of one place with those of another, but the villagers of Youlgreave keep up a consistently high standard year by year and their mosaics are certainly among those most worth seeing in the Peak.

The steep lane starting opposite the Old Hall leads down into Bradford Dale (420363), which is among the shorter and least known of the Peakland dales, but is delightfully wooded. The river, dammed into several ponds to feed corn mills (now vanished), is followed by a good path that ascends after a mile to the hamlet of Middleton-by-Youlgreave (419363), which has mellow gritstone houses of the eighteenth and early-nineteenth centuries. The Gothic Congregational Chapel of 1826 is unusual in having a house attached to it. In a field behind is the tomb, surmounted by a stone model of a Bronze Age cinerary urn, of Thomas Bateman, a pioneer of Peakland archaeology, who died in 1861 at his home at the nineteenth-century Lombersdale Hall, near the road back to Youlgreave.

The lane going on west of the Bradford, towards Elton, passes near Smerrill Grange (419361), a farmhouse built in the eighteenth century, but apparently incorporating some medieval remains of the monastic grange. Dale End Farm, farther on, built in 1689 (but restored), is at the foot of Gratton Dale. The villages of Gratton and Smerrill, like others in this part of the Peak, were 'deserted' (i.e. the villagers were ejected) when the monastic overlords moved in.

Another road, running west from Youlgreave, passes the Moor Lane picnic site, from which we have a wide view over the Bradford to Stanton Moor and to the limestone uplands as far as Minning Low. The road goes on to follow Long Rake (417364), an old lead rake that is now being worked over again for calcite. A cart-road farther on leads down west of Cales Dale, an arm of Lathkill Dale, to One Ash Grange (417365), a farmstead with a remarkable history. There was a village here in the early Middle Ages, but it was deserted when the land was taken over as a sheep run by Roche Abbey, in south Yorkshire. Part of the present farm, which appears to be in the style of a longhouse, probably dates from this time. With the dissolution of the abbey, the lands passed into private ownership, and the farmhouse was partly rebuilt in 1747 for the Bowmans, a Quaker family. John Bright, the Liberal statesman and free-trade reformer, son of a Quaker millowner, spent his honeymoon here. The farm buildings, including the piggeries, at the back, are particularly interesting.

To the south of the road from Youlgreave is Arbor Low (416363), the most interesting survival of the New Stone Age in the northern half of England, dating from about 1800 B.C. It stands on an exposed ridge at a height of 1230 feet, near the top of the watershed separating the catchment areas of the Bradford and the Lathkill, and commanding a very expansive view, extending north as far as Kinder Scout in clear weather.

Arbor Low consists of a circular plateau, about 160 feet across, surrounded by a ditch or fosse which is itself enclosed by a circular vallum or bank, some 250 feet in diameter. The ditch has an average depth of 5 feet 6 inches, though it is partly silted up and has been proved by excavation to have been at least 11 feet deep. The earthern bank is about 7 feet high, but considerable erosion has taken place and it was originally much higher. The ditch and bank are interrupted on opposite sides to form two entrances to the central plateau, on which rest over forty slabs of limestone, irregular in shape and of different sizes. Some of the stones are broken, and the exact number depends on how many we consider to have once formed part of larger stones. The largest slab is 14 feet long, the widest over 6 feet, and the heaviest must weigh not less than nine or ten tons. All the stones, except one (which rests at an angle) now lie flat on the ground, but it is generally agreed from this one exception that they must once have stood upright. Most of the stones

Lyme Park

Eyam, Plague Cottages

are arranged in a large circle of about 150 feet in diameter, but a few are grouped in the centre and may once conceivably have formed part of an altar place.

This type of monument is now usually called a 'henge' monument. Stonehenge in Wiltshire is the most famous example, but a much closer parallel to Arbor Low is the great stone circle at Avebury, also in Wiltshire and contemporary with Arbor Low, and likewise enclosed by a ditch and that by an earthen bank, though at Avebury the surviving stones stand upright. The position of the ditch inside the bank almost certainly disproves a military origin for these monuments, and it would seem that they served some religious purpose, but what sacred ritual went on within the circle, no-one has the slightest idea.

Overlapping the bank near the south-west entrance at Arbor Low is a large mound of earth and stone, now standing 7 feet 6 inches high. It was made partly with material from the bank and is therefore later. A cremation burial was found, with food vessels and other remains, in a chamber, paved and roofed with stones. Burials of the New Stone Age were all inhumations, not cremations, so this in itself would date the mound to the Bronze Age (from about 1600 B.C).

From the south of the bank, another low bank of earth and stone, now less than 1 foot 6 inches high, stretches out for over 1000 feet. This has been proved by excavation to be of the same age as Arbor Low, but its purpose remains obscure. It is no longer thought that this earthwork has any connection with Gib Hill, a large conical mound just over 1000 feet away from Arbor Low to the west. Though much eroded, this mound still stands about 17 feet high, and near the top an interment of the Bronze Age was discovered and removed in 1848 by Thomas Bateman. The rectangular burial chamber, which has a capstone 4 feet square, has been restored to its original position.

Gib Hill is only one of the great many burial mounds ('tumuli' on the Ordnance Survey map) to be seen scattered around on the neighbouring limestone uplands. Indeed, the existence of so many might point to Arbor Low as a centre of religious ceremony in New Stone Age and Bronze Age times. Two good examples of New Stone Age burial mounds are Lean Low (414362) and End Low (415360). Both lie west of the Ashbourne-Buxton road, to which the road from Youlgreave leads out near Parsley Hay (Chapter 12).

Lathkill Dale, which lies to the north of Youlgreave, is one of the quietest and most charming of the limestone dales, and worth exploring all the way by footpath from the medieval Conksbury Bridge (421365), on the Bakewell road. The dale is gay with flowers in summer, and the river cascades over little weirs (as in Dovedale) constructed to improve the fishing. It was Charles Cotton who wrote that the Lathkill "is, by many degrees, the purest and most translucent stream that ever I saw either at home or abroad". (As a Peakrill, or Peaklander, he may have been slightly biased.) The path, running partly through woods with a rich variety of trees, passes below Over Haddon (420366), a limestone village stretched out along the hillside high above the dale. (Over Haddon is so named to distinguish it from Nether Haddon, a deserted village which lay somewhere to the east, probably near Haddon Hall, but whose site has not been located.) The south side of the dale, west of the steep twisting lane from the village, is now a Nature Reserve and therefore inaccessible to the general public. The path lies on the north bank throughout, however, and the Peak Park Planning Board have produced an excellent Nature Trail following this.

Larkhill Dale is not only delightful for its natural scenery, it is interesting for the many remains of the lead-mining industry that flourished in and around the dale. The path from the lane below Over Haddon, passing two small trial levels made by the miners in their search for ore, follows the leat or outlet (usually dry) of the Mandale Sough, a drainage channel constructed between 1797 and 1820, and after entering a wood we can see the 'tail' or outfall of the sough, which penetrates into the hill for more than a mile.

To the right from here can be seen the surface remains of the Mandale Mine, built after 1820, but abandoned in 1851, after incurring a loss, it is said, of £36,000 (not everyone made a fortune out of lead mining). Beyond the ruins of the engine house is the gaping opening of the pumping shaft (dogs and children should be kept under control!) and beside this is the housing for the water wheel, which measured 35 feet in diameter. On the shelf of the valley side above are a small shaft, still open, and an inclined plane which was the principal entrance to the mine. Some remains can be seen, too, east of this point, of the flue which led from the boiler house (now vanished) straight up the hillside to a small chimney at the top.

On the other side of the open shaft begins the leat or channel which brought water in to the mine buildings. This crossed the path and the river farther upstream by a wooden aqueduct, built in 1810, of which the massive stone supporting pillars remain. The leat can be seen (when the leaves are off the trees) running horizontally along the hillside beyond the river and passing behind the ruined Bateman's House, as it is usually called. James Bateman was agent or overseer to the Lathkill Dale Mining Company from 1836 until the mine was closed in 1842. The Lathkill Dale Vein, which comes down the valley side east of this point, was worked at least as early as 1770. On the right of the path before this we can see the hollows which mark the shafts of an old level that drained the Vein.

The Lathkill itself has been raised artificially here, with the object of sealing off the mines below ground, but in dry weather the river disappears among the reeds. Farther up, a branch of the Lathkill Dale Vein can be seen, striking up the hillside to the right, before we emerge from the wood to the site of Carter's Mill. Here the river has been dammed to provide power for a corn mill, recorded in 1862. The path up a charming little dale with no stream leads towards Haddon Grove, a farm on a lane leading east (to Over Haddon) from which the line of hummocks marking the position of the Mandale Rake can be seen.

The path going on up Lathkill Dale passes a small natural weir made of tufa. We continue below serried grey-white crags of the limestone, which are interspersed with layers of softer material (limestone shale) and which in places send down fragmented rocks (screes or slitherbanks), as in Wolfscote Dale. The valley floor is rich with flowers in summer: meadow sweet, herb robert and (in June) the rare blue Jacob's ladder, found nowhere else, I believe, in the Peak District. Beyond Cales Dale, which comes in on the south, the main dale narrows and the valley floor is usually completely dry, as the river runs below ground, but after wet weather it may emerge from the wide mouth of Lathkill Head Cave. Farther up, the dale, whose upper sides are lined by beautiful crags, divides into two. The path up the main branch, to the left, leads out from the dale head to the Bakewell road short of Monyash.

Monyash (415366; pronounced 'Mon-ne'), in a hollow of the limestone plateau, was granted a charter for a market and fair in 1340 and was long a centre of lead mining. The Barmote Court for dealing with mining disputes (as at Wirksworth) was held in the seventeenth-century Bull's Head Inn, beside the green, around which most of the village is scattered, in charmingly haphazard fashion. The restored church, founded about 1198, has Transitional Norman sedilia and piscina, with 'dog-tooth' moulding, in the chancel, and an Early English tower, one of whose buttresses is pierced by a window. The nave arcades were rebuilt in the fourteenth century and the aisles and transepts have those straight-headed Decorated windows that are a feature of Derbyshire churches. In the nave is an iron-bound chest, 10 feet long, perhaps as old as the thirteenth century.

The road to Bakewell passes below Bolehill Farm, a reminder that a 'bole', or early lead smelter, once stood on the hill above. At one time there were as many as 700 smelters to be seen in Derbyshire, but nearly all signs of them have disappeared. The early smelters were invariably placed in exposed positions to ensure a good draft of air over the lead ore, as it was being smelted. The ore consists largely of lead sulphide, and by heating it over coke, the carbon in this combined with the sulphur in the lead and left almost pure lead behind.

To the north-west are the prominent buildings of the Magpie Mine (417368), the best-preserved lead-mining buildings in the Peak, now the field-centre of the active Peak District Mines Historical Society. I have, unfortunately, no space to delve into the long and complicated history of lead mining, but in any case this has been done already in the excellent booklet on *Lead Mining in the Peak District* edited by Trevor D. Ford and J.H. Rieuwerts, and published by the

Peak Park Planning Board, and in several other works, notably *Derbyshire Lead Mining*, by Nellie Kirkham, and the *Industrial Archaeology of Derbyshire*, by Frank Nixon.

The Magpie Mine has been worked, according to local tradition, for over 300 years. It is certainly recorded as being operated in 1795, though not on any large scale, as after 1801 it was sold for one shilling. By 1824 mining had developed considerably, for a new pumping engine was provided and a new main shaft sunk, at a cost of £1000. The mine workings were frequently sold, and new capital provided meant that new equipment was bought; sometimes the mine was closed, only to open again 'under new management'; and new soughs were constructed to combat the everlasting problem of draining or 'unwatering' the mine. Lead mining finally ceased in 1924.

To the left of the entrance (from the south) is a house of about 1864, with the blacksmith's shop on one side and a weigh house on the other. To the left, as we approach the main buildings, in an engine house of about 1870 (it contained a Cornish horizontal-beam engine), with the boiler house at the back and a drum at the front, over which the wire cable passes to the head of the winding gear. This still stands complete above the main shaft into the mine (which reaches 728 feet below ground). The building in front of this was a new winding-engine house, put up only in 1951 (and never used), while the large building behind contained the Cornish pumping engine installed in 1824 and replaced about 1840. Farther over are another building, probably for a 'whimsey' or steam-winding engine, built in 1830, and the building for treating the lead ore, of about 1868.

The limestone uplands in the vicinity of the Magpie Mine are criss-crossed by the hummocks of old lead rakes. One of these, the Dirtlow Rake, to the east of Kirk Dale, is now being extensively reworked, but for fluorspar. Sheldon (417368), to the north of the mine, is one of those villages that have no notable buildings, but that are satisfying for the way in which the houses are grouped around the single street. By skirting round the head of Deep Dale, which descends to the Wye valley, we can reach Taddington (Chapter 17), near the main road from Bakewell to Buxton.

15 Haddon Hall

At Rowsley (Chapter 11) the Matlock-Buxton road (A6), leaving the Derwent valley, turns up the valley of the Wye, and a 'millstone' symbol tells us that we are in the Peak District National Park (the Derwent itself is the boundary). To the left rises the wood-capped conical hill of Peak Tor, backed by the northern slopes of Stanton Moor, and farther on (beyond the junction of the road from Youlgreave and Winster) we skirt the wooded grounds of Haddon Hall, with just a glimpse of the house when there are no leaves on the trees.

Haddon Hall (423366) is one of the best-loved houses in England, and the one that best fits the romantic conception of the medieval castle, not the formidable fortress rising abruptly from a dominating crag, but the rambling, mellowed dwelling of gallant knights and their gracious ladies. Recalling the background of some illuminated manuscript, it fits convincingly into the vision conjured up in the popular imagination (however falsely) of the Middle Ages as an era of chivalry and valour. No other house in England suits this role so perfectly as Haddon: the charm of its surroundings, the Wye, meandering below, the green meadows beyond, the woods rising above the Hall; the house itself, on a low limestone platform above the river, in a varied and picturesque array of towers and battlemented grey-brown walls, seemingly arranged on no architectural plan whatever.

This apparent lack of any architectural system is in fact the outcome of many buildings, alterations and enlargements made from the twelfth century onwards by succeeding owners, the Peverels and Avenels, and especially the Vernons and the Manners, until the original modest house had developed into the present complex series of buildings. No fundamental alterations have been made to Haddon since the death of Sir John Manners in 1611, so on coming down to the bridge (of 1663) over the Wye, we see the house almost exactly as it was in the sixteenth century. In its final form it is a splendid and perfect example of a large Tudor manor house.

The first house or stronghold on this site (we have no idea what it looked like) was built by William Peverel or Peveril, a natural son of William the Conqueror who held the manor of Haddon in 1086 and who built Peveril Castle on the hill above Castleton (Chapter 24). When his son, also William, was disinherited in 1155, the estates were granted to William Avenel, already the tenant here, and in about 1170 he divided the manor between his two sons-in-law, Richard Vernon and Simon Basset.

Vernon, who acquired the Haddon property, built the older part (the nave walls) of the chapel, at the south-east corner of the lower courtyard of the house. The curious position of the chapel, at an acute angle to the rest of the building, would perhaps indicate that Haddon was at this time much smaller, and that when it was enlarged the house had to be twisted round to get it on the sloping plateau on which it stands. The chapel, which contains a round Norman font, was enlarged probably in the thirteenth century (it has lancet windows in the style of this period) by the addition of a south aisle almost as large as the original nave.

Under a licence of about 1195 from Prince John (later king), Richard Vernon was permitted to build a wall, 12 feet high, round his house. The lower part of the mis-called Peveril Tower, near the north-east corner, with its flanking walls, seems to date from this time, and at least part of the wall on the west of the lower courtyard, facing the Wye; but if so, this would indicate that the house was indeed already of its present size (or nearly so) by the end of the thirteenth century. The battlements, which are of the fourteenth century, were added at a time when private houses no longer required to be fortified, and are more picturesque than functional.

Little further building seems to have been done at Haddon for nearly two hundred years after the time of the first Richard Vernon. In about 1370 Sir Richard Vernon IV built the cross-wing between the two courtyards which contains the Great Hall (or Banqueting Hall, as it is called at Haddon), the kitchens and other domestic apartments, as well as some at least of the buildings round the walls, so that Haddon assumed the plan it has today, resembling a flat-sided figure eight, with two roughly rectangular courtyards and the main apartments in the cross-bar of the 'eight'. The plan of the Great Hall and kitchen range is indeed typical of the later Middle Ages and can be paralleled for instance at Wingfield Manor in Derbyshire (though here the great hall range is on one side of one of the courtyards) and at Ashby-de-la-Zouch Castle in Leicestershire, which by this time had become a manor house rather than a fortified castle (but the north courtyard at Ashby has now disappeared).

The Banqueting Hall is of the characteristic medieval pattern, with a raised platform or dais at one end, for the table of the lord of the manor, his family and important visitors (once lighted by a large oriel window on the lower courtyard side, such as can be seen at Wingfield Manor), with a hearth in the centre (such as still exists at Penshurst Place, in Kent) and a hole in the roof through which the smoke from the fire escaped (if you were lucky) and with little or no protection from the wind blowing in through the door into the courtyard. Most of the household spent much of their time in the Banqueting Hall (when they weren't actually working or sleeping) and they ate from long tables extending down the length of the hall, on either side of the hearth. Such halls in the Middle Ages must have been cold, draughty and cheerless, and probably damp.

By the late fourteenth century the prosperity of the Vernons was increasing. The wealth gained from their many estates could be augmented by the profits from the lead mines they owned, and the results can be seen in the additions and embellishments made by almost every succeeding generation. Sir Richard Vernon VI, grandson of the builder of the Banqueting Hall, held no less than thirty-seven manors, mostly in Derbyshire and Staffordshire, but ranging from Buckinghamshire to Pembrokeshire and Westmorland. He also occupied the office of forester in the royal Forest of Macclesfield. He built new apartments round the upper courtyard and on the west side of the lower courtyard, and he added a long chancel to the chapel in 1427, the year after he was appointed Speaker of the Parliament held by Henry VI at Leicester. The glass in the east window of the chapel commemorates Sir Richard and his wife.

The fifteenth-century alabaster reredos above the altar, carved by the Nottingham School with scenes from the Passion, is completely in keeping, though in fact it was introduced only in the present century. The wall paintings in the chapel, mostly of foliage patterns, dating from the late fifteenth century, include a large figure of St Christopher in the usual position opposite the doorway. A porch was added to the great hall range in about 1450 and a fireplace built in the south wall of the Banqueting Hall, with the result that the light is rather excluded from the fourteenth-century window between the porch and the massive chimneybreast.

Sir Richard's grandson, Sir Henry Vernon, Lord of Haddon from 1467, was Treasurer to Prince Arthur, the elder brother of Henry VIII. He built the upper part of the Peveril Tower, over what was then the main entrance to the house, added the buildings along the adjacent east front, and after 1500 contrived new private rooms for himself by erecting a partition across the Banqueting Hall. Behind this he constructed two rooms, a parlour or dining room on the ground floor and a drawing room, the Great Chamber, above.

The Dining Room, completed about 1545 by Sir George Vernon (Sir Henry's grandson), has panelling showing portraits said to be of Henry VII and Elizabeth of York (in the bayed recess), the Tudor royal arms (with the griffin as a supporter) and the Vernon crest, the boar's head. The fireplace and some of the furniture are contemporary, and above the fireplace is carved the family motto, 'Drede God and Honor the Kyng'. The remarkable ceiling paintings are mostly in a chequer pattern of red and white, but panels depict the Tudor rose and the Talbot dog (Sir Henry married Anne Talbot, daughter of the Earl of Shrewsbury). They may be what art critics call 'local work' (which means that they don't think much of them), but they are among the very few painted ceilings of the Tudor period in England.

The Great Chamber upstairs has an early sixteenth-century

fireplace, bayed recess and timber roof, but the plaster frieze looks later (it doesn't fit the room), the panelling was introduced in the early seventeenth century and the tapestries of woodland scenes are of seventeenth-century Flemish workmanship. The Earl's Bedroom next door to it was probably designed by Sir Henry Vernon as a long gallery when rebuilding the south side of the lower courtyard, but it was converted as one of the suite of rooms some time after 1641, when the title of Earl of Rutland passed to the Haddon branch of the Manners family.

Sir George Vernon, who inherited in 1515, was known as the 'King of the Peak' from his large estates, the splendour of his mode of living and his dominating personality (we shall see his effigy in the parish church at Bakewell). He often took the law into his own hands, and on one occasion, it is said, had a murderer hanged by his own retainers without the benefit of a trial. Before 1530 Sir George built the Vernon Tower at the north-west corner of the lower courtyard, but as the slope up through this was too steep to admit a coach (there are several steps, too, up to the courtyard level), new stables had to be built outside at the foot of the slope. The building of the tower created a problem where it encroached on the west wall rooms, the upper parts of these having to be 'squinched' out above the entrance. The worn step below indicates how many feet have passed through this doorway since the early sixteenth century. The kitchens, though still basically medieval, with their original fittings, were probably altered at this time; the timber-framed screen that divides them seems to be of Tudor construction. They may well be compared with the great Tudor kitchens at Hampton Court, though that of course was a royal palace.

Sir George has been cast by tradition to play the heavy father in the celebrated legend of the elopement of Dorothy Vernon, his heiress, with Sir John Manners, son of the first Earl of Rutland, who lived at Belvoir Castle in Leicestershire. It seems likely that Sir George would not wish his daughter to marry John, who was only the second son of the earl and at that time not even a knight. But there are no contemporary records of an elopement and, indeed, the first printed account of the story was not published until 1822.

The marriage certainly took place, reputedly at Aylestone, near Leicester, another Vernon estate (why not at Belvoir, if not at Haddon?). On the death of Sir George in 1567 the property passed to Sir John and Dorothy (whom we shall meet again at Bakewell) and Haddon became part of the Manners estates.

Sir John Manners altered the Long Gallery, within the medieval walls, a light and airy room, 110 feet long. He added large new windows, in about 1600, and introduced the plaster ceiling and the silvery-grey limewood panelling with its early examples of Renaissance features. The boars' heads and peacocks in the frieze indicate the alliance of the Vernon and Manners families, while the roses and thistles, each pair growing from a single stem, no doubt commemorate the union of the English and Scottish crowns in the person of James VI and I, who knighted John Manners after he crossed the border in 1603.

Sir George Manners, who succeeded his father in 1611, re-roofed the chapel (in 1624) and installed the box-pews, the three-decker pulpit and other woodwork, but after his son, another John, succeeded to the Earldom of Rutland in 1641, the family lost interest in Haddon. A dukedom was conferred on the ninth Earl in 1703, but by this time the family was concentrating its activities on Belvoir. Belvoir Castle was entirely rebuilt in the early nineteenth century, and for this we may count ourselves extremely fortunate in the Peak. If the Dukes of Rutland had decided to live at Haddon instead of Belvoir, Haddon (basically medieval as it is) and not Belvoir would have been rebuilt. In the event, Haddon remained practically untouched for about two hundred years and indeed not lived in for any length of time.

Haddon Hall became an object of romantic wonder in the eighteenth and nineteenth centuries. Horace Walpole, that lover of the picturesque, found it "an abandoned old castle of the Rutland, in a romantic situation", and Ebenezer Rhodes wrote in 1819 in his *Peak Scenery*, "A gloomy and solemn silence pervades its neglected apartments, and the bat and the owl are alone the inmates of its remaining splendour". It is not surprising that the story of the elopement of Dorothy Vernon should have caught the popular imagination.

Haddon, though neglected, never fell entirely into ruin, but when the ninth Duke of Rutland decided on a restoration in 1912, he was set with a considerable task. He had to strengthen the walls, renew the roofs (the Banqueting Hall has massive beams with the date of 1926) and reset the windows, all with the object of returning the house to its former appearance, a task in which, I may say, the duke eminently succeeded. The restoration work has now mellowed into the earlier work, so that it is almost impossible to tell the old from the new. The present Duke of Rutland (the tenth), however, continues to live at Belvoir, while his brother, Lord John Manners, lives at Haddon (in apartments round the upper courtyard).

In an ante-room to the north of the Long Gallery is a doorway through which Dorothy is supposed to have escaped when she fled from Haddon. She then, says tradition, hurried down the steps from the upper terrace and through the gardens, and down a long flight of steps and over a packhorse bridge across the Wye, where John was waiting with the horses. It seems reasonable that she should wish to leave by the back door to escape Sir George's eagle eye, but then she must have slid down the bank to the river, for the terraced gardens were built up only in the eighteenth century and the packhorse bridge, it seems, was not built until the seventeenth century. We can go on conjecturing about the elopement, but whether we believe the story or not, we can all enjoy the beautiful rose gardens, looking down the delightful valley of the Wye to its junction with the Derwent.

16 Bakewell: Capital of the Peak

Bakewell (421368) is a delightful stone-built market town in the Wye valley, in a bowl surrounded by finely wooded hills, less than two miles above Haddon Hall and about three-and-a-half miles above the junction of the Wye with the Derwent. It is famous for its tarts, or 'puddings' as they are called locally, and for its agricultural show, held on a Thursday early in August and claimed to be the largest one-day show in England. A well-dressing festival has been held every July since 1971, in the Bath Gardens and in front of the Old Town Hall.

The name of the place was originally 'Badeca's wells', the wells or springs belonging to a Saxon overlord. These number about twelve, in and around the town, and their chalybeate or iron-bearing water has a constant temperature of 59°F. They have never been exploited in the mannor of Matlock or Buxton, and most of the wells have now dried up and have been filled in. There is no evidence that the Romans knew of the wells, though a Roman altar stone was dug up between Bakewell and Haddon Hall (it now stands in the porch to the Banqueting Hall at Haddon). Earlier inhabitants seemingly avoided the valley and kept to the high ground of the limestone uplands. The ramparts of an Iron Age fort, for instance, can be seen near Ball Cross, above the valley to the east.

The Saxon town would begin to develop around the ford over the Wye near the fine bridge built about 1300 (but widened in the nineteenth century). From here it grew across the level ground beside the river to the present town centre (before the Rutland Arms Hotel) and then up the hill to where the church now stands, a prominent landmark in the vicinity. In the churchyard is a fine cross-shaft, about 10 feet high, with a small part of its cross-head remaining and with animals and defaced human figures, as well as the spiral decoration that dates it to the late eighth century.

These Saxon crosses and cross-shafts of Peakland and the surrounding area I have divided into two groups. The earlier group, which I call Mercian, are distinguished by their spiral vine-scroll decoration and all date from the late eighth and early ninth centuries (when the Peak District was part of the kingdom of Mercia), but the only ones in the Peak are at Bradbourne, Eyam and here at Bakewell. The later group, which I call Viking, date from the tenth and eleventh centuries (by which time the Peak was under the Viking administration). These I divide again into two further groups: those of the tenth century, which have interlace decoration (a sort of woven pattern) and of which there are examples at Leek, Ilam, Hope and, again, here at Bakewell, and those of the eleventh century, which also have interlace decoration, but are to be distinguished by a single or double band round the shaft, about half way up, the section of the shaft usually being square below this and round above. Examples of these in the Peak are to be seen at Ashbourne, Leek, Ilam, Cleulow (near Wincle), Macclesfield and Whaley Bridge. Many other Saxon crosses are to be found in the North Midlands, especially in Derbyshire and Staffordshire, but also in the neighbouring counties.

In the church porch at Bakewell are collected, in haphazard fashion, other cross-shafts and tombstones, some of them Saxon, while others are stacked inside the west wall of the church (all these need tabulating and displaying in better fashion), and many were used in a considerable rebuilding of the church in the nineteenth century. The stump of the tenth century cross near the porch, already mentioned, was brought from Two Dales, near Darley Dale.

Edward the Elder (901-25), the son of Alfred of Wessex (Alfred the Great), after pushing back the Viking invaders in the North Midlands, ordered a borough (a 'fortified place') to be built here in 924, as recorded in the *Anglo-Saxon Chronicle*, the first mention of Bakewell; and a meeting was held here at which the Scots, the Northumbrians and the Strathclyde Welsh (as they were called) "chose Edward as father and lord". On Castle Hill, west of the bridge, are the motte-and-bailey earthworks of an early stronghold (and fields nearby bear such names as Castle Field, Warden Field and Court Yard), but it is very doubtful whether these earthworks were part of Edward's fortifications (as sometimes claimed), as no Saxon mottes have been dated as early as this, and in fact a recent theory is that no mottes at all were thrown up before the Norman Conquest.

A minster church (like that at Ashbourne) was founded at Bakewell in 920 or 930. The church was made collegiate (that is, it had a college of priests attached to it) in the twelfth century, and a large new building was begun at this time. Of this church, only the west front, with unusual decoration on its doorway, and the first bays of the north and south arcades of the nave survive (or perhaps were ever built). Arches inside the west front led into towers that were never completed. If the Norman church had been finished and still stood, it would look very much like that at Melbourne, in south Derbyshire, though even here the towers were never taken to their full height.

In 1192 Prince John gave the church into the keeping of the Dean and Chapter of Lichfield (in whose diocese it was) and it seems likely that a rebuilding was begun sometime after this. The long south transept was built about 1220-40, with tall lancet windows (all renewed in the last century), and the chancel was rebuilt in the late thirteenth century. The two-light lancets here and the sedilia and double piscina date from this time as do the widening of the north aisle and the peirs of the crossing tower, but the upper part of the tower and the spire were raised in about 1340, and the nave, too, was probably rebuilt in the fourteenth century. The south porch, the clerestory and the battlements are additions of the fifteenth century, when some of the windows were inserted; but the history of the church is obscured by a drastic restoration undertaken between 1841 and 1852, when the nave arcades were refashioned "in a lighter style", the transepts almost completely rebuilt and the tower and spire re-erected.

Though rather too well restored, the church still has much of interest. The early fourteenth-century font, carved from a single block of gritstone, is the finest in the Peak District. In the south aisle is a wall monument to Sir Godfrey Foljambe, who died in 1377, and his wife, showing the half-figures upright, as though they were looking out of a window. This is the earliest alabaster monument in the Peak District, though alabaster, quarried along the Trent and lower Dove valleys (it is still quarried, or rather mined, here, but we now call it gypsum), had been used for monuments, mostly of more important people, such as Edward II (at Gloucester), since the beginning of the fourteenth century.

The most interesting monuments are in the aisle of the south transept, usually called the Vernon Chapel. The oldest effigy here is that in alabaster of Sir Thomas Wendesley (perhaps Wensley, near Winster), who was killed at the Battle of Shrewsbury in 1403. The alabaster tomb-chest without effigy is that of John Vernon of Haddon Hall, who died in 1477. Between these two, on a massive tomb-chest, lies Sir George Vernon, 'King of the Peak', who died in 1567, and his two wives, an early and splendid work in alabaster (still with traces of colouring) by Richard and Gabriel Royley, who had their workshops at Burton-on-Trent and later churned out monuments in mass-produced fashion, with stock figures.

At the south end of the chapel is the rather poor monument of Sir George's famous daughter, Dorothy, who died in 1584, and her husband Sir John Manners, a characteristic standing wall monument with the pair kneeling and facing each other across a prayer-desk; the curiously disproportionate children underneath might have been taken from other monuments. Sir John sports a formidable black beard, but looking at Dorothy's features makes one wonder why he wanted to elope with her, if indeed he did. (Sorry! I will say no more.) At the other end of the chapel is a large wall monument to their son, Sir George, who died in 1623, and his wife, Lady Grace Manners (formerly a Talbot), the founder of the Grammar School at Bakewell that bears her name.

Up the hill behind the church is the Old House, one of the few genuinely medieval houses in the Peak District. It was built in the fifteenth century, when it was called the Parsonage House, and came into the hands of the Dean of Lichfield before 1549, after which an extension was added

Tideswell Church

Chatsworth House

on the east. The house was purchased by Ralph Gell, the dean's bailiff (we have seen his alabaster tomb-slab in Wirksworth church) and in 1777 it was leased by the Gells to Sir Richard Arkwright for housing workers in his mill at Bakewell. In 1796, when it was described as being "in ten dwellings", it was bought outright by the Arkwrights, who owned it until 1860. After this the house passed through various hands until 1955, when it was scheduled for demolition, but it was happily saved from this fate by the Bakewell Historical Society, which indeed was formed for this purpose. The society have since carefully restored the house to its appearance in medieval times, as far as possible, and it now contains their interesting local history museum, including many old 'bygones' and costumes, and relics of industrial history, including a loom from the Arkwright mill and a 'fish-bellied' rail from the Cromford and High Peak Railway.

Bakewell is one of the oldest market centres in and around the Peak District, but its original charter (if it ever had one) has been lost. In 1330, however, the right to hold a Monday market was confirmed, according to 'ancient custom', and the town still holds a flourishing market on that day. Its first fair is recorded in 1254; fairs are now held at Bakewell on the Mondays at Easter, the Spring Bank Holiday and the Late Summer Bank Holiday, and these are especially animated occasions.

The site of the market was transferred in 1826 to its present location behind the Market Hall, in Bridge Street, and in 1897 the rights were bought by the town council from the Duke of Rutland, the land-owner. The livestock market is the largest in Derbyshire (after that at Derby). The Market Hall was rebuilt in the late seventeenth century, but inside are to be seen the arches, probably older, that were once open to the street and that were brought to light when the building was being renovated (in 1968-71) for use as an Information Centre for the National Park, and a very good information centre, too, with exhibits and displays relating to old Bakewell.

Until the end of the eighteenth century, Bakewell still had rather a medieval aspect, with narrow streets and timber-framed buildings, some of them with thatched roofs, many of these later to be encased in stone and the roofs replaced by gritstone slabs or tiles. The streets converged on the square (now much smaller than it was) below the old Town Hall, which was rebuilt in 1709. Quarter sessions were held upstairs here until 1786, when there was a riot over the balloting for the North Derbyshire militia. From 1826 until 1874 the Town Hall was occupied by the Lady Manners School, which now has large buildings above the town near the Monyash road.

Uphill from the old Town Hall is St John's Hospital, almshouses built in 1709 for a charity for six single men founded in 1602 by Sir John Manners. Until the building of the almshouses the inmates were lodged in cells below the Town Hall. Beyond Church Alley is an interesting row of seven cottages, formerly thatched, and other good houses of the eighteenth century, with classical features, can be seen in the vicinity.

Fronting the pleasant Bath Gardens, on the north of Rutland Square, is Bath House, built for the Duke of Rutland in 1697 (though altered since). It contains a bath (not accessible to the public), 33 feet long by 16 feet wide, fed by one of the warm springs. White Watson, whom we shall meet again at Ashford-in-the-Water, lived here. Bagshaw Hall, on the hillside north of the church, sometimes called Bakewell Hall (and now the Conservative Club), is a rambling house of 1686 built by Thomas Bagshawe, a lawyer, and later the property of the Fitzherberts of Tissington.

The Rutland Arms, facing the Square (new at that time and now the town centre), was built in 1804, when a row of houses, shown on the town map of 1799, was demolished. Jane Austen stayed at the inn in 1811 and here Elizabeth Bennet met her sister's Bingley in *Pride and Prejudice*. Bakewell is the 'Lambton' of the novel and Chatsworth also comes into it, as 'Pemberley'. Bakewell 'puddings' were first made in the kitchens of the inn about 1859 by accident; a servant, instead of using her egg mixture to make the pastry of a strawberry jam tart, as instructed, apparently poured it over the jam. Bakewell puddings, which have been made this way ever since, can be bought at the 'original' Bakewell Pudding Shop in Bridge Street and elsewhere in the town.

William Graves, born at the inn in 1807, was the landlord for over fifty years, as well as being the postmaster of Bakewell, a 'Contractor for the Queen's Highway' (which involved running some twenty coaches), secretary to the Bakewell Hunt, a member of the North Derbyshire Yeomanry Corps, a member of both the Board of Guardians and the Local Board, and (as if that were not enough) farming some 700 acres. The stables of his time still survive, on the other side of the Buxton road. Graves was related to Sir Joseph Paxton (of Chatsworth), who laid out the garden of Bridge House, a fine building of about 1800, near the river. Other good houses of this period are to be found in the town, including Rutland Terrace, facing the Buxton road, and a terrace in Castle Street, near the bridge.

Pleasant walks follow the Wye downstream to the Recreation Ground (opposite the site of the agricultural showground) and upstream on the north bank of the river towards Holme Hall (421369), a four-square building of 1626 with battlements and a central porch, similar in style to Tissington Hall. Beyond Holme Bridge, a fine packhorse bridge of 1664, is the site of Lumford Mill, a cotton-spinning mill built in 1777 (six years after his first mill at Cromford) by Sir Richard Arkwright and "employing 300 hands, mostly woman and children". Finally sold by the Arkwrights in 1860, it was burned down in 1868, and the building on the site of the mill is now occupied by a firm of machine-knife manufacturers. But the bridge over the Wye survives from Arkwright's time, and the eighteenth-century Lumford House (now three dwellings), near the packhorse bridge, was the home of Richard Arkwright II when he was manager of the mill. Behind the house is an old quarry where chert was dug for use in the pottery industry. Limestone facing blocks are now made here.

The introduction of cotton spinning at Bakewell met with some opposition. Arkwright found himself engaged in a lawsuit with the Duke of Rutland, who claimed that the mill would interfere with the fishing in the Wye. But the building of the mill brought new employment to the town, which no doubt shared also in the prosperity of the lead mining industry of the neighbouring limestone uplands that had reached its peak by about this time. The agricultural pattern was changing, too; the Enclosure Act of 1806 ensured that the Wye valley should not be marred by fences, but should be enclosed with 'Quicksets and Drains'.

Bakewell continued to prosper as an agricultural centre during the nineteenth century. Continued Victorian affluence is demonstrated by such buildings as the Bakewell Savings Bank of 1848, in Bath Street, and the Sheffield and Rotherham Bank of 1838 (now Williams & Glyn's), the Town Hall of 1891 and the Post Office of 1894, all in the road leading to the bridge. The town has so far managed to avoid most of the 'improvements' of the present century and now takes its place naturally as the administrative centre of the national park. The Peak Park Planning Board offices are at Aldern House in Baslow Road, the road to the upper Derwent valley (Chapter 21).

17 The Wye Valley: Bakewell to Buxton

The road from Bakewell to Buxton, part of the Derby-Manchester road (A6), goes up the valley of the Wye at first, passing the factory on the site of Arkwright's mill, and keeping to the south side of the river to by-pass Ashford-in-the-Water (i.e., 'in-the-Wye'). On the other side we have a glimpse of Ashford Hall, begun in 1772, with pleasant gardens landscaped in the mid-nineteenth century.

Ashford (419369; 'in-the-Water' is a late addition to the name) is a delightful village with mellow stone houses, many of them of the eighteenth century, well situated below the gap through which the Wye emerges from a narrow valley in the limestone hills. The church, mostly rebuilt in 1870, has a Norman doorway the tympanum of which is carved with curious animals on either side of the tree of life, a boar or hog on the left and a dog or wolf on the right. The tower may be of the thirteenth century, but the tower arch and the north arcade are of the fouteenth century. The font is of the fourteenth century, too, with the head and tail of a dragon (an evil spirit?) on either side of the bowl, as though the creature were creeping through it.

In the north aisle hang four 'crowns' of paper on wooden frames. These are maidens' garlands, or "virgin crants" as they are called in *Hamlet*, where they were brought to Ophelia's burial (v. 1). Two at least date from the eighteenth century, and it was once the custom to carry such a garland before the coffin in the funeral procession of a betrothed maiden who had died before her wedding day.

On the south wall of the church is a tablet in 'black marble' to Henry Watson of Bakewell, who in 1748 opened the quarries near Ashford from which this mineral was obtained. Ashford black marble is an impure limestone containing a high proportion of carbonaceous and argillaceous (clay-like) matter;

it is a darkish grey when it comes out of the quarry, but turns a shiny black with frequent polishing. Columns of grey (unpolished) marble can be seen on either side of the fireplace in the High Great Chamber at Hardwick Hall, completed in 1597 (the first known use of the marble), and we shall see large columns of polished marble in the chapel at Chatsworth (Chapter 22), where the building accounts record that quarries were opened on Sheldon Moor in 1687.

Henry Watson, who died in 1786, was the grandson of Samuel Watson, who was responsible for the splendid wood carving at Chatsworth, and uncle of White Watson, who first worked out successfully the geological system of the Peak District. Henry devised a machine for cutting and polishing the marble, and was the first to make ornaments from it. In the nineteenth century the marble was very popular for vases and other ornaments, jewellery, table-tops, fireplaces and the like; and inlaid work became fashionable, using coloured stones (mostly from the Peak District, but some from elsewhere, even from the Continent) in floral or geometrical patterns. Examples are on display in the Buxton Museum and elsewhere. A fine collection made by Robert Thornhill of Great Longstone, together with the tools of the marble cutters (which he found thrown away on a rubbish heap), have been given by him to the Derby Museum. The marble mills at Ashford closed about 1905, though inlaying was regularly done at Buxton until about 1920. Other decorative stones were obtained from the Wye valley above Ashford, and in the church is a table made in 1882 of Rosewood and other coloured marbles.

The Wye is crossed near the church by the seventeenth-century Sheepwash Bridge, which is unique in having a stone pen attached to it that is still used in washing sheep. The sheep are driven through the gap on the road side of the pen and can only escape through the gap on the river side, where they are well and truly dipped. Ashford still has a well-dressing festival (like Tissington) and here the ceremony takes place on Trinity Sunday or the first Sunday after Trinity.

The road through the village rejoins the Buxton road as it crosses the Wye near a small building which is all that remains of Henry Watson's marble works. The road up Kirk Dale to the

The Wye Valley: Bakewell to Buxton

south towards Sheldon (Chapter 14), passes one of the Ashford marble quarries (now inaccessible). The main road runs below the beautiful Great Shacklow Wood, where the water can be seen issuing from the 'tail' of the Magpie Sough, begun in 1873 to 'unwater' the Magpie Mine over a mile and a quarter away. The road recrosses the Wye to the foot of Deep Dale, well named, then leaves the river and makes the long winding ascent through the delightfully wooded Taddington Dale (416371), now partly owned by the National Trust, to reach the limestone uplands short of Taddington.

A charming footpath, starting from the bridge, follows the Wye upstream through Monsal Dale (417371), which makes a great sweep round under the steep flanks of Fin Cop (1072 feet). The level top of this is crowned by the ramparts of an Iron Age promontory fort, probably of the first century B.C. The dale sides are partly covered by woods, and through these the path climbs to Monsal Head (418371; sometimes called Headstone Head), which can be reached more directly from Ashford by road. This is one of the finest viewpoints in the Peak District, though for this reason much too congested at weekends and in the summer. The noble prospect extends both up and down the river, which just below us makes an acute bend to pass under the great viaduct on the railway from Bakewell to Buxton against which John Ruskin thundered when it was opened in 1863. Shooting out from the tunnel on to the viaduct high above the Wye was one of the most dramatic moments in the journey from London to Manchester, but the railway is now closed. The suggestion that the viaduct should be demolished, however, met with another great outburst. It has now become part of the landscape!

The road to the east from Monsal Head goes through Little Longstone, a charming hamlet with the eighteenth-century manor house of the Longsdons and other limestone dwellings. Farther east is Great Longstone (420371), a characteristic limestone village mainly stretched along one street, with several eighteenth-century houses and with medieval cross steps on the small green near one end. The Crispin Inn, with its sign of the patron-saint of shoemakers, reminds us that the village was once engaged in this industry, though the lead-mining industry was far more important. Near the inn is the restored manor house, partly medieval (with remains of cruck frames inside) and partly of the eighteenth century, and opposite this is the approach to Longstone Hall, long a home of the Wright family, a stone house probably of the fifteenth century but with a brick façade added in 1747.

The well-restored thirteenth- to fifteenth-century church has fourteenth-century nave arcades and good fifteenth-century roofs with bosses carved mainly with arms and flowers, though one (difficult to see) shows a lead miner. The modern pulpit has a small pillar of Duke's Red Marble, an iron-stained limestone which was mined at Alport, near Youlgreave, from 1831 onward. The entire deposit is said to have been worked out on the instructions of the landowner, the Duke of Devonshire, who stored the marble in the cellars at Chatsworth and sold small quantities occasionally for inlaying and other decorative work.

Above the village to the north stretches Longstone Edge (420373; 1284 feet), a bold ridge of the limestone etched with old lead rakes. High Rake, right along the top of the escarpment, is being scored out again in an enormous trench for the yellow-brown fluorspar, which is taken away by a succession of lorries to Sheffield for use as a flux in the making of steel.

The road descending into the Wye valley from Monsal Head takes us to Cressbrook Mill (417372). The original cotton mill here was built about 1783 by Sir Richard Arkwright, and the first manager was William Newton, the carpenter-poet whom Anna Seward dubbed 'the Minstrel of the Peak'. Because of the isolation of the site, the mill had to depend for its labour on workhouse boys, or 'parish apprentices' as they were called, who lived in cottages near by (since pulled down). Cressbrook was then a comparatively small mill and there were at the most only about sixty apprentices. Newton found his post at the mill hard and tedious, and the hours long, but he treated his apprentices well, unlike the owner of Litton Mill farther upstream. When Sir Richard died in 1792 the mill was sold by his son, Richard Arkwright II, and the large building in a classical style, rather like a great country house, was built in 1815 by the new owner.

A delightful footpath, starting behind the mill, ascends

The Wye Valley: Bakewell to Buxton 139

through Millers Dale (416373; formerly Millhouse Dale), where the river makes a great S-bend under fine limestone crags on its way to Litton Mill. Roadusers will have to tackle one of the steep roads up to the hamlet of Cressbrook and go on via Litton (Chapter 21) and Tideswell Dale to reach the main dale again.

Among the more modern buildings at Litton Mill (416373) can be seen the original mill built in 1782 by Ellis Needham, one of the most notorious of the early millowners, or factory masters, as they are often called. When Needham and his partner, Thomas Firth, attempted to dispose of the mill in 1786, their advertisement declared that it was "well supplied by Hands from the neighbouring Villages at Low Wages". This supply of cheap labour was presented as one of the attractions of the site, but when he failed to sell the mill Needham changed over to parish apprentices. His evil reputation in the use of these boys, mostly from London, was made public in a Memoir by one of them, Robert Blincoe, published in 1832.

Robert Blincoe was employed at Litton Mill from 1803 to 1814. He had received no education, he could not read or write, and his Memoir was written down by a John Brown, who has been accused of distorting the facts. The style of the publication, says one writer, "with its Dickensian pathos and tedious repetition", is not calculated to appeal to twentieth-century readers", and the Memoir, published some eighteen years after Blincoe had left the mill, has been regarded by some as propaganda for the Factory Act of 1833. Nevertheless, Blincoe's recollections seem to me to have been borne out by the comments of other, perhaps less-biased observers. The case has been argued by Stanley Chapman in *The Early Factory Masters* and Miss M. H. Mackenzie in the *Derbyshire Archaeological Journal* (1968-70).

The lane going upstream from the mill passes below a sheer limestone crag where the black deposits of volcanic outpourings referred to in Chapter 2 can be well seen. The lane passes the foot of Tideswell Dale (415373), rich with many varieties of flower in summer (the Peak Park Planning Board has produced a Nature Trail). A path ascends the dale to a picnic place near the road coming from Tideswell (Chapter 21). As this road takes us back into Millers Dale, we have a good view of a large quarry of dark-brown dolerite on the other side of Tideswell Dale, before passing the beautifully-situated youth hostel of Ravenstor, a National Trust Property.

The road reaches the deep-sunk valley floor at the hamlet of Millers Dale (414373), beyond which it crosses the Wye. From the bridge an excellent path follows the north bank of the river into the well-wooded Cheedale, rounding the huge upstanding limestone crag of Chee Tor (412373), one of the most impressive in the Peak District. The path passes below the entrance to Great Rocks Dale, up which the railway ran for Manchester, and comes out on to the Bakewell-Buxton road in Wye Dale.

Another road from the bridge in Millers Dale climbs up to Wormhill (412374), sheltered in an upland hollow on the north side of Chee Dale. The Hall, built in 1697, is a fine example of the transition from the vernacular style of the period between 1540 and 1700 to that of the eighteenth century. The house has double gables and mullioned and transomed windows, but it also has a segmental pediment over the doorway and other features that are more commonly met with in the eighteenth century. Its predecessor, Old Hall Farm, farther up, is of the sixteenth and seventeenth centuries. The church, mostly rebuilt in 1864, has a gabled top to the tower that was probably inspired by the famous Saxon helm-tower of Sompting, in Sussex.

On the green is a well which is dressed each year on the Saturday before the Late Summer Bank Holiday. The well is a memorial to James Brindley, who was born in 1716 a mile away to the north-west, at Tunstead (411375), a hamlet of only two or three farms. His cottage birthplace has disappeared and of an ash-tree that forced its way through the floor only the stump now remains. Brindley, who as a lad sometimes worked at Old Hall Farm at Wormhill and led the waggons taking sacks of grain down to the grist mill in Chee Dale, moved away when he was seventeen to be apprenticed to a millwright at Gurnett, near Macclesfield (Chapter 5). In Great Rocks Dale (410374), to the west of Tunstead, is the largest limestone quarry in Europe.

The road south from Millers Dale climbs out to join the Bakewell-Buxton road west of Taddington (414371), an impoverished-looking village standing on a shelf of the limestone at about 1100 feet and commanding a splended view north over the deep-hewn gorge of the Wye to the distant moorlands of Kinder Scout. The restored fourteenth-century church has tall arcades and square-headed chancel windows, as well as a contemporary stone lectern or book-rest built into the chancel wall, a feature to be found only in Derbyshire (which has five of these). The tower is built of gritstone, the body of the church of limestone, with gritstone dressings. In the churchyard is a remarkable shaft, 6 feet high, carved with chevron and saltire decoration. "Is it Norman?" asks Dr Pevsner; well, it certainly doesn't have any features corresponding with the Peakland Saxon crosses, and there seems to be no indication that it even bore a cross-head.

To the west of Taddington rises a long ridge of the limestone, the eastern part of which is called Taddington Moor (though moor is a term better suited to the gritstone country), while the western part is known as Chelmorton Low. On the saddle of the ridge is the so-called Five Wells (412371; Long Cairn on the Ordnance Survey map), a chambered tomb of the New Stone Age, the highest in England at over 1400 feet. This has been completely revealed by the erosion of the mound that once covered it, and the arrangements have been laid bare by the loss of the capstones. The tomb consisted of two burial chambers, wedge-shaped in plan and placed back to back, reached from the outside by passages. Both chambers and passages were lined by large, upright, roughly-dressed stones, with two pillar-like stones defining the break between the chamber and the passage. Some twelve inhumations were found in the chambers, together with fragments of pottery and flint tools. The mound which covered the tomb could hardly have been less than 20 feet high or 90 feet across, and must have been a distinctive landmark on top of the hill.

Chelmorton (411370), on the west side of the Low, is the highest village in Derbyshire, at about 1200 feet, and the second in England (only Flash is higher). It still follows the pattern laid down in Saxon times, with about a dozen farmsteads spaced along either side of the single street and the former crofts or individual holdings of the farms appearing as long, walled fields behind. It must have retained its Saxon and medieval appearance later than most villages (the outer fields in the parish were enclosed only in 1805). The church, at the upper end, has a Norman south arcade, an unusual north arcade, perhaps of the thirteenth century, a tower of the thirteenth century and a fourteenth-century chancel, but the upper part of the tower is of the fifteenth century, as is the unusual stone chancel screen.

Calton Hill, to the north of Chelmorton, is gradually being quarried away to extract the dolerite, an intrusion of volcanic rock into the limestone that is now used in road building. The northern foot of the hill is skirted by the Buxton road before this descends into Wye Dale, reaching the valley floor below Topley Pike, where the oldest deposits of the limestone come to the surface. The road up Wye Dale passes the entrance to another Deep Dale (410371), now partly occupied by a large quarry. Farther up this dale are caves where prehistoric finds have been made. The winding road goes on beside the Wye through Ashwood Dale to reach the main street of Buxton (Chapter 18).

18   Buxton: the Peakland Spa

Buxton (405373) has the highest market place in England, standing well over 1000 feet above sea-level and about fifty feet higher than that of Alston in Cumberland, often claimed to be the highest. The probable reason for this confusion is that the market place at Alston is pitched high up on the steep side of a hill, whereas at Buxton the town is completely surrounded by higher hills. Set in a great bowl formed by the head reaches of the Wye valley, it has limestone uplands on the south side and gritstone moorlands on the north. The wonderful position of Buxton would have demanded that a town be established here, quite apart from the development as a spa that resulted from the presence of its warm springs.

The waters of Buxton, famous for their healing virtues and unchanging at all seasons at a temperature of 82°F, were known to the Romans, who called their settlement here *Aquae Arnemetiae*. The second part of the name was perhaps adapted from the name of a local deity (as at Bath); 'aquae' of course means water. Many Roman roads led to the spa; that which came from Doncaster and Brough is still called Batham Gate, the 'road to the baths'. But we have no idea what the settlement was like, though Roman bricks and tiles and Roman coins have been found (and can be seen in the Buxton Museum) and the remains of a bath have been discovered (and, unfortunately, destroyed). In Saxon times, when Buxton became part of the Royal Forest of the Peak (Chapter 21), the waters appear to have been neglected, but one can imagine the king's deer (which appear on the town's arms) drinking the warm water that trickled from the springs into the river.

The tradition of the springs, at least, was not entirely forgotten. In the Middle Ages, in spite of Buxton's remoteness and its lack of accommodation, pilgrims sought out the well. Buxton had no parish church (it was included in the huge parish of Bakewell), but near the springs a chapel had been built, dedicated to St Anne, patron-saint of cripples. In the sixteenth century the chapel walls were hung with "crutches, shirts and shifts". Sir William Bassett, one of Henry VIII's commissioners, confiscated these as "being things that entice and allure the ignorant"; he also removed the image of St Anne and finally sealed the wells and the chapel.

By the time of Elizabeth I, the wells were open again and in fact were being visited by a great concourse of poor people, who created a problem for the legislators. The Poor Law of 1572 declares that "a greate number of pore and dyseased people do resorte to the . Towne of Buckston . for some Ease and Releife of the Diseases at the Bathes there, and by meanes thereof the Inhabitauntes . of Buckstone are greatly overcharged". As a result "no dyseased or ympotent poore person living on Almes" should be permitted to visit the place unless he had received a licence from two Justices of the Peace and was provided for by the place from which he came.

The first house for the benefit of bathers was built by George Talbot, sixth Earl of Shrewsbury. It is described in a tract by Dr John Jones, 'The Benefit of the auncient Bathes of Buckstones', published in 1572, and is depicted on John Speed's map of Derbyshire, published in 1610. In addition to the "very goodly house, foure square, foure stories hye", there were in Buxton other "goodly lodgings to the number of 30", as well as "necessaries most decent", all "defended from the ambyent ayre". Charges for using the baths varied, according to rank, from £5 for an archbishop and £3 10s. for a duke down to 12d. for a yeoman.

From 1573 on Mary, Queen of Scots, who was under the charge of the Earl of Shrewsbury, was brought over from Chatsworth several times for the benefit of the waters. The poor lady, who suffered from rheumatism (and apparently "found some relief"), stayed at the Earl of Shrewsbury's house, now called the Old Hall (and a hotel, facing the Pavilion Gardens). This was rebuilt in 1670 and altered again in the eighteenth century, so nothing is now to be seen of Mary's time. After her last visit in 1584 (three years before her execution), she is said to have inscribed, on a window pane of the hall, a Latin couplet which can be translated as: "Buxton, whose fame thy milk-white waters tell, Whom I, perhaps, no more shall see, farewell".

Other great personages also visited Buxton at this time. William Cecil, Lord Burghley, called "the greatest statesman of his age", was here in 1575, not for the first time, though Elizabeth suspected he came for political reasons and was scheming on behalf of Mary, Queen of Scots. On a later visit, in 1577, he was "thoroughly licensed by her Majesty to come thither". The Earl of Leicester, too, came here in 1577; he had been ordered by his physician to "drink Buxton water twenty days together", though the Queen of Scots thought that his real motive was to sound out the opinion of the nobility concerning his proposed marriage to Elizabeth. The Earl of Sussex, soldier and patron of men of letters, was here in 1577 and again in 1582.

Queen Elizabeth herself projected a visit to Buxton, but she never came, and after the close of her flamboyant reign, the spa's popularity waned and its facilities declined. Charles Cotton included St Anne's Well in his 'Wonders of the Peake', published in 1681, and the bath-house was rebuilt by the third Earl of Devonshire. The baths were "much frequented, especially by the Northern Nobility and Gentry", but they would have been more popular with society "were there better conveniences of lodging and entertainment". Joseph Taylor, visiting Buxton in 1705 on his way to Edinburgh, describes it as "a poor little Stony Town" and although Defoe acknowledged that in the Bath House there were "convenient Lodging and very good Provisions", he thought the most remarkable thing about Buxton was that natural opportunities superior to those of Bath could be so much neglected.

The old village, clustering round what is now the Market Place and along the High Street stretching south, continued its separate existence. (Even today, Buxton is divided into a higher town and a lower town which seem largely to ignore each other's existence.) The market cross is said to date from the fifteenth century, though there is no record of a market at this time. Tucked away out of sight off the High Street is St Anne's Church, a low, chapel-like building, with no tower, no aisles and no structural division between the nave and the chancel and with the massive tie-beams only about seven feet from the floor. The date of the church itself is probably earlier than that of 1625 given on the porch. In the Market Place the Duke of Devonshire built the large Eagle Hotel in the early eighteenth century, and there are other, humbler inns and houses of this period in the vicinity.

Buxton continued to decline during much of the eighteenth century, and its real development as a fashionable spa began about 1780, when the fifth Duke of Devonshire, who was the landowner, conceived the idea of converting Buxton into a second Bath. By this time the growing use of stage coaches was resulting in the replacement of old packhorse routes by relatively better-made roads; travelling was becoming safer and places like Buxton rather less inaccessible.

For the fifth Duke, the architect John Carr of York designed The Crescent, completed in 1786, at the foot of St Anne's Cliff, close to the original well. Carr modelled his crescent on the Royal Crescent at Bath, which had been completed only five years before. The rather cramped position did not permit him the grand sweep or the wonderful vista of John Wood the younger's crescent at Bath, but as architecture Carr's more classical and elegant crescent is the finer work. Building problems were caused by the fact that the river Wye runs below the Crescent; it had to be tunnelled beneath the foundations, which were then supported on piles.

The Crescent is in the form of a segment of a circle of 200 feet span, with a wing some 58 feet long projecting at either end, making a total length of about 316 feet. A paved walkway on the ground floor, 11 feet high and 7 feet wide, is raised above the level of the road on steps and divided from it by an arcade with a series of forty rusticated pillars. These support the façade, two tall storeys high, which has fluted Tuscan pilasters rising to the frieze and the balustrade, where the Cavendish arms are displayed in the centre. The Assembly Room inside is a splendid apartment with a richly decorated ceiling, large Corinthian pilasters and alcoves at each end screened off by Corinthian columns, rather in the manner of Robert Adam. The Crescent was originally occupied entirely by hotels (one of which survives), with shops at the front; all were owned by the duke, and visitors had "the exclusive privilege of bathing before nine o'clock".

Calver Mill

Froggatt Edge

Up the slope behind the Crescent, Carr built for the fifth Duke in 1786 the large Stables and Riding School, with a covered circular courtyard for riding exercise and with stalls (for 110 horses) which can still be seen inside, round the courtyard. These, with the Crescent, cost the duke £120,000, a sum said to have been provided by the profits of his copper mines at Ecton. In 1858 these stables and riding school were converted by the sixth Duke of Devonshire into a hospital (now the Devonshire Royal Hospital) and in 1880 the architect Henry Currey covered the central courtyard with a large iron-framed dome, the widest unsupported dome in the world, with a span of 154 feet (St Peter's in Rome has a span of 142 feet, the Reading Room of the British Museum is 140 feet in diameter, and St Paul's Cathedral is a mere 112 feet).

To the north of the Old Hall, John Carr built The Square (in about 1786), a block of accommodation designed with an arcade all round on the ground floor so that residents could pass from house to house without going out in the rain.

By the time of the sixth Duke of Devonshire, Buxton had developed into a fashionable health resort. The 'Bachelor Duke' called in Sir Jeffry Wyatville, who was to work for him at Chatsworth, and he provided a new parish church for what had become a New Town. St John's, built in 1811, is in an Italianate style, with a massive portico and a tower rising to a domed top. Wyatville also began to lay out St Anne's Cliff (now usually called The Slopes) facing the Crescent. The large stone vases here are original, but the design was modified in the 1840s by Sir Joseph Paxton, the duke's gardener at Chatsworth, who also developed a new area of building, known as The Park, to the west of the church and the hospital. This had a circular open space in the centre, with the houses spaced around it, rather resembling John Nash's much larger conception for Regent's Park in London, begun in 1820. Some of the elegant villas in The Park, built between 1845 and 1850, still survive.

New Thermal Baths were built in 1851-53 to the east of the Crescent, to the designs of Henry Currey, who was apparently influenced by Paxton's new lily-house at Chatsworth. The Pump Room, opened in 1894, opposite the Crescent, is also by Currey, though originally it had an arcaded front and the interior was reconstructed in 1912. It is now a Peak National

Park information centre, but you can still sample the water here (at a small charge). The water, though warm, is not unpleasant; indeed it is much more palatable than that of Harrogate or Tunbridge Wells, which tastes like rotten eggs. You can also drink the water (free) from a fountain outside the Pump Room to the west. A well-dressing festival is held here in July, as well as in the market place at the top of the hill.

Further development began with the coming of the railways. The Midland Railway from Derby arrived in 1863 and the London and North Western Railway from Manchester in the following year. The trains ran side by side into identical stations, but this symmetry has been destroyed now that the gable end of one of the stations has been removed. The large Palace Hotel was built in 1868 by Henry Currey in a dominating position above the stations. In 1871 was formed the Buxton Improvements Company, to which the seventh Duke of Devonshire gave land along the banks of the Wye for the laying out of the ornamental Pavilion Gardens. The designer of these was Edward Milner, who had been associated with Paxton in the layout of the Crystal Palace grounds around the great Hyde Park exhibition building when it was removed there. The Pavilion, an iron and glass structure built in 1871 by R.R. Duke and flanked by a long conservatory, was enlarged in 1876 by an octagonal concert hall with a large dome.

Building has continued into the present century with the Opera House (now a cinema), designed by Frank Matcham and opened in 1903, adjoining the Pavilion Gardens. The interior, with a lavish use of marble and with ceiling paintings by Italian craftsmen, is by our time quite a period piece. The Natural Baths, adjoining the Old Hall Hotel, were reconstructed in 1924, but have now been closed. The newest of Buxton's municipal buildings is the Swimming Pool opened in 1972 at the west end of the Pavilion Gardens. The two baths here are filled with water pumped from the natural springs near the Crescent.

The waters of Buxton are of two kinds, the chalybeate or iron-bearing waters and (far more important) those from the radioactive thermal springs on which the fame and prosperity of the spa have depended. The thermal waters rise from an estimated depth of about 5000 feet in the limestone substrata and reach the surface in nine springs in or near the Crescent. The springs are identical not only in their constant temperature, but in their mineral and gaseous content, and they have a regular output of some 200,000 gallons per day. The water is notable for its pale-blue colour and for its clarity; bubbles of gas can be seen rising to the surface. The predominant mineral constituent is calcium and the gas is mainly nitrogen, with a mixture of carbon dioxide and certain radioactive gases such as argon and helium. It can now be sampled only in the former Pump Room and seen only here and in the new swimming pool.

Buxton is an excellent centre for walks. To the south of the Pavilion Gardens, we can follow Broad Walk, then continue past Buxton College, founded in 1674, to the entrance to Poole's Cavern (closed at the time of writing), another of the Seven Wonders of the Peak and one of the sources of the Wye, which flows through an underground chamber about 700 yards long, noted for its stalagmites and stalactites. The cavern penetrates into the northern face of Grin Low (405371), a limestone hill which is topped by a tower sometimes called Solomon's Temple, after Solomon Mycock, who built it in 1896 to provide employment for out-of-work men. The view extends over the limestone uplands to the south and east, south-west to Axe Edge, north-west to Burbage Edge and northward over Buxton to the gritstone moors of Combs Moss.

The southern end of the wood-fringed Burbage Edge is skirted by the old road from Buxton to the Cat and Fiddle Inn, another good walking route. This leaves the Macclesfield road in the suburb of Burbage (404372) and just beyond the church, rebuilt in 1861 by Henry Currey. The custom of 'clipping', or circumambulating in procession round the church, takes place here every July.

From the Whaley Bridge road above the Devonshire Royal Hospital, paths meander up through the woods to Corbar Hill (405374; 1433 feet), another fine view point, surmounted by a distinctive cross. From the top we can go on north over rough moorland by way of Combs Moss to Castle Naze and descend to Chapel-en-le-Frith (Chapter 19).

19 From Buxton to Glossop

The north-western side of the Peak District is a region of high gritstone moorlands split up by long, deep valleys that are partly given over to industry. Because of the presence of this industry, the boundary of the Peak District National Park follows rather a haphazard line. The boundary has been specifically drawn to exclude not only Buxton and the surrounding limestone quarries but also the towns of Whaley Bridge, Chapel-en-le-Frith, Hayfield and Glossop, mostly textile manufacturing towns of long standing. Though all are in Derbyshire, they are divided from the rest of the county by the central uplands of the Peak and seem in consequence to look naturally in the direction of Manchester and the Lancashire cotton towns.

The Manchester road (A6), starting from the east end of Spring Gardens, the main street of Buxton, and passing under an imposing railway viaduct of 1863, climbs out of the bowl of the Wye to Fairfield (406374), now no more than a suburb, but once a separate community. It faces an open, breezy common with a golf course which must be one of the highest in England, at over 1050 feet. At Town End, on the south side, are some interesting houses, including the Old Hall of 1687 (now three dwellings), with mullioned windows and with the flattish gables that indicate that it was built towards the end of the seventeenth century.

The main road crosses the common, with Black Edge, the eastern rampart of Combs Moss, rising to the left. It passes an enormous heap of lime waste to reach Dove Holes (407378), an uncompromising quarrying village. Behind the church to the east of the road is Bull Ring, a New Stone Age earthwork whose plan was similar to that at Arbor Low. The circular bank, about 250 feet in diameter, and the ditch remain, with two opposite entrances, but the stones have long since been broken up and used for building. A large mound, 8 feet high, to the south-west, seems to occupy a position analogous to that of Gib Hill near Arbor Low.

To the east of Bull Ring is the northernmost and highest in a series of huge limestone quarries that stretches down through Peak Dale and Great Rocks Dale (Chapter 17). The quarries at Dove Holes were formerly served by a tramway that carried the limestone and lime down to the Peak Forest Canal at Buxworth. The tramway, 7 miles long, with plate rails (not the usual edge rails) and a wide gauge of 4 feet 2 inches, was built by Benjamin Outram of the Butterley Company in 1794-96. Its trade was eventually destroyed by the more convenient road transport and it closed in 1921. The course of the tramway can clearly be seen to the left of the Chapel road before it reaches a road junction.

The road on the right here ascends to Sparrowpit (Chapter 21) on its way to Castleton or Peak Forest. On the right again in half a mile, opposite Bennetston Hall (now a hotel) and partly enclosed by a wall, is the Ebbing and Flowing Well, one of Charles Cotton's Wonders of the Peak. Because of movements in the limestone strata below, it no longer ebbs or flows.

The A6 descends the wooded valley of the Barmoor Clough to Chapel-en-le-Frith (406380), the 'chapel in the forest'. The frith of Saxon times became the Royal Forest of the Peak (see Chapter 21). The small town, in a hollow almost entirely surrounded by high gritstone moorlands, has had a market at least since Tudor times. The forest estates were held by William de Ferrers, Earl of Derby, in the thirteenth century, but in 1372 the manor passed to John of Gaunt and so became a possession of the Duchy of Lancaster. In the seventeenth century, when most of the district was disafforested, the freeholders retained the right of electing the vicar.

In the market place is the restored market cross and the old stocks are preserved here. As we approach it from the market place, the church appears to be entirely in the classical style of the eighteenth century; the west tower and the south aisle were rebuilt in 1733 by George Platt, a Rotherham architect. But the interior reveals a medieval church, though it was heavily restored in 1890. The first church was consecrated in 1226 as a chapel for the foresters and verderers in the royal forest. It was rebuilt in the Decorated style in the fourteenth century, and the red sandstone piers to the nave arcades are of this time. Across the tower arch are altar rails carved by a vicar in the seventeenth century and the Flemish candelabrum in the nave was given to the church in 1731.

In 1648 some 1500 Scots, supporters of Charles I who had been defeated under the Duke of Hamilton at the Battle of Preston, were brought here as prisoners and crowded in the church for sixteen days. Unable to lie down and with not enough air to breathe, it is not surprising that over forty of them died before the door was opened and the survivors began their forced march back towards Scotland.

In the chancel is buried William Bagshawe, the nonconformist minister known as the 'Apostle of the Peak', who died in 1702 and whose arms are on the wall. Ejected from the living of Glossop in 1662, after the Restoration of Charles II, he carried on his work in the wilder, less-frequented parts of the Peak, where several chapels were built for him. Warrants were issued from time to time for his arrest, but they were never enforced.

William Bagshawe lived at Ford Hall (407382), a seventeenth-century house with a fine Georgian façade of about 1727, in a deep valley below the gritstone moorlands that extend north to Kinder Scout, and well seen from the Castleton road. The road goes along Rushup Edge towards the head of The Winnats (Chapter 24). The building that looks like a large shooting box on the moors is in fact the top of a ventilator from the Cowburn Tunnel (pronounced 'Co-'), which is 2 miles 182 yards and was driven in 1892-95. It takes the Sheffield-Manchester railway right through the gritstone from Edale to the Chinley valley.

The A6 from Chapel, on its way west to Whaley Bridge, runs south of Eccles Pike (403381; 1213 feet), an elongated cone whose summit is owned by the National Trust. It affords a remarkably varied view, to the moorland heights of Kinder Scout on the one hand, and across the industrialised lower valley of the Goyt on the other. On the southern slopes is Bradshaw Hall, a seventeenth-century manor house, now converted into two farmhouses. The fine gateway bears the date of 1620 and the arms of the last of the Bradshaw family to live here.

The Whaley Bridge road skirts the dam of Combs Reservoir (403379; pronounced 'Coomz'), built to feed the Peak Forest Canal and now a popular venue for sailing. From the hamlet of Combs, in a secluded valley above the head of the reservoir, a narrow, twisting lane climbs over the northern flanks of Combs Moss. It passes below Castle Naze (405378), a buttress of the moors named from an Iron Age promontory fort on the plateau above. The north and west sides of the enclosure are protected naturally by the gritstone crags, partly quarried (and now a favourite climbing ground), but on the summit plateau it is defended by two ramparts, each with a ditch outside. At the north-west extremity a hollow way climbs up through a gap in the rocks to reach the enclosure. A fine moorland walk leads south from Castle Naze to the ridge of Black Edge (1662 feet) and thence down to Buxton.

Another steep lane from Combs runs south up the valley below Combs Edge (404376), the northern escarpment of Combs Moss, a name, however, which is often applied to the whole of the triangular mass of moorland in the angle between the roads from Buxton to Chapel and Whaley Bridge. The lane climbs steeply out of the valley to reach a narrow road on the course of the Roman road that connected Buxton with Manchester. To the south along this is an entrance to White Hall (403376), a house taken over in 1950 by the Derbyshire County Council as a centre for open country pursuits. Young people go out from here to be trained in walking, rock climbing, sailing and other outdoor activities. The Roman road descends north to Whaley Bridge, and runs south as a track to join the Buxton road on Long Hill (403375), from the top of which (1401 feet), the watershed between the Wye and the Goyt, the road on the west goes down to the dam of the Errwood Reservoir in the Goyt Valley (Chapter 8). The Whaley Bridge road makes a wide circuit round the head of a valley below White Hall (hidden among trees); the old road (once the post road to Manchester) crosses the valley more directly but considerably more precipitously. One can imagine the coaches toiling up the hill on either side, with the less affluent passengers struggling up on foot behind them.

Whaley Bridge (401381) is an old established cotton-weaving town which now has clothing and engineering factories. It has characteristic gritstone houses and inns, and is well situated at the entrance to the wooded upper valley of the Goyt, with its charming reservoirs. The track of the Cromford and High Peak Railway (Chapter 12) runs through the town, passing under the A6 by a short tunnel, and ends in the dock house beside the terminal basin of the Peak Forest Canal, north of the town centre.

The Peak Forest Canal was built in 1794-1800 by Benjamin Outram, mainly to take limestone and lime down to the Mersey from the west side of the Peak. At Dukinfield, in the Tame valley, it was connected with the Ashton-under-Lyne Canal, which itself was linked with the Mersey at Manchester. The distance from Dukinfield to Whaley Bridge is 14½ miles and the locks limited the width of the boats to 7 feet (so it is a 'narrow' canal). Like other canals, the Peak Forest felt the impact of the new railways in the mid-nineteenth century; in 1846 it was leased by the Sheffield, Ashton-under-Lyne and Manchester Railway (later part of the London and North Western system). The canal was finally closed to goods traffic in 1959, but it now belongs to the British Waterways Board and is open for pleasure craft.

About half a mile below Whaley Bridge the canal is joined by a branch from Buxworth (402382) or Bugsworth, as it used to be spelt, at the lower end of the tramway from Dove Holes. Near by are lime kilns and other buildings associated with the canal, and farther down the derelict wharves are being restored. Buxworth Hall, a manor house of 1627, much renewed, stands above the road, which goes on to Chinley (404382), a settlement that grew up beside the station on the Manchester–Sheffield railway near the junction of the line to Bakewell and Derby (now closed). Above rise the steep slopes of Chinley Churn (403383; 1480 feet), a western outlier of the Kinder Scout massif with a large gritstone quarry in its side. Whitehough (403382), a hamlet on the other side of the Black Brook valley from Chinley, has a rambling manor house, probably of the late seventeenth century, despite the date of 1559 inscribed above the entrance.

The Hayfield road, leaving Chapel-en-le-Frith on the north, passes the large works of Ferodo, the brake-lining manufacturers, established here by Herbert Frood as long ago as 1897.

The well-designed research laboratories were opened in 1958. The road passes under the imposing double viaduct at the junction of the lines from Manchester, Sheffield and Derby, and climbs at length to the saddle (1077 feet) connecting Chinley Churn with the prominent South Head (1622 feet), the south-western buttress of the Kinder Scout moorlands. As we descend on the north to Hayfield, we have a fine view forward into the valley of the Sett.

Hayfield (403387), a small textile-manufacturing town that also makes paper and prints calico, has some houses of the seventeenth and eighteenth centuries, and is the best starting-point for the exploration of the western side of Kinder Scout. It has often suffered from the floods brought down from the moorlands by the Sett, and in 1818 the church was swept away. Rebuilt on its old foundations, it was raised so that the piers of the old arcade were shortened to serve as supports for the new floor. In the church is a marble bust (by John Bacon the Elder and brought from Glossop church) to Joseph Hague, who was born here and who became a pedlar, carrying his wares on his back until he could afford a donkey. In 1717 he went to London, where he made a fortune, but returned to live at Park Hall, an early eighteenth-century house near the Glossop road, and here he died in 1786.

A road penetrates into the narrow upper valley of the Sett for nearly a mile and a half, and is the beginning of the walking routes to Edale and the Snake Inn (Chapter 25). The road continuing up the valley ends at the gates of waterworks (where there is a mountain rescue post), but a track goes on above the north side of the Kinder Reservoir (405388) built in 1912 (for the Stockport Corporation), beyond which we have a fine view of the western escarpment of Kinder Scout, broken effectively by Kinder Downfall when there is sufficient water in it. The lane crossing the Sett and ascending past Booth Farm, of the eighteenth century, continues as a private road to Kinder Upper House, among woods on the south side of the reservoir. At the house, built in the seventeenth century but enlarged and modernised in the last century, Mrs Humphry Ward wrote much of her novel, *David Grieve*, which is set in this moorland region. A path bearing to the right above the woods is the continuation of the walk to Edale.

The road north from Hayfield passing the grounds of Park Hall makes another long ascent, with the sharp peak of Lantern Pike (402388; 1177 feet) rising to the west. Part of the top was given to the National Trust as a memorial to Edwin Royce, a president of the Manchester Ramblers' Federation. The prospect from the summit, across to the Downfall and the rock-lined western edge of Kinder Scout, is most impressive. The road, passing above the fine seventeenth-century farmhouse of Brookhouses, climbs up to the ridge between the valleys of the Sett and the Glossop Brook. Here the Monk's Road (why is it so called?) leads to the left near the Abbot's Chair, perhaps the base of a medieval boundary cross, and round the north end of Cown Edge (402392), with a wide view over Glossop to the moorlands of Bleaklow, before going down to Charlesworth (Chapter 20). The main road from Hayfield descends to Glossop past the farm of White House, built in 1699 and whitewashed (unusually for the Peak District).

Glossop (403394), the north-west gateway to the High Peak, is a textile-manufacturing town below the gritstone moorlands, on streams which descend from the western slopes of Kinder Scout and Bleaklow. It has cotton mills, rayon printing works and canneries, and manufactures rope and paper. The 'new' town was mostly laid out after 1830 on a regular plan around the crossing-point of important roads, one of which goes on north for Longdendale (Chapter 27), while that to the east climbs over the Snake Pass to the Ladybower Reservoir and the road to the west descends Dinting Vale, the valley of the Glossop Brook, towards Manchester.

The old village of Glossop, which had a market and fair from 1290 onwards, is grouped round the parish church in a valley to the north-east of the town centre. It has some good seventeenth-century houses, but practically nothing remains of the old church; the tower and spire were rebuilt in 1855, the nave was rebuilt in 1914 and the chancel in 1924. Glossop Hall, built in 1850 and once a mansion of the Duke of Norfolk, is now a school. The Roman Catholic church to the north of this was built for him in a Grecian style in 1836.

The Manchester road through Dinting Vale passes under a lofty viaduct of 1842. Beside Dinting Station (402394), on the north side of this, is the Dinting Railway Centre, a disused locomotive depot and sidings which from 1968 onward have become the nucleus of a facinating museum, with many old locomotives and other relics of great interest to railway enthusiasts.

To the west of Dinting Vale, above the point where the Glossop Brook emerges into the valley of the Etherow, are the rectangular earthworks of the Roman fort of Melandra (400395), or Melandra Castle, as it is often called (leading the unwary to expect a medieval stronghold). The fort stood in a good strategic position, on a promontory above the valleys, and on the road from Brough to Manchester which crossed the Snake Pass (Chapter 27). Excavation is still going on each summer, but nothing except the earth-covered ramparts are to be seen, apart from some lower courses of the corner turrets. The name of the fort has not been positively established, though the Ordnance Survey (on their map of Roman Britain) have suggested *Ardotalia* as a possibility.

20 Lyme Park, and thence to Glossop

The main road between Buxton and Manchester, followed by the Peak Forest Canal, descends the valley of the Goyt, now sadly industrialised, from Whaley Bridge (Chapter 19) to Disley (397384), a large village much patronised by commuters from Stockport and Manchester. The church, on a hill to the south, was built in 1510-24 by Sir Piers Legh III of Lyme Park, but largely recast in the early nineteenth century. It retains its fine sixteenth-century roof and much fifteenth- and sixteenth-century stained glass, some of it from Continental sources. The much-restored Wybersley Hall (396385), to the north-west on a road to Marple, was possibly the birthplace in 1602 of John Bradshaw, the regicide, though he may have been born at Marple Hall, since demolished.

On the Manchester road to the west of Disley is the entrance to Lyme Park (396382). The name is applied to both the house and the grounds, so the house is sometimes called Lyme Hall (as on the Ordnance Survey map) to make the distinction. 'Lyme', according to Eilert Ekwall, the chief authority on English place-names, was "the old name of a large royal forest district" which included Macclesfield Forest. The name occurs also in Newcastle-under-Lyme (in Staffordshire) and Ashton-under-Lyne (in Lancashire), and from the position of these places it would appear that the forest extended down the western side of the Peak District. Another derivation of the name is from the Latin 'limes', meaning a border or boundary, and this may have applied to the western boundary of the Peak. It seems to me unlikely, however, that a Latin name would be added to a Saxon one unless it were of Roman origin.

The house of Lyme Park stands on a spur of the Peak, in Cheshire, over 800 feet above sea-level, its park extending to nearly 1250 feet on the moorlands beyond. Its beautiful situation was not always so regarded; one eighteenth-century visitor described it as "by no means well chosen, as the surrounding country is bleak, moorish and unfruitful".

Lyme remained the seat of the same family for exactly 600 years, from 1346 until 1946. Sir Thomas Danyers, of Bradley within Appleton (in Cheshire), who had rescued the Black Prince's standard at Caen and captured the Constable of France at Crécy, was rewarded by Edward III in 1346 with a grant of land at Lyme (then called Lyme Handley). In 1388 his daughter and heiress married Sir Piers or Peter Legh, eldest son of Robert Legh of Adlington (also in Cheshire). Sir Piers, like his father-in-law, had fought at the Battle of Crécy; he was granted arms in 1397 by Richard II, whom he supported, but two years later he was beheaded at Chester by Henry Bolingbroke (soon to become Henry IV). His son, Sir Piers Legh II, who accompanied Henry V to France, was present at the Battle of Agincourt and died of wounds received at Meaux in 1422. Sir Piers Legh III fought for the Lancastrians at the Battle of Towton and his grandson, who succeeded in 1478, won his spurs at the Battle of Hutton Field. He built the church at Disley and the watch-tower in the park known as Lyme Cage (though this was altered in 1720). Piers VI, who came into the estates in 1527, had fought against the Scots in 1513 on Flodden Field.

Sir Piers VII, who inherited the property in 1541, took part in the Earl of Hertford's invasion of Scotland and was present in 1544 at the sacking of Edinburgh. In 1587 he contributed a considerable sum towards equipping the fleet that defeated the Spanish Armada. The house at Lyme, first recorded in 1465 (when the family probably moved from Bradley Hall, in Lancashire), was rebuilt for him in about 1570. Of this building, the entrance gatehouse remains and the outer walls are incorporated in the present house, so Sir Piers' house, like the present building, was rectangular in plan and built round an open courtyard. The gatehouse, the only visible external part of the Elizabethan house, is an architectural feature of some interest, consisting of four superimposed stages displaying the four classical orders of Tuscan, Doric, Ionic and Corinthian. The shell ornament above the clock, an earlier example of that on the Bodleian Library at Oxford, was inspired by a treatise published in 1563, and this would date the gatehouse to about

1565-75. The figure of Minerva within the broken pediment at the top was added in the early eighteenth century.

The principal rooms surviving practically unaltered from the Elizabethan house are the Drawing Room and the Long Gallery. The Drawing Room, dating from about 1580, has panelling of oak, inlaid with various other woods. The large chimneypiece of stone and plaster reaches from floor to ceiling, with an overmantel that bears the arms and supporters of Elizabeth I. The bay window is filled with heraldic glass of the sixteenth and seventeenth centuries, originally placed by Sir Piers VII in the east window of Disley church, but brought here in the early nineteenth century. The small Stag Parlour next door has a wooden chimneypiece with a plaster overmantel bearing the arms of James I. Above this is a plaster panel in low relief showing the house as it was in Sir Peter Legh VIII's time. Around the room runs a frieze with medallions of coloured plaster showing the stag at different stages of its growth.

The Long Gallery, which may be compared with that at Haddon Hall, is 120 feet in length and occupies the entire second storey of the east wing. It likewise has oak panelling, a chimneypiece of coloured plaster and a large overmantel with the arms of Queen Elizabeth. The floor is of elm boards, laid rather unevenly across the apartment.

Sir Piers was succeeded in 1590 by his grandson, Sir Peter VIII, who is thought to have accompanied the Earl of Leicester on his abortive expedition against the Spaniards in the Netherlands. He in turn was succeeded, in 1635, by his grandson, Peter IX, who was elected Member of Parliament for Newton (Lancashire) at the age of sixteen, but died two years later of wounds received in a duel. Richard Legh, who inherited the estates in 1643 and enjoyed them for forty-four years, made many alterations to the Elizabethan house after 1660, providing, for instance, new roofs and windows. Lead rainwater conduits with heads of beautiful design, the arms of Richard and his wife and the date of 1676 appear on the north front. In this year he entertained the Duke of York (later James II), who slept in the Yellow Bedroom, in the great four-poster bed, which is carved with the Prince of Wales's feathers. For this occasion the Yellow Bedroom and the two adjacent rooms were redecorated; all are hung with sixteenth- and seventeenth-century tapestries. The marble chimneypieces in the two larger rooms, made in 1675, cost Richard Legh £35 the pair.

Richard Legh died in 1687 and was succeeded by his son, Peter X, who in 1720 commissioned Giacomo Leoni, the Venetian architect (brought to England by Lord Burlington) to carry out very considerable alterations. Leoni completely recased the outer fronts of the rectangular Elizabethan house and after 1725 added the splendid classical portico on the south front. He also refashioned the inner courtyard, providing it with classical features, and altered many of the state rooms, on the first floor of the house.

The Hall here, reached from the courtyard by a double flight of stone steps, was lowered 12 feet from its original level by Leoni, and has a passage end divided from the main part of the room by a colonnade of four Ionic columns. The decoration was probably finished in 1723, but the chimneypiece has an overmantel inserted in the late nineteenth century. On the walls are three panels of tapestry, part of a series depicting the story of Hero and Leander, woven in the royal factory at Mortlake, on the Thames, between 1623 and 1636, to designs by Francis Clein or Cleyn, the German artist. On the north wall hangs a portrait of the Black Prince, eldest son of Edward III, bought by Piers Legh I from St James's Palace. It is curiously hinged to open inwards and reveal a secret opening (probably the position of the former doorway) between the Hall and the Drawing Room.

The Grand Staircase, introduced by Leoni, is of imposing proportions. On the walls are portraits of the Leghs and the ceiling of the stairwell has plasterwork probably executed by Italian craftsmen. The Saloon beyond has tall windows inserted by Richard Legh and a gilt plaster ceiling. The walls are covered with six large panels of oak between fluted Corinthian pilasters and decorated with beautiful limewood carvings, among the most splendid wood carvings in England. Measuring 8 feet 8 inches in height, they are said to represent the Four Seasons, Music and Painting. The carvings, formerly attributed to Grinling Gibbons, who died in 1720, are now thought to be later than this, though they do resemble the carvings of Samuel Watson at Chatsworth in their delicacy and craftsmanship.

Thomas Legh, who inherited Lyme in 1792, was a friend of

Lord Byron and a noted archaeologist who travelled extensively in Greece, Egypt and the Middle East. Further alterations were made to the house for him in about 1816. The work was carried out by Lewis Wyatt, cousin of Sir Jeffry Wyatville who built the long north wing at Chatsworth. Wyatt added rooms on the east front, redecorated the library and the dining room (not usually shown to visitors), and built the curious box-like structure on the roof of the house (as servants' quarters). The Orangery on the east terrace, which contains a fine camellia, is also probably by him.

William John Legh, who succeeded in 1892 and was created the first Lord Newton, laid out the attractive Dutch Garden to the south-west of the house. In 1946 the third Lord Newton transferred the house and 1323 acres of the park and moorland to the National Trust, at the same time leaving some of his pictures, furniture and tapestries on loan. The house (carefully renovated in 1973) and the grounds are both administered for the Trust by the Corporation of Stockport, which is only a few miles along the Manchester road and for which the grounds serve as a very fine public park.

The park, formerly part of the royal forest already mentioned, still contains a herd of some 200 red deer. The Lyme deer have been distinguished for their size and fierceness, and it was once the custom to 'drive the stag' every midsummer across a pond (which no longer exists). Stag hunting at Lyme is referred to by Sir Walter Scott in *Peveril of the Peak*. Sheep Dog Trials are now held in the park, in August.

The park climbs up on to the moorlands to the north of the road from Macclesfield to Whaley Bridge. Just outside the boundary, and reached by a lane from Higher Disley passing near the Moorside Hotel, are the Bow Stones (397381), two standing stones that are probably parts of Saxon cross-shafts of the 11th century. A track goes on from them along the ridge of Sponds Hill (1348 feet), with a wide view over Stockport and Manchester to the moors above Bolton and west to the Clwydian range in North Wales. We can descend south from the hill to reach the road between Kettleshulme and Pott Shrigley (Chapter 8).

New Mills (399385), on the other side of the Goyt, upstream from Disley, is a small industrial town which has long

Castleton, from Peveril Castle

Peveril Castle, the Keep

established textile printing and engraving works, as well as other textile, metal and engineering works, and which also makes confectionery. A lane above the north side of the valley leads to Brook Bottom (398386), a hamlet secluded in the Strines valley, with interesting weavers' houses, one of them five storeys high.

Farther north, by a roundabout road, is Mellor (398388), an old textile manufacturing village that has become a favourite place of residence for workers in and around Manchester. The parish was transferred from Derbyshire to Cheshire in 1936. The church, on a hill to the north, with a fine view east towards Kinder Scout, was rebuilt in the early nineteenth century, except for the Perpendicular tower. It contains an early Norman font, sculptured with animal figures, and a unique fourteenth-century pulpit, perhaps the oldest in England, carved from a single block of oak. Mellor Hall, on the hill slope to the north-east, is a fine late seventeenth-century house.

Marple Bridge (396389), to the west from Mellor, is on the road from Stockport to Glossop at the point where it crosses the Goyt. Marple (396388), beyond the river, is a market and residential town, with engineering works. Here the Peak Forest Canal (Chapter 19) descends 200 feet in a mile and a quarter by a series of sixteen locks, beyond which it crosses the Etherow below its junction with the Goyt by a splendid aqueduct, 93 feet high, built by Benjamin Outram in 1801-08. Old canal warehouses can be seen in St Martin's Road, south of the main road. Samuel Oldknow, an early factory master and one of the promoters of the Peak Forest Canal, built a cotton mill at Marple in 1790. It has disappeared, but lime kilns built by him in 1797 and looking like some medieval manor house, survive at the corner of Strines Road and Arkwright Road, east of the canal.

Devious lanes take us eastward from Mellor to Rowarth (401389), a scattered hamlet in a remote situation, with several old manor houses and farmhouses in the neighbourhood. Long Lee, the best of these, is an interesting house built in 1663, with the hall in the main range, behind a fine three-storeyed porch, and the kitchen and parlour in a large cross-wing. To the north extends the long moorland ridge of Cown Edge (401391), on the west side of which, near the farm of Far Slack, are Robin

Hood's Picking Rods, two standing stones of unknown origin (what are 'picking rods'?).

The north end of the ridge is skirted by the Monk's Road (Chapter 19), which descends past a prominent Congregational Chapel of 1797 to Charlesworth (400392), a village which once had a market and fair (under a charter of 1328), on the road from Marple which emerges into Dinting Vale below Glossop.

21 From Bakewell to Castleton via Eyam

The road crossing the bridge at Bakewell (Chapter 16) and turning north is the most direct route to the upper valley of the Derwent. In less than a mile from the town centre the road divides. The branch on the right crosses to the Derwent near the north end of Chatsworth Park; that bearing left goes on past Hassop Station (now an engineering factory), well over a mile south of the village and between the stations of Bakewell and Great Longstone, which are themselves little more than 2 miles apart. Why are the three stations so close together?

When the railway was laid up the Derwent valley it was called to a halt in 1849 at Rowsley, at the junction with the Wye. The Duke of Devonshire refused to have the railway through his park at Chatsworth and the Duke of Rutland refused equally strongly to have it through his park at Haddon. Eventually, after fourteen years delay, a compromise was reached by taking the railway up the Wye but under Haddon Hall by a long tunnel. After this both dukes had a change of heart and both wanted a private station, so the station at Bakewell was made to serve the Duke of Rutland, while the Duke of Devonshire was provided with the station of Hassop, to which he could drive over from Chatsworth, the train being stopped whenever he required it.

Hassop (422372) is a small village below the limestone ridge of Longstone Edge, with a manor house of the vernacular Peakland type, now the village shop. The comparatively flat gables and small mullioned windows indicate that it was built late in the seventeenth century. The classical Roman Catholic church with its large eaves, perhaps modelled on Inigo Jones' church of St Paul's Covent Garden (in London), was built in 1818 by Joseph Ireland for the Eyre family. On the Italian baroque altarpiece is a large painting of the Crucifixion by Ludovico Carracci of Bologna, who died in 1619. For the

Eyres, too, was built the Hall, a large late seventeenth-century house refronted in 1827-33, half-hidden behind a wall in its fine park.

The road from Bakewell skirts the east end of Longstone Edge to reach the cross-roads at Calver (Chapter 23). Here we turn west to Stoney Middleton (423375), picturesquely situated in the limestone depths of Middleton Dale. The church, rebuilt in 1759 (except for the low fifteenth-century tower), is unusual in being octagonal in plan. The village holds a well-dressing festival, at the end of July or the beginning of August, in a delightful corner near the church.

The road for Tideswell and Chapel-en-le-Frith goes on through Middleton Dale, with precipitous limestone crags on either side. The scene is not improved, however, by the white dust created by the huge limestone quarries, which settles on all the greenery, or by the noisy succession of lorries from the quarries. A side road in about a mile takes us away from all this, ascending through the short Eyam Dale to the large village of Eyam (421376; pronounced 'Eem'), which is stretched along a shelf high above the dale, looking out over the limestone country to the south, but backed by the gritstone escarpment of Eyam Edge.

The Saxon (or Mercian) cross in the churchyard is the finest in the Peak District, with its head complete, and perhaps the earliest, as it dates from the eighth century. The cross-shaft is carved with the vine scroll pattern of the period, and both the head and shaft have interesting carved figures. The cross stands some 8 feet high, but the upper part of the shaft is missing, so the head now sits rather uncomfortably on top of the shaft.

On the south chancel wall of the church is an intricate sundial made in 1775. The church has a chancel and north arcade of the thirteenth century, a tower of the fourteenth century with a fifteenth-century top, and a south arcade of the fifteenth century, but the aisles were widened in 1868 and 1882. Inside are two Norman fonts (one of them found in a garden at Hathersage). The nave roof is of the fifteenth century, and above the north arcade are rare sixteenth-century wall paintings, discovered in 1962. In the chancel is a chair with the inscription "MOM 1665 EYAM". This was the chair of the Rev. William Mompesson, rector here at the time of the devastating plague which swept through the village in 1665-66.

To the west of the church is a row of seventeenth-century gritstone cottages, one of which is known as the Plague Cottage. To this, in September 1665, was delivered a box of clothes brought from London (then suffering from the Great Plague). The box was opened by George Vicars, a journeyman tailor who was lodging in the house, and he died within four days. By the end of the month five more were dead and in October a further twenty-three. The pestilence abated during the hard winter months, only to burst out again, with greater violence, in the spring of 1666. One of those who died in April was Emmot Siddal, whose family lived opposite the Plague Cottage. Her father, brother and four sisters had died in the October, leaving only her mother and herself. Emmot was betrothed to Rowland Torre, the son of a flour-miller at Stoney Middleton, and they used to meet secretly in Cucklet Delf, a limestone dell, until she persuaded him that it was too dangerous. After Emmot's death, her mother, demented by grief, lived outdoors in the Delf.

In June nineteen villagers died, in July fifty-six, in August even more. Once the symptoms of the plague showed themselves, few of the victims survived. How strange that the nursery rhyme, 'Ring a Ring o' Roses', is derived from the plague. The 'ring of roses', the scarlet rash that appeared on the victim's chest, was the first visible symptom; the 'pocket full of posies' was the bunch of sweet smelling herbs carried in an attempt to ward off the disease; sneezing ('a-tishoo, a-tishoo') was one of the first symptoms before the plague swelling developed; and then 'we all fall down'. William Mompesson, the young rector, and Thomas Stanley, the minister who had been ejected for nonconformity after the Restoration of Charles II but had remained in Eyam, isolated the village. They arranged with the Earl of Devonshire for food and medical supplies to be brought from outside and left at certain places on the boundaries. One such place was Mompesson's Well, on Eyam Edge to the north, and the coins left in payment were carefully sterilised in the water, which had been purified by the addition of vinegar.

As deaths became more frequent, the churchyard ceased to take the dead. Graves were dug in fields and gardens, and those that were spared had to bury their own relations. The Riley Graves, on the open hillside east of the village, above the Grindleford road, commemorate one such family. Enclosed within a low wall (built later) is a group of six headstones and a tomb. The tomb marks the grave of John Hancock, the headstones (collected from elsewhere) are to his three sons and three daughters. All died in just over a week (3rd-10th August) and all were buried with her own hands by the mother, who then escaped to her surviving son in Sheffield. In the orchard of Riley House Farm, farther up, is the family grave of the seven Talbots who died, and many other graves are to be found around the village.

Eventually the church was closed and services were held out of doors in Cucklet Delf or Delph, below the Hall west of the church. Catherine Mompesson, the rector's wife, died on 25th August and her tomb is in the churchyard. By October 1666, more than twelve months after the outbreak of the plague, the last victim died, by which time the pestilence had claimed more than 250 of the villagers, out of a population estimated at some 350 (though probably more). The two ministers survived, but Mompesson left the village shortly afterwards to take the living of Eakring, in Nottinghamshire. Thomas Stanley, the ejected minister, stayed on at Eyam until his death in 1670. He is commemorated in the churchyard, though the whereabouts of his grave are unknown.

A plague memorial service is held every year in Cucklet Delf (now often called Cucklet Church) on the last Sunday in August, and a well-dressing festival (the last to be held each year in the Peak District) takes place on the Saturday before the service. The principal floral design usually relates to some aspect of the village's history.

The Rectory to the east of the church, where Anna Seward, the 'Swan of Lichfield', was born in 1747, has been rebuilt; but Eyam Hall still stands, set back behind a walled garden. The home of the Wright family, it was built in 1676, and the tiny gables on the front (no more than decorative features) and the relatively small windows are indicative of its late-seventeenth century date. Opposite, on the small green, are the village stocks, and near by is an eighteenth-century house with a brick façade, one of the very few in the Peak District.

Eyam has other houses of the eighteenth century, when it was a centre of lead mining. The Glebe Mines whose surface buildings are in the centre of the village are now being worked again, but for fluorspar. To the north of Mompesson's Well are the ruined early nineteenth-century engine house and chimney of the New Engine Mine, and farther north-west can be seen the buildings of the Ladywash Mine, which is being exploited for fluorspar and barytes. When the mine was sunk, a thickness of 796 feet of gritstone had to be bored through to reach the lead ore in the limestone below. The mine lies on the side of Sir William Hill (421378; 1407 feet), named after Sir William Cavendish, grandson of Bess of Hardwick, who owned Stoke Hall in the Derwent valley.

Farther north stretches the heather-covered Eyam Moor (422378), high above the valley. On a spur of the moor, overlooking the tributary valley of the Highlow Brook, is the Bronze Age circle of Wet Withens, consisting of twelve blocks of gritstone (originally there were more) set to form a circle nearly 100 feet in diameter, within a circular bank of earth up to 12 feet wide. In the vicinity other small earthen circles can be seen, some with and some without stones, and many more are mentioned in the nineteenth century. Some of these had mounds at the centre which were found to contain pottery vessels.

At the Black Hole Mine, west of Eyam and below the Edge, magnesium and fluorspar are processed. Foolow (419376), farther west, is collected attractively around its green, on which are the village pond and a fine fifteenth-century cross, once probably a boundary cross of the Royal Forest of the Peak, like that at Wheston. On the south side are the Hall, an irregularly-planned seventeenth-century building, and the Manor House, which dates from the eighteenth century.

Farther north-west is Great Hucklow (417377), another limestone village, once well known for its Village Players, a company formed in 1927 by L. du Garde Peach, the playwright, and directed by him until he retired in 1972. The performances of the players drew enthusiastic audiences from a wide area of south Yorkshire and the North Midlands. The theatre was formerly a lead-smelting mill, built about 1900. Above the village rises Camp Hill (about 1300 feet), the westward extension of Eyam Edge. The summit plateau is the launching-ground of the Derbyshire and Lancashire Gliding Club, whose gliders can be seen on fine Sundays in the summer, swooping out over Bradwell Dale.

Turning south from Great Hucklow over the limestone plateau, and crossing the Calver-Chapel road, we come to Litton (416375), which has good seventeenth- and eighteenth-century houses spaced round a green that is exceptionally large for the Peak District. At the west end are the steps of a market cross, though there is no record of Litton having a market charter. It had, however, a flourishing stocking-making industry in the eighteenth century, a 'cottage' industry not connected with the cotton factory at Litton Mill, in the Wye valley (Chapter 17). Litton now has a well-dressing festival, at the same time as that at Tideswell. Peter's Stone, to the east at the head of Cressbrook Dale, is a detached block of limestone which has been weathered away from the outcrops that line the head of the dale.

Tideswell (415375), hidden away in a fold of the uplands near the head of its dale, is a large village with characteristic old limestone houses. It was a place of some importance in the Middle Ages and the principal courts of the Royal Forest of the Peak were held here. A charter for a market and fair was granted in 1251 and Tideswell still had a market in the seventeenth century, at least. It is not the most attractive place in the Peak District, but it has the largest and finest church, often called the 'Cathedral of the Peak'. This was rebuilt entirely in the fourteenth century, but during two periods. The nave, with the aisles and transepts, and a two-storeyed porch on the south, were begun about 1320. The nave arcades have tall piers, and the aisles and transepts have windows of the reticulated pattern that mark the mature Decorated style; that of the south transept is particularly elegant. This phase of the building was completed about 1350, but then work was apparently interrupted, perhaps by an outbreak of the bubonic plague known as the Black Death. The chancel arch has imposts similar to the nave piers and is obviously of the same time, but the tall unaisled chancel, like a great lantern, was rebuilt from about 1360 onward and has the finest examples of those square-headed windows, with late Decorated tracery, that are a feature of fourteenth-century Derbyshire churches. The vaulted tower, the last part to be built, was completed about 1400, by which time we had changed over to the Perpendicular style of architecture. It has a very tall arch to the nave and large angle turrets rising to rather curious pinnacles.

The north transept, which contains the old oak stalls (moved from the chancel), is the chapel of the Guild of St Mary, founded about 1349 and refounded, as a craft guild, in 1953. The chancel has fine sedilia and piscina, and behind the high altar is an unusual stone screen that shuts off the vestry. The chancel stalls of 1880, with their well-carved bench ends, are the work of Suffolk craftsmen, but the choir stalls outside the chancel, the splendid vicar's chair and the carvings on the organ case and the north transept screen are all the work of Advent Hunstone, a local craftsman, and members of his family. The Hunstones still have their workshops in Tideswell.

The church contains many interesting monuments. In the north transept are two stone effigies of women of the thirteenth and fourteenth centuries, and in the south transept is a table-tomb with fifteenth-century alabaster effigies, claimed (very doubtfully) to be those of Sir Thurstan de Bower and his lady. In the centre of the chancel, on a modern tomb-chest, is the brass of Sir Sampson Meverill, with an unusual representation of the Trinity. He was lord of the manor, Knight Constable of England, served the Archbishop of Canterbury and fought eleven great battles against Joan of Arc, so his inscription tells us, and he died in 1462. Below is his cadaver, a corpse-like figure intended as a reminder of mortality. In the chancel floor is the splendid brass, still medieval in conception, of Robert Pursglove, who was born at Tideswell, founded the Grammar School (the old building is near by) and died here in 1579. He became a Protestant bishop under Edward VI, a Roman Catholic under Mary Tudor, but in 1559 lost his appointment for refusing to take the oath of supremacy. In the sanctuary is the brass of Sir John Foljambe, who died in 1383 and who seems to have been responsible for the chancel.

The George Inn, east of the church, has a grand display of eighteenth-century Venetian windows. Tideswell has a well-dressing festival each year in June, when Oliver Shimwell and his team of helpers portray one of our great English cathedrals, on the tiny green in the main square.

Wheston (413376), to the west of Tideswell, has no less than six farmhouses which appear to be of the longhouse type. In the farmyard of the Hall is a fine fifteenth-century cross, with a Crucifixion on one side of the head and a figure of the Virgin on the other. This was most likely a boundary cross of the Royal Forest of the Peak.

A 'Forest' was a tract of land set apart for hunting by the kings of England; a 'chase' was a similar tract, but in private hands (Sherwood Forest was a royal property; Cannock Chase was not). Though this part of the Peak District seems to have been preserved as a hunting ground by the later Saxon kings, it was not until the Norman Conquest that a regular system of administration was introduced, with forest laws enforced by a system of courts and a staff of officials. The deer and the verdure on which they fed ('vert and venison') were strictly protected for the monarch's pleasure. The Keeper of the Royal Forest of the Peak was usually the Custodian of Peveril Castle, an office established by William the Conqueror.

The exact boundary of the Forest, which covered an area of nearly 180 square miles, was defined in 1305, during the reign of Edward I. The boundary followed the Goyt and the Etherow on the west and north, then crossed to the head of the Derwent, which it followed down to the foot of Bradwell Dale. It went on southward across the limestone country to reach the Wye below Tideswell, then followed the river up to its source and on to reach the Goyt again. The Forest was divided into three wards: Hopedale in the south-east, Campagna in the south-west and the largest, Longdendale, in the north. 'Campagna' means 'open country', so presumably the other wards were comparatively well wooded at that time. Longdendale, indeed, is described in the Domesday Survey as being 'waste'. From the fourteenth century onward the Forest seems to have lost favour as a hunting ground, the rigid laws were relaxed, and by the end of the Middle Ages much of the land had passed into private hands. It was finally disafforested in the seventeenth century and today there are few reminders of the existence of the Royal Forest.

One reminder, however, is the village of Peak Forest

(411379), on the Chapel road, which runs north of Tideswell and Wheston. The church, founded in 1657 by Christian, second Countess of Devonshire, as a private chapel, but rebuilt in 1877, is one of the few churches in England dedicated to King Charles the Martyr. The minister held the title of 'Principal Official and Judge of Spiritualities in the Peculiar Court of Peak Forest'. Until the early nineteenth century he enjoyed the special privileges of being able to grant marriage licences and prove wills, and at one time, it is said, the runaway couples who came to be married averaged one a week (it was farther to Gretna Green). An act of 1753 limited the hours during which such marriages could take place, but the vicar went on performing the ceremony for another fifty years.

Chamber Farm, rebuilt in the eighteenth century, to the south of the Chapel road, was one of the places where the Swainmotes or Forest Courts were held. These comprised a Steward of the Forest and not less than twenty foresters. The road goes on to the rather curiously-named hamlet of Sparrowpit (409380), on the road from Buxton to Castleton. The Wanted Inn here was originally named the Devonshire Arms; it was put up for sale, but as there were no offers it became known as the 'Unwanted Inn'; then it was sold, so the name was promptly changed.

About a mile to the north of Peak Forest (no path leads to it) is Eldon Hole (411380), one of the 'Wonders of the Peak' and known as the Bottomless Pit until 1780, when the bottom, 245 feet down, was first reached. The chasm, 110 feet long and 20 feet wide, is the largest open pot-hole in the Peak District, and from the bottom cave-explorers can reach a great cavern some 90 feet high. The Hole is in the southern slopes of Eldon Hill (1543 feet), the northern side of which, eaten into by a great quarry, is skirted by the road to the Winnats and Castleton (Chapter 24).

22 Chatsworth

Coming up the Derwent valley from Rowsley (Chapter 11) through the village of Beeley (426367), which has some seventeenth-century houses and others built about 1840 in the 'estate' style, and crossing the river by a graceful seventeenth-century bridge to enter the beautiful deer park, one already has a sense of expectancy, indeed of well being, though the great house of Chatsworth remains out of sight until we breast a rise, when it bursts into view in all its splendour — the 'Palace of the Peak'.

Chatsworth House (426370) has been the seat of the Cavendish family since the sixteenth century. The first house on this site was begun in 1552 by Sir William Cavendish and his second wife, Elizabeth Hardwick, three years after they had bought the estate. 'Bess of Hardwick', as she is better known, was born about 1520, if we are to believe her monument in Derby Cathedral, which says that she died in February, 1607, in about the eighty-seventh year of her life. She was born at Hardwick (in Derbyshire) in the old manor house the ruins of which still stand, close to the magnificent Hardwick Hall, built by Bess in 1591-97.

Bess of Hardwick had four husbands, each one richer than the last. She was first married in 1532, when she was only twelve, to Robert Barley of Barlow (west of Chesterfield). He was only fourteen, so it was patently a marriage of convenience, aimed at bringing two estates together. Robert Barley died in the same year, and Bess remained a widow until 1547, when she was married to Sir William Cavendish, who had played an important part in the dissolution of the monasteries under Thomas Cromwell.

Bess and Sir William had ten years of married life together, producing three sons and three daughters, but when he died in 1557, the house was by no means completed. Nothing survives of Bess's Chatsworth, but we have some idea of what the house looked like from a needlework panel, previously at Hardwick but now back at Chatsworth again, and from a landscape by Richard Wilson which, although it was painted in the eighteenth century (by which time Bess's house had been demolished), made use of a contemporary drawing. The house, like the present Chatsworth, was almost square in plan and built round a central courtyard. It had square towers at the four corners and a large gatehouse-tower facing the Derwent, with towers or turrets on either side of it projecting above the roof line by a further storey. The layout was in fact very similar to that of Burghley House, built between about 1575 and 1587 for William Cecil, Lord Burghley, so this, too, gives us a good impression of what Bess's Chatsworth looked like.

Two buildings in the park at Chatsworth do survive from Bess's time. One is the Hunting Tower, or Stand as it is sometimes called (a kind of lookout post for locating the deer in the park), which stands high on the hill-top north-east of the house. It appears to have been rebuilt, or at least remodelled, but if so, is still in the same style as its forerunner, judging from an old print. The other building is a kind of summer retreat, surrounded by a moat (now dry), which is called Queen Mary's Bower and is said to have been used by the Queen of Scots. She was several times at Chatsworth between 1570 and 1581, while in the charge of the sixth Earl of Shrewsbury, who had the responsibility of looking after her for nearly fifteen years. Though much restored, the Bower greatly resembles the building shown on a print of 1773.

Two years after the death of Sir William Cavendish, Bess married Sir William St Loe, 'grand Butler' of England, who brought her estates in Gloucestershire (Bess always managed to secure the estates in her own name). St Loe died in 1565 and three years later Bess married as her fourth and last husband, George Talbot, sixth Earl of Shrewsbury, perhaps the wealthiest man in England, with whom she had twenty-two years of married life (mostly unhappy). Bess grew suspicious of her husband's relationship with Mary, Queen of Scots, and at the same time she was often suspected by Elizabeth I of conniving on Mary's behalf (Bess spent some months in the Tower of London as a result).

In 1584 Bess finally left her husband and moved back to

Hardwick with the idea of rebuilding the old manor house, her birthplace. Though the earl had more than sufficient houses for himself (in Sheffield, near Worksop and elsewhere), Bess was not permitted to live at Chatsworth as it had become the subject of a protracted lawsuit. Bess claimed that as she had built the house, it was hers, but the earl said that as she was married to him, the house was his (legally, if not ethically, he seems to have been right). The lawsuit was not resolved until after the earl had died in 1590, by which time Bess (now the richest woman in England, apart from Queen Elizabeth herself) had decided to stay on at Hardwick and build the great house there.

William Cavendish, Bess's second son, moved to the Old Hall (as it is usually called) when her grand new house was completed, but after her death in 1607 he moved again, into the new house. Chatsworth passed to Bess's eldest son, Henry Cavendish, who had married Grace Talbot, one of the Earl of Shrewsbury's daughters. (One of Bess's daughters married one of the earl's sons, but the estates both remained with the Cavendishes, not the Talbots.) Henry, called by Bess 'my bad son' and referred to by his contemporaries (less politely) as 'the common bull of the Midlands', died in 1616 and as he had "no legitimate issue" (so the inscription on Bess's monument tells us), Chatsworth passed to her second son, who was created Earl of Devonshire in 1618. (Why Devonshire? No-one seems to know, but it has been suggested that some Jacobean clerk wrote Devonshire when he was supposed to have written Derbyshire). William died in 1626 and he and his brother share a rather grandiose monument (attributed to Maximilian Colt) in the church of Edensor, on the other side of the valley.

The Tudor Chatsworth survived seemingly untouched until 1687, when William Cavendish, fourth Earl of Devonshire, decided to add two new ranges of building on the south and east sides of his great-great-grandmother's house to provide large state rooms. The new work was carried out in the classical style which had been reintroduced to this country from Italy by Inigo Jones and was now in its heyday. The architect employed was William Talman (two years later appointed Comptroller of the King's Works) and the work was completed in 1696. Another drawing, done in 1699, shows the new south range attached to the west wing of the existing house and so gives us an excellent idea of the size as well as the design of Bess's house. The earl had already begun to lay out the gardens anew and in 1699 he commissioned Kniff to paint a perspective view of the house and grounds which is a valuable record (allowing for some artistic licence).

In 1694 the fourth Earl had been created the first Duke of Devonshire for his leading part in bringing William of Orange over to this country and putting him on the throne as William III. In 1699 the duke got the building bug again; he decided to pull down Bess's house (antiquated by late seventeenth-century standards) and build two new wings in its place to match his existing design. Work was begun on the west front, which became the principal façade of the house, but by this time the duke had fallen out with Talman (who had a reputation as a quarrelsome individual) and it is not known whom he called in as architect, if indeed he had an achitect at all. The late Francis Thompson, the librarian at Chatsworth (who, it can safely be said, knew more about the house than anyone), has suggested that the duke may have been his own architect. After all, he had some nine years experience of building and its problems by this time and he may have thought that he could dispense with an architect and supervise the job himself. If this be so, it may be the duke's fault that the inside of the west range doesn't match the outside, and the north end of this range doesn't line up with the north end of the east range.

Be that as it may, the duke appointed Thomas Archer in 1704 to design the north range and so complete his new house. Archer (then little known) had to provide a large bowed section in the middle to hide the fact that the east and west ranges do not match up. (The main entrance at Chatsworth remains on the west side; the visitors' entrance hall, in the north range, was formerly a kitchen.) The house was finally completed in 1707, but the first Duke didn't enjoy it long, for he died in the same year. In his will the duke left £200 to Archer, and Francis Thompson has suggested that he had been advised by the architect on the west front, but had not in fact paid for the advice.

If the exterior of Chatsworth is magnificent, the interior is even more magnificent. As Sacheverell Sitwell has said in his *British Architects and Craftsmen*, "The apartments are not to be surpassed in any house in Europe", and Chatsworth "is a worthy frame for the most superb collection of works of art in private hands". The interior was decorated by artists, mostly Continental, some of whom worked at Hampton Court (then being extended by Wren for William III). The Painted Hall, the principal apartment, in the east range, has scenes from the life of Julius Caesar painted in 1692-94 by Louis Laguerre, the French artist. The proportions of the hall, unfortunately, have been upset by the grand staircase, introduced by the sixth Duke (but rebuilt in 1912) merely as a more convenient way of getting upstairs.

The Chapel, completed in 1694, has wall and ceiling paintings by Laguerre, but the painting (of the Incredulity of St Thomas) on the altarpiece is by the Italian, Antonio Verrio. The altarpiece, of alabaster with columns of Ashford black marble, was designed by Caius Gabriel Cibber, the Danish sculptor who worked on St Paul's Cathedral, and he also carved the two white marble figures above the columns. Two other black marble columns support the Duke of Devonshire's private pew at first floor level. The altarpiece itself was carved and the splendid wood carving in the Chapel was executed, not by Grinling Gibbons (as was long thought), but by Samuel Watson, a Derbyshire craftsman who was born at Heanor. Watson, twenty-five years old when Chatsworth was begun, worked here throughout the building of the house, so he was forty-five when it was finished. He died in 1715 at the age of fifty-three and is buried in Heanor church, where his memorial declares, with delightful doggerel: "Watson is gone Whose skilfull Art display'd To the very Life W^{t}ever Nature made. View but his wondrous works In Chatsworth Hall Which were so gaiz'd at And Admired by all. Yow'l say 'tis pity He should hidden lye And nothing said T'revive his Memory." Watson was also responsible for the stone carvings around the courtyard walls and the large trophy of arms (also in stone) in the pediment of the west front.

A staircase, in a well which has a ceiling painting by Sir James Thornhill (who came here in 1706), ascends to the second floor, where the Sabine Room in the west range has walls and a

The Winnats

Mam Tor

ceiling so brilliantly painted by Thornhill that they look more real than reality. The State Rooms in the south range, designed by Talman, mostly have ceiling paintings by Laguerre and carvings (on the doorcases, the overmantels, etc.) by Samuel Watson. In the first of the rooms is the bed in which George II died in 1760. The fourth Duke of Devonshire was Lord Chamberlain and he claimed the bed as one of the perquisites of his office. On an inner door of the State Music Room hangs a famous violin and bow, except that it does not 'hang', it is painted, and on a flat board at that (not even the door is real!). It used to be said that Antonio Verrio was so exasperated by the praise accorded to Grinling Gibbons' carvings at Chatsworth, he determined to do a painting that would deceive the eye. But the carvings at Chatsworth are not by Gibbons, the painting is not by Verrio, and indeed it was not here in Verrio's time. Painted by Vandervaart, a little-known Dutch artist, it hung in the Duke of Devonshire's London house in Piccadilly and was removed to Chatsworth when that house was demolished.

The State Drawing Room has a portrait of the first Duke (on the overmantel) and is hung with Mortlake tapestries of about 1635 from cartoons by Raphael depicting scenes from the lives of St Peter and St Paul. The cartoons were purchased in 1623 by Charles I (when prince) and are now the property of the Queen, but are on permanent loan to the Victoria and Albert Museum in London. The large State Dining Room, at the east end, has some ponderous furniture made about 1735 by William Kent, the protégé of the third Earl of Burlington, the architect (whose daughter married the fourth Duke of Devonshire). The ceiling painting here, by Verrio (who has a lighter touch than Laguerre), includes a witch shown cutting the thread of life. This is apparently a representation of the housekeeper of the time, with whom Verrio had disagreed. The gilt-iron balustrading of the Great Stairs was made for the first Duke by Jean Tijou, the great French ironsmith who worked in St Paul's Cathedral and under whom Robert Bakewell of Derby may have learned his craft.

The gardens, on which the first Duke spent £662, were laid out from 1685 onward by George London and Henry Wise, the royal gardeners who worked at Kensington Gardens and

Hampton Court for William III. Features of this time which survived a second layout include what is now the private garden, on the west side of the house. The Cascade, a kind of water staircase, was constructed in 1694 by Grillet, a pupil of the great French gardener, Le Nôtre, and enlarged in 1702. The water is channelled off the moor above the east side of the valley into a pond, from which it falls over a large gritstone crag, comes to the surface again in the Cascade House or 'Temple', built by Thomas Archer in 1702, and at the bottom of the cascade disappears underground to find its way into the Derwent. The scrolls and festoons on the Cascade House were carved in 1707-08 by Samuel Watson. Flora's Temple, originally called the Bowling House, was built in 1693-95 and removed to its present position, now the entrance to the gardens, in 1750. The Old Greenhouse nearby was built by Grillet in 1698 (but rebuilt in 1750). The Seahorse Fountain, on the lawn south of the house, has sculpture by Cibber, who was also responsible for the trophies of arms on the huge pedestals at the corners of the private garden. The Canal Pond farther south was made in 1703 by removing a hill which obscured the view from the house on that side.

The second and third Dukes of Devonshire made few changes at Chatsworth, but the fourth Duke, who succeeded in 1755, did far more to the grounds than he is usually given credit for. In 1760 he engaged Lancelot 'Capability' Brown to landscape the park. Brown planted the valley slopes to the east of the house (until that time bare of trees), he dammed up the Derwent to form a long narrow lake and he rebuilt the corn mill farther downstream (its ruins remain). The elegant classical bridge over the river by which we approach the house was built after 1765 by James Paine, who also built the fine Stable Block farther up the hill. Part of the large village of Edensor was in sight from the house, so the fourth Duke had this part demolished and its inhabitants moved up the hill to the west to a new village at Pilsley (Chapter 23).

The sixth Duke of Devonshire, who acceded to the title in 1811, enjoyed his estates for forty-seven years. Apart from his large properties (which extended from Hardwick Hall to Buxton) he had interests in the prosperous lead and copper mining industries and he was unmarried (he is often called the

'Bachelor Duke'). Having no wife to spend his fortune, he lavished it on improving the house and grounds at Chatsworth. His architect was Jeffry Wyatt, who changed his name to Wyatville at the request of George IV when he began a great restoration of Windsor Castle for the king in 1824. Wyatville, who began work at Chatsworth in 1820, built a new entrance gateway and lodges to the north of the house and closed in the colonnades round the courtyard to form corridors. He redecorated the Queen of Scots' Rooms, in a late Regency style (they are supposed to occupy the site of the rooms in which the queen stayed when she was at Chatsworth). He also remodelled the Long Gallery built for the first Duke in the east wing, turning it into a library (the ceiling paintings, by Verrio, are original). Chatsworth possesses the largest and finest collection of books in private hands, numbering some 17,500 volumes.

Sir Jeffry Wyatville (he was knighted in 1828) also added the long north wing to the house, rather upsetting its symmetry. The sixth Duke was a great collector of works of art and particularly of sculpture, which requires a lot of space. So he had a sculpture gallery provided in his new wing, with the Great Dining Room on one side and the Orangery on the other. Some of the most valuable paintings are in this wing: four characteristic Van Dycks in the dining room, as well as a portrait of the first Duke by Kneller, the court painter; and Rembrandt's superb 'Portrait of an Oriental' in the gallery, which also has sculpture by Canova, Thorvaldsen and other contemporaries of the sixth Duke. At the north end of the range is the prominent Theatre Tower, containing a charming little theatre which is now used each summer for a special exhibition on some aspect of Chatsworth. Wyatville's work was completed in 1827 and the duke lived on in splendour until 1858.

The gardens were also laid out afresh for the sixth Duke, though incorporating the many features of the first Duke's time mentioned above. The work was first begun under Wyatville, but in 1826 Sir Joseph Paxton, then a young man of twenty-three came from Kew Gardens. He introduced much of the statuary in the gardens, and in 1843 he constructed the Emperor Fountain in the Canal Pond (so called because it was got ready for a visit of Tsar Nicholas I, who never came). The fountain, the highest in Europe when it is going full blast, can throw a jet of water 290 feet, and it then appears high above the tree-tops. In 1836-40 Paxton built the Great Conservatory, a structure of iron and glass which inspired the idea for his Crystal Palace at the Great Exhibition held in Hyde Park in 1851. Unfortunately, it was found impossible to heat the conservatory effectively during the First World War; the plants died and the conservatory was demolished in 1920, but the foundations remain and can be seen to cover a considerable area.

No important changes have been made at Chatsworth since the time of the sixth Duke of Devonshire. But when the tenth Duke died in 1950, the death duties on the estate were so enormous that the family had to give up not only Hardwick Hall but some of the treasures out of Chatsworth, which are now rather lost in the national collections in London. To avoid this happening again, the estate is now administered by the Chatsworth Trust. The yew maze within the foundations of the Great Conservatory was laid out by the Dowager Duchess (the present Duke's grandmother), who died in 1960. A serpentine beech-hedge was planted by the present Duchess, and a fine new greenhouse, completed in 1972, may be compared with the greenhouses put up for those intrepid builders, the first and sixth Dukes.

The Chatsworth Horse Trials, which take place in the park on the second Saturday in October, are often patronised by royalty.

23 The Derwent Valley: Chatsworth to Hathersage

The road running up the Derwent valley through Chatsworth Park passes the estate village of Edensor (425369; pronounced 'En-sor'). The original village lay along a hollow on the other side of the road; the lower part, in view from Chatsworth, was demolished in the eighteenth century by the fourth Duke of Devonshire, and the job was completed by the Bachelor Duke, who demolished the rest of the village, except for one house, in its small walled garden, and the former inn.

The new village, laid out by Sir Joseph Paxton, was built in 1839. The architect was John Robertson, who had been assistant to J.C. Loudon, author of the famous *Encyclopaedia of Cottage, Farm and Villa Architecture,* and the houses show almost every conceivable stylistic feature, mostly based on a pattern-book design. Twenty years ago everyone thought this architecture was ghastly; now it is the fashion to praise such early Victorian work, but I think with justification here. The houses ('cottages ornée' is the usual term for this style) are set along two lanes curving up from the small green, which is reached through an imposing gateway. The church, rebuilt in 1867 above the green by Sir George Gilbert Scott, rather obtrudes on the scale of the village.

Outside the park gate on the north is the Edensor Inn, an elegant brick house of about 1775 with Venetian windows (now the estate office and institute). A road on the left ascends to Pilsley (424371), the village created by the fourth Duke of Devonshire, some of whose houses are still to be seen, while other houses and the school (of 1849) are by Paxton. Pilsley now has a well-dressing festival, in July.

Baslow (425372) is pleasantly situated in a wide stretch of the Derwent valley, enclosed on the east by part of the long series of gritstone edges. The village comprises two groups of houses, one of which is at Nether End, round a green near the tributary of the Bar Brook, where Thatch End not only has a thatched roof (an unusual sight in the Peak District) but also has cruck frames inside. The Chatsworth Park lodges, near the Sheffield road, were designed by Wyatville and completed after his death in 1840 by Paxton. The other group of houses is round the church, whose graveyard is washed by the Derwent. Though much restored, the church has a thirteenth-century tower and spire and fourteenth-century nave arcades. Near the south door are a whip used for driving dogs out of church and a pitch-pipe used for tuning the organ after it was installed in 1856. Above the church is a footbridge with a diminutive toll-house at one end, and farther upstream, on the west bank, is the restored seventeenth-century Bubnell Hall, once a home of the Basset family.

On Gardom's Edge (427373), between the roads to Chesterfield and Sheffield, a millstone-maker's smithy has been excavated. In the Millstone Grit escarpment are several quarries, and the working areas are on the scree-covered slopes below. Grooves in the rock made by sharpening chisels or wedges may be seen, and several millstones are in the vicinity, some broken or unfinished, others buried under the scree. One quarry has the date of 1803 carved in its face, but some of the millstones may be much older.

The road ascending the east bank of the Derwent from Baslow passes Cliff College, a Methodist training college founded (at Rochdale) in 1885, then crosses the river near Calver Mill (424374), a textile mill founded in 1785 by John Gardom, a yarn and cotton merchant of Bakewell, and rebuilt after a fire in 1804. Its great, gaunt, seven-storey façade will be familiar, though unknowingly, to countless television viewers, as it served as a background for some of the scenes at Colditz Castle. The mill was still in service for cotton spinning until 1920, but it now produces stainless-steel sinks.

Above the mill is Curbar (425374), a village that is growing in popularity with commuters from Sheffield. It stands high up, with a fine outlook over the valley to Longstone Edge and the hills above Eyam. At the upper end is an eighteenth-century lock-up, with a conical roof on square walls. The road climbs steeply to a dip in the gritstone escarpment from which we can walk along Baslow Edge (426374), passing the Eagle Stone, a great mass of hard gritstone that has been left behind when the surrounding deposits have been eroded. From the south end we have a delightful view down the Derwent valley into Chatsworth Park.

In the other direction we can walk along Curbar Edge, where the marks of glaciation from the Ice Age can be seen on some of the rocks, and continue along Froggatt Edge (424376), which commands a splendid view across the Derwent to Middleton Dale and the heights above Eyam. To the east of the broad path is a Bronze Age circle consisting of two concentric rings of stone uprights set on the inner and outer edges of a low bank, with entrances on opposite sides.

From the cross-roads at Calver (423374) one road goes on into Middleton Dale for Eyam and Tideswell (Chapter 21), but we keep to the right, continuing up a beautifully wooded reach of the Derwent valley past Stoke Hall, a fine classical house of 1757, a home of the Bridgeman family and then of the Arkwrights, until 1840 (and now a hotel).

From Grindleford (424377) the road continues up the narrowing valley, passing below the grounds of Leam Hall (423379), a large, plain, eighteenth-century house, completely hidden among its woods. Steep by roads on the left farther on ascend to a beautiful (and little visited) section of gritstone moorland in the angle between the Derwent and Bradwell Dale. Near the first of these roads is Hazelford Hall (423380), a seventeenth-century house in the vernacular style, while the other road takes us up to Highlow Hall (421380), a sixteenth-century house of the Eyres, unusual in having battlements and a square porch, but half rebuilt in the eighteenth and nineteenth centuries. The hall or house place, in the older part, is a very large room with an oriel window and has a large solar over. The farm buildings, probably also of the sixteenth century, are interesting.

To the north of Highlow Hall (by a farm road) and overlooking the Derwent above Hathersage, is Offerton Hall (421381), a fine sixteenth-century house of the 'hall and double-cross wing' plan, with alterations made in 1658. The road past Highlow Hall goes on to Abney (419379), a hamlet surrounded by quiet uplands dissected by deep wooded 'cloughs' or valleys. A narrow lane takes us up to the open, breezy Abney Moor, where we have a choice of tracks, equally fine. That on the right goes over Shatton Edge and down to Shatton in the Derwent valley. The track to the left runs along the ridge of Bradwell Edge, and then goes down to Brough. On the left, before the track begins its descent, is an earthwork known as the Grey Ditch, consisting of a rampart made by digging out a ditch on its north or vulnerable side. It descends steeply into Bradwell Dale and may have been constructed (like Carl Wark) as part of a defensive system protecting Mercia from the expanding kingdom of Northumbria.

The Sheffield road, crossing the Derwent from Grindleford, ascends towards the wooded valley of the Burbage Brook, where it passes the approach to Grindleford Station (425378), on the Sheffield-Manchester railway. The station stands at the west end of Totley Tunnel, driven in 1893 and 3 miles 950 yards long, which makes it the second longest railway tunnel in England (only the Severn Tunnel is longer).

A cart-road goes on to Padley Hall (424378), a site of great interest. The old hall range was converted in 1933 into a chapel in memory of two Roman Catholic priests, Nicholas Garlick and Robert Ludlam, who were discovered in hiding here in 1588, taken to Derby and hanged. This hall range, though restored as a chapel (where a pilgrimage takes place each year on the Thursday nearest 12th July), still has its original windows and its original timber roof, with carved angels on the hammerbeams, indicating that part of the upper floor has always been a chapel. Behind this building is the courtyard round which the house was extended in the fifteenth century, when a new hall range was built on the farther side. In a cross-wing to the left of this was the kitchen, with a solar or drawing room over and a parlour at one end. Only the lower courses of these buildings survive, but we can see hearth stones and the steps of a newel staircase that led to the solar. The Hall passed from the Padleys to the Eyres when Joan Padley married Robert Eyre (their tomb is in Hathersage church) and then to Sir Thomas Fitzherbert, who died in the Tower of London in 1591 after twenty years' imprisonment for his faith.

The Sheffield road continues up the lovely wooded valley of the Burbage Brook, skirting the Longshaw Estate (426374) of the National Trust, an area of moor and woodland, from the

The Derwent Valley: Chatsworth to Hathersage

upper part of which we can enjoy a wide view over the Derwent valley towards Mam Tor and Kinder Scout. Longshaw Lodge was built in the last century as a shooting lodge by the Duke of Rutland. The Longshaw Sheep Dog Trials are held on the pastures near by during three days early in September. Above the lodge is the Fox House Inn (426380), a well-known hostelry near the meeting place of roads from Chesterfield, Sheffield and Hathersage. The Chesterfield road crosses the north end of Big Moor, a vast tract of featureless moorland, to reach Owler Bar (429378), with the Peacock, another noted inn, on the road from Baslow to Sheffield.

From Fox House the Hathersage road crosses the upper waters of the Burbage Brook near a signpost that tells us that we are on the boundary of the City of Sheffield, though we are surrounded by moorlands and the city is nowhere in sight. On the other side of the bridge is the Toad Rock, or Toad's Mouth, so called from its resemblance to that reptile. On a rock-bound hill to the north, west of the Burbage Brook, we can see the prominent but mysterious fortification of Carl Wark (426381). The natural defences formed by the edges of the summit plateau are strengthened by walls of gritstone, while across the neck of the plateau, where this is joined on to the main body of the moorland, the fortification is protected by a massive wall of gritstone boulders, partly squared and standing 10 feet high and about 30 yards long, backed by an earthen rampart. At the south end of this wall is a well-preserved entrance, with remains of a guard chamber. The entrance is of the double-inturned type to be seen on Mam Tor, but the wall with its earthen rampart is unique and suggests that the fortification does not belong to the Iron Age, as was once generally supposed. It may indeed be as late as the sixth century, when the frontiers of Mercia and Northumbria were being established, though excavations carried out in 1950 produced no evidence of this. Farther north from Carl Wark is Higger Tor (1261 feet), which has curious weathered rocks around the escarpment top.

An interesting walk, starting at Burbage Bridge or the Fox House Inn, leads down beside the Burbage Brook and through the wooded Padley Gorge (425379) to Grindleford Station (the Peak Park Planning Board has published a Nature Trail). The road over the moor from the Toad Rock reaches the escarpment of Millstone Edge (424380), where the 'Surprise View' opens up the Derwent valley and that of its extension, the Noe (the Hope Valley), with a background formed by the heights of Bamford Edge (to the right), Win Hill, Lose Hill and Mam Tor, and by Kinder Scout, rising over the ridge connecting these. Millstones can still be seen in the old quarry here.

The road descends steeply to Hathersage (423381), finely situated in the Derwent valley below the gritstone moors, at the place where the river turns from an easterly course to a southerly one. The village has spread in recent years to serve commuters from Sheffield, whose houses are rather too much in evidence along the hillside. The Hall (behind the George Inn) is a simple classical building with a front of 1820 and a Roman Catholic chapel attached to it.

Hathersage had an ironworking industry from the sixteenth century onward. In 1566 Christopher Schutz came here from Germany and set up works to draw iron wire, mainly for knitting needles and for the sieves used in washing lead ore. In 1740 Benjamin Huntsman, a clockmaker of Doncaster, developed the crucible method of casting steel, at Sheffield, for the springs of clocks and pendulums, and in about 1770 he sought the help of Robert Cocker of Hathersage in drawing cast steel. The Cockers were still making needles at Hathersage in 1857, while Samuel Fox of Bradwell began by making umbrella frames here before moving his works to Stocksbridge in the Don Valley.

Hathersage church, on a hill above a side valley, east of the village street, is characteristic of Peakland churches, with fifteenth-century battlemented porch, aisles and clerestory, and a tower whose crocketed spire is recessed behind the battlements. The church was built mainly in the fourteenth century, though restored by Butterfield in 1852. The north chapel was added as a chantry for the Eyre family in 1463. In the chancel are fifteenth- and sixteenth-century brasses of the Eyres, the finest being those on the tomb of Robert Eyre, who died in 1459, and his wife Joan Padley (we met them at Padley Hall). The fifteenth-century arms of the Eyres are on the porch and the font. The east window of the chancel was brought in 1949 from Derwent church, drowned when the Ladybower Reservoir was filled.

Under a yew tree in the churchyard is a grave claimed to be that of Little John, the lieutenant of Robin Hood who is supposed to have been a native of Hathersage, to have worked in the nail making industry here, to have fought in 1265 in the rebel army of Simon de Montfort at the Battle of Evesham, to have been outlawed as a result and so to have joined Robin Hood and his 'merry men' in Sherwood Forest. When the grave was opened in the late eighteenth century, a human thigh bone about 30 inches long is said to have been discovered. The distance between the head and foot stones of the grave is 11 feet.

Hathersage is the 'Morton' of Charlotte Brontë's novel *Jane Eyre*. At the Vicarage, half hidden behind its garden wall, west of the church, Charlotte stayed for three weeks in 1845, helping her friend Ellen Nussey get the house ready for her brother and his bride. Henry Nussey, the vicar, became the model for St John Rivers in the novel (he had proposed marriage to Charlotte in much the same way that Rivers proposed to Jane). It was up to the Vicarage that Jane struggled after her night on the moor near Whitcross (possibly Moscar Cross; Chapter 26).

Dale Mill, an old button factory (now engineering works), in the valley below the church, is probably the early nineteenth-century mill that comes into *Jane Eyre*. Moorseats (423382), on the hillside among the trees north-east of the church, is a house built in 1682, though much altered later. This best answers the description of 'Marsh End' (or 'Moor House') in the novel, where the Rivers family lived, though the old woman at the Vicarage told Jane that it was "happen three mile" away. For this reason a claim is made for North Lees Hall (423383), among trees farther north, below the escarpment of Stanage Edge. (It seems likely that Charlotte, employing 'literary licence', took Moorseats as her model, but moved it to the site of North Lees.) The Hall, one of the many homes of the Eyres, is a four-square building resembling a tower-house. It was rebuilt in 1596 and has been attributed to Robert Smythson, the architect of Hardwick Hall. 'Vale Hall', the home of the Olivers in the novel, has been identified with Brookfield Manor (423382), a sixteenth- to seventeenth-century building masked by a Gothick façade of 1825, in the valley below North Lees.

Stanage Edge (423384) has a gritstone escarpment over 3 miles long (a favourite climbing ground) and rises to 1502 feet in High Neb. The whole length of the escarpment top makes an exhilarating walk, starting from the southern end (where discarded millstones can be seen), easily reached from the old road between Hathersage to Sheffield, and going on to the Sheffield-Ladybower road near Moscar Lodge. The wide-spreading view extends in one direction over the broad Hallam Moors towards Sheffield, in the other over the upper Derwent valley to Shatton Edge, the Hope Valley, Win Hill and the moors of Kinder Scout. Stanage Edge is crossed by the Long Causeway, a trackway of Roman origin on the route from Brough to Templeborough (near Rotherham). The causeway winds up to a gap in the escarpment by means of a flagged path, then continues eastward across the moor. The flat stones, of which there are two rows in places, are certainly not Roman and are probably not earlier than the eighteenth century, when the causeway was used as a packhorse route. From Stanage Pole, at over 1450 feet, on the boundary between Derbyshire and Yorkshire, the causeway descends to the Redmires Reservoirs (426385), constructed in 1836-54, at the head of a branch of the Rivelin Valley and just inside the boundary of the national park.

24 The Hope Valley and Castleton

From Hathersage the Hope and Castleton road (part of the Sheffield-Chapel road) runs west across a level stretch of the Derwent valley which has Offerton Moor rising to the left and the hills of the High Peak ahead: Lose Hill is straight in front, with Win Hill and Bamford Edge to the right. The road to the Ladybower Reservoir in the upper Derwent valley (Chapter 26) turns off to the right opposite the Marquis of Granby Inn, while our road continues on the north of the river Noe into the Hope Valley. On the right beyond the junction are the popular High Peak Rose Gardens; Shatton (419382), on the other side of the river, has some attractive eighteenth-century houses.

A road on the left farther on, opposite the Traveller's Rest Inn, ascends into Bradwell Dale, crossing the Noe to Brough (418382) and skirting the east side of the field which contains what little is visible of the Roman fort of *Navio*. This small military settlement has been excavated in recent years, but only the earthen ramparts which enclosed the fort can be distinguished.

To the west of the Bradwell road are the unsightly buildings of the Hope cement works, which make use of the limestone shales here, soft beds of the limestone which were probably laid down as mud banks. The huge quarry carved into the hill behind has been landscaped so that only the narrow entrance can be seen from the valley. A lane farther on, starting near the Bowling Green Inn, ascends steeply past Smalldale Hall, a characteristic house of 1670, and follows the course of Batham Gate, the Roman road that ran from Brough to Buxton.

Bradwell (417381) is a large, plain, quarrying village and a former lead-mining centre, in the valley between the limestone uplands of Bradwell Moor, to the west, and the gritstone heights of Bradwell Edge. Bagshaw Cavern, on the west of the dale above the south end of the village, was discovered in 1806 by lead miners and has fine stalactites, but is not generally accessible. Bradwell has a well-dressing festival, on the first Saturday in August.

The Tideswell road continues through Bradwell Dale, with its towering limestone crags. At the upper end is the farmhouse of Hazlebadge Hall (417380; pronounced 'Haz-zel-' locally), which has the arms of the Vernons and the Swynnertons in the gable. It is said to have been part of the dowry brought by Dorothy Vernon to Sir John Manners, and may once have been larger. Also in the gable is the date of 1549, which makes the hall the earliest datable example of the vernacular style of manor houses in the Peak District which lasted for 150 years, until about 1700. Characteristic features are the steep gable and the long mullioned windows, and the windows here have pointed arches in the medieval manner. The building has not been improved aesthetically by the roughcasting of the exterior or by the slate roof. The contemporary farm buildings show the natural limestone walls and still have their gritstone slab roofs.

A lane on the right of the Castleton road, west of the Bradwell turning, ascends to the hamlet of Aston (418384), well situated on the lower slopes of Win Hill (Chapter 25), which appears from this side as a long ridge. Aston Hall, a most interesting small house of the Balguy family, is dated 1578, though some of the features, such as the doorcase and the strapwork cartouche above containing the date, may well have been added later. If not, they are certainly the first example in the Peak District of such Renaissance features, which can be seen, in more grandiose form, on Wollaton Hall, near Nottingham, built in 1580-88.

The village of Hope (417383) stands at the junction of the Peakshole Water, coming from Castleton, with the Noe, which descends on the north from Edale (Chapter 25) through the gap between Win Hill and Lose Hill, heights which are fancifully supposed to have been named from two armies that opposed each other in battle hereabouts. 'Hope' really means 'an enclosed valley' (a good description of its situation) and the name was only later applied to the village; it was 'at Hope' in A.D. 926. The church was once the centre of a very large parish extending beyond Castleton and across Edale to the wilds of Kinder Scout.

The church is mainly of the fourteenth and fifteenth centuries. It has a porch with a room over, and in the aisles are two coffin slabs carved with the horns of foresters of Peak Forest (Chapter 21) and four large eighteenth-century paintings of Moses and Aaron, Time and Death. The walls of the chancel are lined with the backs of sixteenth- and seventeenth-century pews of the Balguys and of the Eyres, who lived at the eighteenth-century Old Hall opposite, now an inn. In the churchyard is a tenth-century Viking cross-shaft, carved with interlace and foliage decoration, pieced together after being found in the walls of the old school. A well-dressing festival takes place at Hope, on the last Saturday in June, and the Sheepdog Trials and Agricultural Show, on the Late Summer Bank Holiday, are also well worth seeing.

The road going on up the valley passes the Hope Valley College, a foundation for adult and further education on the lines pioneered by the Cambridgeshire village colleges. On the north rises Lose Hill (415385; 1563 feet), generally pronounced 'Luce', though sometimes 'Loaze' in Derbyshire. From here we can see that it is the end of a long ridge extending east from Mam Tor, which stands up impressively at the valley head. The top of Lose Hill was given to the National Trust in 1945 in memory of G.H.B. Ward of Sheffield, an indefatigable fighter for the rights of walkers to go on to Kinder Scout and other privately owned grouse-moors. On the right of the Castleton road is the drive to Losehill Hall, a late nineteenth-century house taken over by the Peak Park Planning Board as a residential educational centre and opened in 1972. Courses are held here regularly on many aspects of Peakland life and landscape.

The road crosses the river to Castleton (415382), a compact village with its narrow streets arranged in a square, dominated by Peveril Castle on the hill above. It is finely situated towards the head of the almost enclosed dale, between the limestone country, to the south, and the gritstone ridge connecting Lose Hill with Mam Tor. The village takes its name from the castle; it is not mentioned in Domesday Book, though the castle is. But it soon began to grow in importance under the patronage of the Peverels and later of the Crown. Castleton was created a borough in 1196, when a payment of four marks for the year is recorded "de cremento burgi de Alto Pech", i.e., of the High Peak, to which the name of the Hundred of Bakewell was changed at this time. It was granted a charter for a weekly market in 1222-23 and for a second market in 1245 (an acknowledgement of its growth), and in 1255 the borough records forty-three burgages (properties held for a small yearly rent) and seventy-one stall-holders. On the south-east of the village are some remains of the Town Ditch perhaps dug at this time; to the north-west this function is performed by the Mill Race.

The old market place, between the church and the castle hill, was once much larger, but it has been encroached on by the churchyard. The church has a fifteenth-century tower and a fine early Norman chancel arch (effectively dating the foundation of the village soon after 1086), but the chancel was rebuilt, new windows were inserted and the nave arcades were removed in a restoration of about 1837, so the roof is now supported on the outer walls, which are 3 feet 6 inches thick. The seventeenth- and eighteenth-century box-pews, with their names and initials, were retained at the restoration. In the vestry beside the chancel is a library of early books left by a vicar in 1817.

Castleton observes a Garlanding Ceremony each year in the evening of Oak Apple Day, 29th May (or the following evening, if that day be a Sunday). A 'king', his body completely covered by a massive bell-shaped garland of flowers, and accompanied by his 'queen', both in seventeenth-century costume, rides in procession to the church. Here the garland is hoisted by a rope to the top of the tower, where it is left until the flowers wither. Among the old houses in the village is the restored Hall, basically of the seventeenth century and now a youth hostel. It stands on the west side of the square, near the approach to the footpath ascending to Peveril Castle, and in the road to the north is a national park information centre.

Peveril Castle (414382), often called Peak Castle formerly, stands in a strong position at the extremity of a long limestone ridge, cut off from the main part of the ridge by the ravine above the entrance to Peak Cavern, and with a precipitous crag on the south towards Cave Dale. A Norman motte-and-bailey type castle, it was begun soon after the Conquest by William

Kinder Scout, the plateau

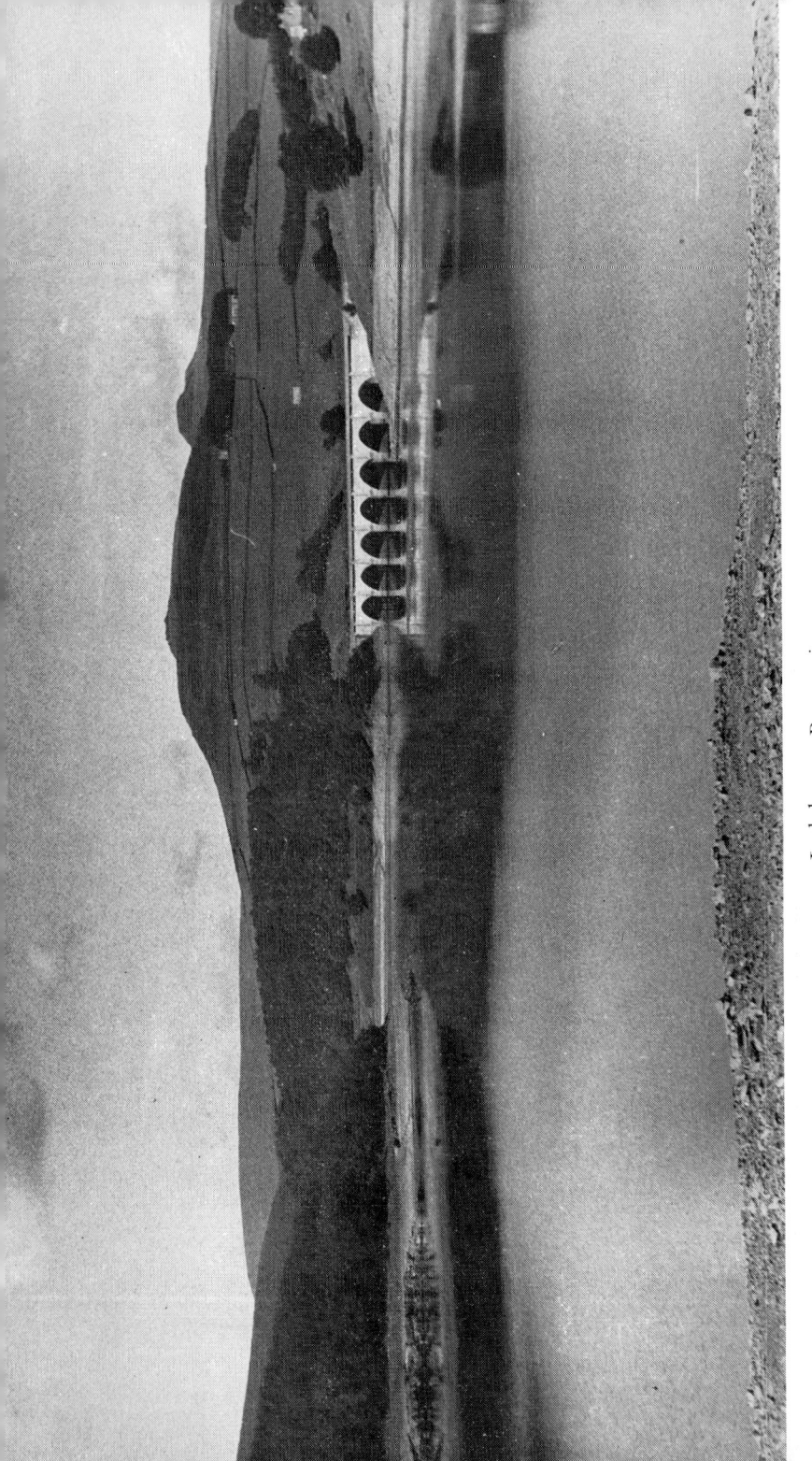

Ladybower Reservoir

Peverel or Peveril, a natural son of William I, by whom he had been made bailiff of the royal manors in north Derbyshire. The surrounding part of Peak Forest was important for its lead, and the Normans would no doubt wish to secure a tight control over this. Peverel also built strongholds of some kind at Haddon (where the hall now stands), at Bolsover Castle and at Nottingham Castle.

Unlike most early Norman fortifications, Peveril Castle was built in stone from the beginning. The outer or curtain wall encompassed a large courtyard or bailey, and the existing wall on the north side, at least, was completed in the late eleventh century. On Peverel's death in 1114, the property passed to his son, also named William, who seems to have raised the west wall of the steeply sloping bailey, but there is no evidence for a keep at this time.

William Peverel II was disinherited in 1155 on a charge of poisoning the Earl of Chester and his estates passed to the Crown. Henry II was at the castle in 1157, when he received the submission of Malcolm IV of Scotland (often called 'the Maiden'), and again in 1158 and 1164, and work is recorded on the castle ('Castellum de Pech', or Peak Castle) for 1173-77. The keep, built in 1176 in the highest part of the bailey, is typical of the many erected during the troublesome reign of Henry II. It is square in plan and stood three storeys high, with the main entrance, as was usual, at the first floor level. The roof was covered with lead, one of the earliest known uses of lead for this purpose. The keep stands on no motte or mound, as an outcrop of the natural rock sufficed for this purpose. The gatehouse (now much-ruined) at the east end of the castle and a turret on the north curtain were added to the defences at this time.

At his accession in 1189, Richard I gave the castle to his brother, Prince John, whose son Henry III stayed here in 1235. The great hall and other buildings in the north-west corner, of which little more than the lower courses remain, seem to date from about this time. Edward III was at the castle in 1331, but later gave both the castle and the manor, with other properties, to his brother, John of Gaunt, Duke of Lancaster, in exchange for the Earldom of Richmond, in Yorkshire. In 1399, when the duke's son, Henry Bolingbroke, became king as Henry IV, the castle reverted to the Crown, but by this time it was no longer of any importance, and by the seventeenth century at least it was in ruins. In 1932 the castle was placed in the care of the Office of Works (now part of the Department of the Environment).

Castleton is famous for the underground limestone caverns in its neighbourhood. The nearest of these, Peak Cavern, one of the Seven Wonders of the Peak, is reached by a lane starting south of the Hall and a path beside the Peakshole Water. This issues from the yawning mouth of the cavern, over 100 feet wide, at the foot of a sheer precipice in the wooded limestone ravine which isolates Peveril Castle, whose keep can be seen high above. The mouth of the cave has been used as a ropewalk for over 400 years, but as the sole surviving ropemaker is now approaching ninety, this craft may not continue much longer. The dark patches on the roof inside the entrance are of soot from the chimneys of the houses which were built in the cave for the ropemakers. Visitors are conducted through winding passages and galleries into great natural chambers, one of which is 150 feet high and 90 feet broad. At one place, where the roof shelves down nearly to the floor of the cavern, the rock has been blasted to give more space. Before this was done, visitors had to lie flat in the bottom of a punt while the guide pushed them through. Lord Byron and Queen Victoria were taken through in this manner.

To the west of Castleton, the Chapel road bears to the right towards the foot of Treak Cliff, a reef-formation of the limestone which effectively blocks the end of the Hope Valley. The old coach road to Chapel branches to the left to ascend The Winnats (413382), sometimes called the Winnats Pass, a steep and narrow ravine in the limestone hemmed in by jagged outcrops. The derivation of the name from 'Wind Gates' will be appreciated by those who stand in the ravine when the west wind is blasting through on a cold winter's day.

At the foot of the ravine is the entrance to the Speedwell Mine, a lead mine that was unique in being specifically planned to utilise boat haulage underground. The lead ore was removed in boats which were pulled through a circular tunnel half filled with water, the water being diverted from that in the natural cave system beyond. The idea itself was not original, as James

Brindley in 1761 had built a tunnel at Worsley, near Manchester, so that the third Duke of Bridgewater could carry away coal from his mines to the Mersey. The agent at the Speedwell Mine was John Gilbert, who had been associated with Brindley's scheme at Worsley, and the Speedwell Level was constructed between 1774 and 1781. Visitors are now taken through the half-filled tunnel, half-a-mile long through the solid limestone. The boat is usually propelled by 'legging'; the operator lies on his back at the stern of the boat and propels it forward by pushing with his feet on the tunnel roof. The level ends in a vast cave extending 70 feet below the tunnel (though often claimed to be bottomless), but of unknown height, the roof being lost in the darkness.

Above the main road, north of the Winnats, is the entrance to Treak Cliff Cavern (413383), a series of caves worth visiting for their blue john strata, but even more remarkable for their beautiful stalactites and stalagmites. The best of these are in the inner caves discovered only in 1926, when miners seeking blue john blasted their way through from the Blue John Caverns on the other side of the hill.

Farther on, the road passes the impressive entrance to the Odin Mine, a lead mine which was first worked at least as early as the seventeenth century (though certainly not as early as Viking times, as its name might seem to imply). From the early eighteenth century it began to be worked beneath the gritstones of Mam Tor; the workings proved to be extremely rich and the mine eventually extended for about three-quarters-of-a-mile under the hill. Several natural caverns were intersected and in times of flood great volumes of water poured in. This led to considerable pumping problems and a sough to drain or 'unwater' the mine was cut some time after 1772. Below the road and the mine entrance can be seen an early nineteenth-century crushing wheel, with its iron tyre, and a circular iron track. These are the remains of the horse-gin used for reducing the lead ore to more manageable proportions. The mine ceased working in 1846.

The road winds steeply up below the foot of Mam Tor (412383), another of the Wonders of the Peak, rising to 1696 feet above the valley head and capped by the double ramparts and ditches of an Iron Age hill-fort of the first century B.C.

These have been partly destroyed by the breaking away of the hill on the side facing down the valley towards Castleton. Mam Tor is made up of successive bands of hard Millstone Grit and the softer and more friable shales, and the constant crumbling of this softer material, which slips down the precipitous face, has given the hill its popular name of the Shivering Mountain. From the road below the hill we have a splendid view down the Hope Valley past Castleton to the gritstone edges beyond the Derwent valley.

An even finer view is obtained from the top of Mam Tor, which is easily reached by a path from Mam Nick, on the west side. It extends not only eastward down the Hope Valley, but southward over Treak Cliff to the rolling limestone country and, much more significant, northward over the Vale of Edale to the moorland plateau of the Kinder Scout massif, whose southern flanks are spread out beyond the valley with panoramic effect. An exhilarating walk takes us from the top of the hill along the elevated ridge of the gritstone to its lowest point at Hollins Cross (413384), where the ridge is crossed by the old coffin track from Edale to Castleton, and then over the wooded crag of Back Tor for Lose Hill and the descent to Hope. Both Mam Tor and The Winnats belong to the National Trust.

Facing the southern foot of Mam Tor is the entrance to the Blue John Caverns (413383), which are partly natural caves and partly old lead workings. They are famous for their banded veins of the blue, purple and yellow fluorspar known as blue john. The origin of the name is uncertain; it may have been given by early miners in opposition to 'black jack', their name for zinc blende (also once mined in the Peak); or it may have been adapted from the French 'bleu-jaune', meaning 'blue-yellow', as many early pieces were cut and polished in France and fitted into ormulu mounts.

The origin of the formation of the blue john is uncertain, too. One theory is that it was caused by hot gaseous material, probably in a semi-plastic state, being forced up into cracks and joints of the surface crust, there combining chemically with the limestone. Another theory is that oil accumulated on a reef of the limestone of Treak Cliff while the gritstones were being laid on top, and this oil seeped into the hill to combine with the limestone during the subsequent earth movements. The first part of the word 'fluorspar' comes from a Latin word meaning 'to flow', and this may indeed be the origin of all fluorspars.

Blue john is generally supposed to have been first worked by the Romans, on the strength of two vases of stone resembling the fluorspar which were unearthed during the excavation of the buried city of Pompeii, but there is not the slightest evidence that these vases (or the stone) came from the Peak District. The existence of blue john in the Peak is not recorded until the late seventeenth century. It was first used for ornaments about the middle of the eighteenth century, when Matthew Boulton, the engineer, made ormulu ornaments and Robert Adam employed it as an inlay for fireplaces in Kedleston Hall near Derby, completed in 1770.

Blue john was popular for vases and other ornaments through the nineteenth century and until the 1930s, when the veins began to run thin. It is now found in veins averaging 3 inches thick, so only jewellery and small ornaments can be made from it. The stone has to be mined by hand, as blasting disturbs the crystalline structure and shocks out the colouring, and it is very difficult to work because of its brittleness and crystalline nature. So the fluorspar is expensive to mine and the craftsmanship is even more costly. Specimens of blue john vases and other ornaments can be seen in the Geological Museum and the Victoria & Albert Museum in London, in the Manchester, Sheffield, Buxton and Derby Museums, in the Stockport Museum in Vernon Park (which has a window of twenty-four varieties) and at Chatsworth, where the Tazza vase is the largest object ever made from the fluorspar. Nearer to the caverns, you can see a priceless private collection of blue john in a shop in Castleton.

Beyond the entrance to the Blue John Caverns, the road divides: the left branch, for Buxton, leads near the top of the Winnats and skirts the north side of Eldon Hill (Chapter 21), while the other road continues along the side of Rushup Edge at a high level for Chapel-en-le-Frith (Chapter 19). In the angle between the two roads is Windy Knoll, where rhinoceros, bear and wolf bones were found in a cavern, and farther west is the entrance to Giant's Hole (411382), which is 495 feet deep, one of the deepest pot-holes in Britain. Some 2 miles of caves and passages have been explored below ground by pot-holers.

Lord's Seat, on the ridge of Rushup Edge, is a Bronze Age burial mound, 7 feet high, owned by the National Trust. A narrow, twisting road climbs over Mam Nick, between Mam Tor and the east end of the Edge, before descending into the Vale of Edale.

25 Edale and Kinder Scout

The road opposite Hope church (Chapter 24), followed by the Sheffield-Chinley railway, leads north towards the gap between Lose Hill and Win Hill. In three-quarters-of-a-mile it crosses the river Noe, which descends from the Vale of Edale (pronounced 'E-dale'). From the farm of Fullwood Stile, east of the bridge, we can follow the Roman road that ran from Brough to Melandra up the western slopes of Win Hill (418385; 1523 feet), which is capped by a distinctive knob of the hard Kinderscout Grit. The track takes us up to the narrow ridge between the Vale of Edale and the Ashop or Woodlands Valley (Chapter 27), and from the top we have a fine view over the two arms of the Ladybower Reservoir to the enclosing moorlands. The track passes the remains of Hope Cross (416387), probably once a boundary stone of the Royal Forest of the Peak, before descending into the Woodlands Valley opposite the foot of Alport Dale.

The valley of the Noe turns from a northward course to a westerly one, still with Lose Hill on the left, but with the eastern outliers of the Kinder Scout massif extending on the right. The Vale of Edale, which we have now entered, is a wide 'V'-shaped valley, scored out of the soft shales, not a narrow steep-sided ravine like the dales of the limestone. From Clough Farm another track climbs over to join the Win Hill track by way of Jaggers Clough, probably following a packhorse route ('jaggers' were the men who led the teams of packhorses).

Below the prominent nineteenth-century house of Rowland Cote (the Edale youth hostel), delightfully positioned in a fold of the hills, the Edale road goes through the hamlet of Nether Booth (414386), one of five 'booths' in the valley; the others are Ollerbrook, Grindsbrook, Barber and Upper. These originated as farmsteads in the royal forest which were let out by the bailiff to foresters or private landowners. (A path goes through the fields from Nether Booth to the farm of Ollerbrook Booth and on to Edale village.) Beside the Noe, farther west, is a former lace-thread spinning mill, built about 1790 and enlarged in 1795; it has recently been converted into flats.

From a large car-park beside the valley road, farther on, a road goes past Edale Station into the village of Edale (412385). The name of this was previously Grindsbrook Booth (pronounced 'Grynds-') and Edale is properly the name of the valley, but with the growth of the settlement north of the station, the name became attached to the village and the valley is now often called the Vale of Edale (the Ordnance Survey follows this practice). At Fieldhead, near the church, is a national park information centre, a camping ground and a mountain rescue centre, and here, too, are the headquarters of the wardens (most of them part time) who do duty on Kinder Scout at weekends and in the holiday seasons, putting wanderers right when they go astray and finding them when they get lost, which happens all too frequently. It is amazing how many people come out from the cities to spend a day on Kinder Scout without any knowledge of the mountains and their moods and without being properly equipped.

The church at Edale, rebuilt in 1885, is the third on the site; the first church was built in 1633. Before the churchyard was dedicated, coffins had to be taken by the 'coffin track' over Hollins Cross, for burial in the churchyard at Castleton. In the small square at the end of the road past the church is the charming Nag's Head Inn, built in 1577, and Edale village has other old houses of the local gritstone.

The village is surrounded on almost every side by steep slopes rising to moorland heights. To the south is Mam Tor, with its Iron Age ramparts, and towards the east the crag-faced Back Tor, on the ridge extending to Lose Hill, is a prominent feature. To the west the hills close in round the head of the Vale. To the north rises the rounded hill of The Nab, with a line of dark outcrops known as Ringing Roger; to the north-west is the bulky hill of Grindslow Knoll, and the steep valley coming down between this and The Nab is Grindsbrook Clough.

Edale village is the starting point of the Pennine Way, the long-distance walking route established in 1951, mainly through the efforts of Tom Stephenson and other enthusiastic walkers and seekers after liberty, and extending right along the Pennines and over the Border hills to Kirk Yetholm, in Scotland. There are two 'official' routes for beginning the walk, though both aim for Kinder Downfall on the western edge of Kinder Scout. One route leads up Grindsbrook Clough (to which the Peak Park Planning Board has produced a Nature Trail) to the plateau of Kinder Scout, the other starts opposite the Nag's Head and crosses open fields below the slopes of Broadleebank Tor, the southern extension of Grindslow Knoll, making for Barber Booth and the upper part of the Edale Vale. The Ordnance Survey indicates the route up Grindsbrook Clough as the recognised route and that through upper Edale as an alternative route to be used in bad weather. But in bad weather it is probably better not to start on the Pennine Way at all. As A. Wainwright says in his excellent *Pennine Way Companion*, "better a postponement than a postmortem"! A third route, up over Grindslow Knoll, is also shown on the Ordnance Survey map, but this is better reserved for a descent after you have wallowed and got lost in the bogs of the Kinder plateau.

Most of Kinder Scout and Bleaklow were once reserved entirely for grouse shooting and walkers were rigorously excluded, a state of affairs that led to much bitterness and sometimes to conflict. The public now have free access to the moors, except that the right is withdrawn on certain areas of moorland on certain days during the grouse-shooting season, which starts on 12th August and goes on, usually, to November. Particulars can be obtained from the Peak Park Planning Board and from the national park information centres.

The main route of the Pennine Way follows a lane north from the inn for a quarter-of-a-mile, then crosses the Grinds Brook by a footbridge to the meadows above the east side of the brook, with a good view back over Edale church to Mam Tor. Beyond a small wood we reach the open moorland and continue by a well-trodden path into the wild secluded recesses of Grindsbrook Clough. The path ascends over alternate bands of the softer shales and the hard Millstone Grit, which can be seen outcropping in the valley sides and which forms a kind of terrace that has to be surmounted. The walking becomes noticeably rougher as we climb; the brook is crossed again and nearly half-a-mile farther on, where the main stream comes down on the right through a stony corrie, we go straight ahead up a tributary stream, when a steep scramble over boulders will bring us out on to the plateau of Kinder Scout.

Kinder Scout (408387; pronounced 'Kin-der'), the highest part of the gritstone country of the High Peak, is a vast plateau covered with a profusion of bilberry, crowberry and other moorland plants, deeply entrenched with peat hags which after wet weather have the consistency of thick treacle. The plateau is no place to cross with comfort in rainy or misty weather, and in these conditions you may well be advised to give up on reaching the edge and to descend to Edale village by the track to the south along the edge and over Grindslow Knoll.

The main route of the Pennine Way keeps almost due west from the Grinds Brook tributary to reach the upper waters of the Crowden Brook, which descends to Upper Booth and provides a useful way off in mist. There are no views, except of the empty moorland all round, and it is easy to lose your way, even on a clear day. The Ordnance Survey map, preferably the two-and-a-half-inch edition (which incidentally shows a path here, though there is none), and a reliable compass are essential. On the one-inch map the route is marked as 'undefined', a glorious understatement.

By continuing along the Crowden Brook in a north-westerly direction we should pick up the head-waters of the Kinder River, which leads on to the Downfall. We are here on the watershed of England, though imperceptibly; all the water flowing off Kinder Scout in a southerly direction finds its way into the Trent and so to the North Sea, all that coming off to the west drains into the Mersey and thence to the Irish Sea. As Mr Wainwright rightly says of this stretch of the plateau, "A line of posts set at 50-yard intervals across this bad half-mile would remove the danger of going astray, assist in forming a defined track, and make unnecessary the alternative bad-weather route".

As an alternative to ascending the Crowden Brook we can continue westward across the highest point of Kinder Scout (2088 feet), if we can find the top; it is marked only by a small cairn or heap of stones and is difficult to distinguish on the uneven surface of the plateau. Eventually, if we keep going westward, we will reach the western edge of the plateau between Edale Cross (to the south) and Kinder Downfall. Then, if we have to get back to Edale at the end of the day, we could return by the alternative route of the Pennine Way, though the Downfall should on no account be missed.

The road up the Vale of Edale continues to Barber Booth (411384), a hamlet where the road over the side of Mam Tor (Chapter 24) comes in. Our road bears right to the farmstead of Upper Booth (410385), in the great bowl that forms the head of Edale. Here we join the alternative route of the Pennine Way and go on by a lane in the delightful valley to Lee House, the last inhabited farm. From here a broad path continues towards the valley head, hemmed in by high moorlands all around. As we ascend the view opens and several weathered tors can be discerned on the skyline. The path crosses the Noe by a seventeenth-century packhorse bridge and we are then confronted by the steep slope known as Jacob's Ladder. The original route no doubt went straight up the direct but very stony path, marked 'Dangerous Ground', but there are now several easier alternatives, that to the left above the ruined farm of Edale Head House being perhaps the best. Once the Ladder has been outmanoeuvred, a wide path goes on (with a fine view of the head of Edale to the right) to reach the watershed at Edale Cross (407386), marking the extent of lands once owned by Basingwerk Abbey (in Flintshire).

The track going ahead here drops down quickly into the upper valley of the Sett, which it descends towards Hayfield (Chapter 19), joining the route to the Snake Inn nearly half-a-mile above the village, where the Kinder River joins the Sett. Another (shorter, but steeper) descent, starting west of the cross, goes down above the woods of Kinder Upper House to reach this point.

The alternative route of the Pennine Way turns north before reaching Edale Cross, by a path over the rise of Swine's Back, after which it is better to keep well to the left of the distinctive gritstone outcrops of Edale Rocks to reach the ruins of a shooting box. We go on west of the trigonometrical point on Kinder Low (2077 feet), then follow the edge overlooking the

Kinder Reservoir, seen far below, to reach the top of the Downfall.

Kinder Downfall (408388) is a great amphitheatre of gritstone crags and tumbled boulders below the point where the Kinder River reaches the rim of the plateau. The river throws itself down successive steps of the rock face in spectacular fashion. In high summer, when there is usually little water in the river, the impression may be disappointing (though the rock scenery is grand under any conditions), but after wet weather it is very dramatic, the water splashing down in a long cascade. It is even more effective when the wind is in the west and the water is thrown back over the edge in a great wave. Anyone going along the edge in thick mist may walk into this spray and get soaked before he can do anything about it. (I speak from experience!) The Downfall is indeed most impressive when the water is frozen into bands of ice. Above the Downfall the Kinder River is in summer the most delightful of moorland streams, but after wet weather it may be difficult to cross. If we have followed the edge of the plateau from the south, this may involve a considerable detour; if we have followed the river from Crowden Head, we shall have taken the precaution of crossing it high up.

The two Pennine Way routes join at the top of the Downfall and the Way continues along the edge to the north, which gives the finest view of the Downfall. A firm path over a bed of sandy gravel and weathered boulders follows the terrace between the peat of the plateau and the gritstone edge. From the western end of the edge a line of cairns marks the way down to a saddle of the moorland crossed by the broad path between Hayfield and the Snake Inn. The Pennine Way goes on from here to the flattish top of Mill Hill (406390; 1761 feet), where it turns sharply to the right along a boggy ridge. The best route is marked by a line of stakes over Moss Castle and Glead Hill; the walking is laborious, but we have a good view across the Ashop Clough to the northern escarpment of Kinder Scout. From the end of the ridge we keep straight on over Featherbed Moss (well named) to the road at the top of the Snake Pass (Chapter 27), which is usually identifiable in the moorland landscape by the line of parked cars.

The walking route from Hayfield to the Snake Inn goes up

the valley of the Kinder River, then climbs by a path above the north side of the Kinder Reservoir (Chapter 19). The path continues steeply up the narrow valley of William Clough (rather fatiguing when the going is soft) to cross the route of the Pennine Way above Ashop Head (406390; about 1650 feet). The Snake Path then descends at length through Ashop Clough, beside the head stream of the river Ashop, with the imposing northern edges of Kinder Scout rising to the right and extending out to the promontory of Fairbrook Naze. The path crosses the Lady Clough to reach the Glossop-Ladybower road just above the Snake Inn (Chapter 27).

Edale village can be regained from the inn by ascending on the north side of the Fair Brook to reach the escarpment top south of Fairbrook Naze (409389; about 2500 feet). From the point where the brook tumbles over the edge in a miniature downfall we can go due south to join the Pennine Way near Crowden Head, but there is no path and the heather and constant peat hags make the going tedious. An alternative route, perhaps easier, is to cross the Fair Brook and continue on the south side of the Ashop to a shooting box, then to climb over the stony edge of the Seal Stones (411388; 1978 feet) and go on across the upper part of Blackden Moor; but again, there is no path. The descent may be made to Grindsbrook Clough or (much better) we can follow a good path along the southern edge of the plateau by way of Nether Tor and Ringing Roger, then go down steeply from The Nab to Edale village.

A complete circumambulation of Kinder Scout from Edale may be made via Edale Cross, the Kinder Reservoir, Ashop Head, the Snake Inn and the Seal Stones. This avoids most of the peat hags of the plateau, but the distance is about 17 miles and much of it is still very hard walking.

26 From the Upper Derwent to the Little Don

The road opposite the Marquis of Granby Inn, on the Hathersage-Hope road (Chapter 24), ascends to Bamford (420383), a village of gritstone houses pitched on the steep slope of a hill below Bamford Edge. The Gothic church of 1861 is by William Butterfield, a Victorian architect whom it is now fashionable to praise; the vicarage close by is his work, too. Near the Derwent is a mill built for cotton spinning by Christopher Kirk in about 1780, and rebuilt after a fire in 1791, when a weir of gritstone from the Edge was constructed across the river. Though the mill changed hands several times, textile manufacture was carried on here until 1965, after which it converted to making electric furnaces. Sheep Dog trials are held at Bamford every year on Spring Bank Holiday Monday.

The road runs below the western slopes of Bamford Edge, from which walkers are fenced out. We look over the Derwent valley to the gritstone cap of Win Hill (Chapter 25) before passing the strangely named Yorkshire Bridge Inn (420385). The nearest point on the Yorkshire boundary is a mile and a half to the east, at Crow Chin, near the northern end of the Stanage Edge escarpment.

Beyond the inn rises the dam, 1250 feet long, of the Ladybower Reservoir (419386), the lowest of the three man-made lakes in the upper Derwent valley which have enhanced the landscape, rather than the reverse, creating a miniature 'lake district' in the Peak. The reservoir was constructed in 1935-39 (though not opened officially until 1945) to supply the needs of Sheffield, Nottingham, Leicester and Derby. It has a storage capacity of 6300 million gallons, and extends for over 3 miles up the Derwent, with an arm of about 2 miles up the Woodlands Valley, the lower valley of the Ashop (Chapter 27). The waters of the reservoir have drowned two villages: Ashopton, which stood just below the place where the road from Sheffield begins to cross the viaduct over the main arm, and Derwent, a mile or more farther up the valley.

The road from Bamford crosses a short arm of the reservoir to reach one of the main roads between Sheffield and Manchester. In the Sheffield direction this ascends through a short but pleasant valley to gain the open moorland north of Stanage Edge and cross the boundary between Derbyshire and Yorkshire near Moscar Lodge (423388). To the north of this is the site of Moscar Cross, which stood near the old coach-road to Sheffield and may have been the 'Whitcross' where Jane Eyre was set down from the coach in Charlotte Brontë's novel, after she had fled from Thornfield Hall and journeyed for two days.

The modern road runs north of the extensive Hallam Moors, a name which reminds us that the area of Yorkshire around Sheffield was formerly known as Hallamshire, and descends at length into the attractive Rivelin Valley, crossing the river and leaving the national park at Rivelin Mill (428387). It is difficult to believe that the centre of Sheffield is only 4 miles from this point. The gritstone outcrops of the Rivelin Rocks, to the north of the road, have become a convenient practice ground for Sheffield climbers.

From a point west of Moscar Lodge, a by road (motorists should be warned of the steep hills and awkward bends farther on) runs at the edge of heather-clad moors to the Strines Inn (422390), beautifully situated high above Bradfield Dale, where the river Loxley has been dammed by Sheffield into several lakes, made more attractive by the wood-fringed shores. A track starting beyond the inn ascends to Derwent Edge (419389), a ridge of the moorland from which we can enjoy a fine view westward, over the reservoirs in the upper Derwent valley, to Kinder Scout. From the Edge we can either descend to the west by Abbey Bank to the Derwent Reservoir or follow the ridge southward, passing several weathered tors which have been given curious names, such as the Cakes of Bread, the Salt Cellar and the Wheel Stones (these last sometimes likened to a man playing the organ), and so down to the Ladybower Reservoir.

From the by road beyond the Strines Inn, steep, twisting lanes go down into the Loxley Valley to meet at Low Bradfield

(426392), which has some three-storey houses reminding us of the former framework-knitting industry of this neighbourhood. From the hamlet an exceedingly steep hill climbs up to Bradfield (426392), a village with interesting houses on a shelf high above the valley. The spacious church, built to serve a very extensive if sparsely inhabited parish, is mostly in the Perpendicular style of the fifteenth century, with large windows, some of them with straight heads, but retaining a fine fourteenth-century tower and other features from the previous church. The roof in the nave is original, and in the north aisle is some fifteenth- and sixteenth-century stained-glass. Bailey Hill, to the north of the church, and Castle Hill, south-east of the village, are the small mottes of two early Norman strongholds.

The road starting to the north from Bradfield bears away westward on to the open moorland. Just before joining the more direct road from the Strines Inn, it crosses the Bar Dyke (424394), a well-defined rampart and ditch which faces north-west and was perhaps intended to cut the line of a route along a ridgeway crossing the boundary between Mercia and Northumbria. The road passes the wooded grounds of Broomhead Hall (424396), built in 1813 and an early example of the gabled Tudor style that was to come into fashion. A track on the left here, leading towards the Ewden Beck, crosses another rampart and ditch, over half a mile long. It is noticeable that these are on the slopes above the south side of the stream (not the north), and it may be that all these earthworks (like the Grey Ditch, near Bradwell) had some connection with the defence of Mercia against the expanding kingdom of Northumbria, though their exact use may always remain a subject for speculation.

The road descends very steeply to cross the Ewden Beck, which lower down is dammed to form two wood-enclosed reservoirs, then climbs equally steeply to the moor again. Where the road forks, the right branch descends to Midhopestones (423399), a hamlet with a tiny church of 1705 which has a Jacobean pulpit and eighteenth-century box-pews and west gallery. The road crosses the Little Don River (sometimes called the river Porter) to reach the Huddersfield road up the valley from Sheffield through the steel-manufacturing town of Stocksbridge. The other branch finds its way through Upper

Midhope and crosses the dam of a reservoir to reach Langsett (421400), a small village which is likewise on the Sheffield-Huddersfield road. At the Flouch Inn (419401), farther on, this is crossed by the road from Penistone going over to Longdendale (Chapter 27) on its way to Manchester.

Returning now to the upper Derwent valley, after our expedition across the moorlands towards the Don, we cross the Ashopton Viaduct (419386) which takes the Sheffield-Manchester road over the longer arm of the Ladybower Reservoir. We then turn right on a delightful by road that runs above the west side of the reservoir through Derwent Dale, as this part of the valley is sometimes called. On the other side the moors rise to the ridge of Derwent Edge, where the old man playing his organ on the Wheel Stones and the other weathered outcrops stand out distinctively on the skyline.

Beyond the head of the Ladybower Reservoir, a lane goes off on the right below the immense dam of the Derwent Reservoir (417389), which was completed in 1916 and has a capacity of 4100 gallons. The dam is best seen when the water cascades over after heavy rain (it is usually dry in summer). The lane turns down the east shore of the Ladybower, passing above the site of Derwent village, which stood below the foot of the Mill Brook. The ruins of the church and village were visible during a great drought in 1959 and this upset so many people that the church spire was thereupon demolished. A farm road continues beside the reservoir to regain the main road near the viaduct.

A track goes upstream from the Derwent Dam, along the east shore of the Derwent Reservoir, crossing the county boundary below the steep Abbey Bank. From this point onward the west side of the Derwent is in Derbyshire, the east side in Yorkshire. The track continues alongside the Howden Reservoir, through fine plantations, to a junction of tracks beyond the bridge at Slippery Stones.

The by road continues on the west side of the Derwent Reservoir, and then follows the shore of the Howden Reservoir (417392), the uppermost of the three reservoirs, completed in 1912 and named from the moors above its head. The road makes a wide detour round the end of an arm of the reservoir that extends up the valley of the river Westend. The track continuing up this valley is an approach to Bleaklow, but the going higher up is very hard and it is perhaps better reserved for the descent on this side. The road beside the reservoir ends nearly half a mile short of its head and if we wish to explore the Derwent valley from this point we must walk.

A track continues from the road head through plantations, beyond the end of which, at Slippery Stones (417395), is an elegant packhorse bridge of the seventeenth century which stood in the village of Derwent, but was taken down when the reservoir was constructed and rebuilt here in 1959. The path to the east from the bridge climbs out of a side valley on to a ridge north of Margery Hill (418395; 1793 feet), the highest point of the moorlands east of the upper Derwent, in the centre of a wild and desolate landscape. The whole of these moorlands, extending from Derwent Edge in the south to Swains Head, above the head of the valley (6468 acres in all), make up the Derwent Estate of the National Trust. From Margery Hill the track, known as Cut Gate (and perhaps a packhorse route), goes on northward to descend east of the valley of Mickleden. It crosses the Little Don above the Langsett Reservoir and comes out on the Sheffield-Longdendale road near the Flouch Inn.

The main track from Slippery Stones continues up the east bank of the Derwent for about 2 miles, but we can follow the river farther upstream and climb out without much difficulty on the north side to Swains Head (413398). Here we are only a mile from the head-waters of the river Etherow at the upper end of Longdendale, and can watch the endless traffic pouring over the Woodhead Pass on its way between Sheffield and Manchester.

Committed 'bogtrotters' will want to continue up the Derwent to its head-streams (it is difficult to decide which is the real source of the river), or, rather better, turn west along the ridge from Swains Head, and then push on in a south-westerly direction (occasional stakes mark the route) to the Bleaklow Stones (411396), one of the two summits of equal height (2060 feet) on the ridge of Bleaklow. It doesn't look very far on the map from the Derwent below Swains Head to the Bleaklow Stones (it is in fact little more than a mile and a half in a straight line), but the going is extremely hard. For the whole of the way we are floundering knee-deep in heather or, worse still, in desolate bogs which are deeper and even more treacle-like than those on Kinder Scout, and the sense of isolation is even more extreme. Since the top of Kinder Scout was first opened to the public, in 1958, many tracks have been worn on the well-used routes, but on Bleaklow there are no tracks at all. My son and I once spent the best part of a day on Bleaklow and during a period of about six hours we did not see a single person, no walkers, not even a shepherd.

27 From the Ashop Valley to Longdendale

Returning from the desolation of Bleaklow to the Ashopton Viaduct over the Ladybower Reservoir (Chapter 26), we take the Glossop and Manchester road, which follows the north shore of the beautiful and often sombre arm of the reservoir that penetrates into the lower valley of the Ashop, usually called the Woodlands Valley. On the other side the plantations rise towards the ridge of Win Hill, with its distinctive gritstone cap. Beyond the head of the arm the road passes below a new hostel and camping site at Hagg Farm (416388), from which a track crosses over to the Derwent Reservoir and a path runs out along a ridge towards Crook Hill, charmingly placed in the angle between the two arms of the reservoir.

Continuing on the Manchester road, we see the Seal Stones, the north-eastern buttress of the Kinder Scout plateau, rising ahead, while the track following the course of the Roman road over Win Hill from Brough can be seen descending across the hillside on the left. Beyond the tiny chapel of Hope Woodlands, the road crosses the river Alport, a tributary of the Ashop which descends through the deep, hidden valley of Alport Dale.

A narrow road ascends the dale for a mile to Alport Castles Farm (413391), where a Methodist Love Feast is held every year on the first Sunday in July. The origins of this go back to the seventeenth century, when acts of parliament were passed in an attempt to prevent freedom of worship according to one's conscience. Alport Castles (414391) are the gritstone outcrops that rise dramatically on the east side of the dale. A steep path ascends from the farm to the southern end of the edge, then runs along the top, with fine views, before descending to the arm of the Howden Reservoir in the Westend valley. Alport Dale goes on towards the innermost recesses of the southern flanks of Bleaklow, which could indeed be approached from this side, but names such as Over Wood Moss, Grains in the

Water and The Swamp give some idea of the difficulties to be encountered.

As the main road continues up the Ashop Valley, we can see that the Seal Stones have fallen away to the left, to give place to Fairbrook Naze, the eastern extremity of the northern edges of Kinder Scout. The road reaches the Snake Inn (411390), over 1000 feet above sea-level at the eastern foot of the Snake Pass. The pass takes its name from the inn (not the other way round) and the inn takes its name from the serpent which is the crest of the Cavendish family. The Duke of Devonshire was the owner of the Hope Woodlands Estate, a vast area of moorland that extends from above Alport Dale to the upper Derwent, Bleaklow and the Snake Pass. But on the death of the tenth Duke the estate was taken by the state in lieu of death duties and in 1959 it was made over to the National Trust.

The head reach of the Ashop opens on the west, traversed by the path to Hayfield over Ashop Head (Chapter 25). The Snake Road ascends the steep tributary valley of Lady Clough, through plantations at first, then climbing out on to the open moorland. The path going off to the right at the uppermost bridge follows the course of the Roman road between Brough and Melandra, here known as Doctor's Gate (409393). The name, it has been suggested, is a corruption of Dog Tor, though I have been unable to find any outcrop that resembles a dog. We could follow Doctor's Gate on foot down through the fine valley of the Shelf Brook to Old Glossop.

The level top of the Snake Pass (408392; 1680 feet) commands as desolate a moorland view as one could wish for; to the south over Featherbed Moss (its name indicates its nature) as far as the northern flanks of Kinder Scout, and in the other direction to the great promontory of Bleaklow Head (this is the only road from which the top can be seen). In a way, the scene is even more impressive when the mists are down over the pass, and the heights can be visualised only in the imagination. The tall poles alongside the road, incidentally, are disused telegraph poles, and are not intended to show the position of the road when it is covered with snow, as I have heard suggested!

At the top of the pass, the road is crossed by the route of the Pennine Way from Kinder Scout (Chapter 25). Continuing towards Scotland, this takes a north-easterly course at first, following a rather haphazard line of stakes and crossing the Doctor's Gate. The section from the Snake Pass to Longdendale, says Mr Wainwright, is "commonly considered the toughest part of the Pennine Way. It is certainly mucky, too, often belaboured by rain and wind, and weird and frightening in mist". The route continues beside the Devil's Dyke, a curiously straight channel in the moor which certainly looks man-made. At the rise of Alport Low, we turn to the north, and it is better to keep to the right of the stakes, crossing the almost imperceptable col between Crooked Clough and Hern Clough, two streams which are only a few yards apart and difficult to distinguish in the wilderness of peat and heather. But the waters of Crooked Clough find their way into the Irish Sea, while those in Hern Clough finish up in the North Sea. The best plan is to make for the outcrops of the Wain Stones which can be seen ahead (except in mist!). Just beyond is the top of Bleaklow Head (409395; 2060 feet), the western end of the long ridge of Bleaklow, sometimes called Bleaklow Hill, an unnecessary duplication, as 'low' means hill. In any case, it is not so much a hill as the highest part of a great waste of peat-hag-ridden moorland of which Bleaklow Head and Bleaklow Stones (Chapter 26), a mile and a half to the east, provide almost the only firm ground.

The Pennine Way ('undefined' again on the Ordnance Survey map) starts off in a westerly direction from Bleaklow Head, leaving the peat hags at length and descending over heather and crowberry to Torside Clough. Above the west slopes of this are the earthworks of Torside Castle (407396), apparently an Iron Age hill-fort, though in a very out-of-the-way position. A good track will be found west of the clough and along the top of Clough Edge, from which the descent is made into Longdendale to join a cart-track to the west of Reaps Farm (406397). This will take us out to the road from Glossop into Longdendale.

To the west of the Snake Pass summit, the Manchester road soon descends into the valley of Holden Clough, then bears to the right to take a winding course down towards Glossop (Chapter 19), which can be seen below with its textile and other factories at the upper end of Dinting Vale. The town centre can be avoided by taking a road to the right into the more interesting Old Glossop, here turning to the left near the church to come out on to the road from Glossop to Longdendale. This road runs round the western flanks of the moors that rise at length to Bleaklow, then turns up the dale and crosses the Manchester-Sheffield railway beyond the end of the track from Reaps Farm.

Longdendale is the long upper valley of the Etherow, a river which joins the Tame lower down to form the Mersey. (As 'den' means valley, 'dale' is an unnecessary addition.) The south side of the valley is in Derbyshire, the north side in Cheshire. One of the eternally busy roads from Manchester to Sheffield runs on the north side of the river. I said river, but for most of its course the Etherow is lost in a succession of large reservoirs, constructed between 1848 and 1862 to supply the requirements of Manchester and its satellites. The reservoirs do not enhance the scene as they do in the upper Derwent valley; they detract from it; in fact, they mar it; they are too obviously man made. Indeed, the hand of man is all too evident here; apart from the reservoirs and their attendant waterworks, the dale is ruined by the telegraph poles, the electrified railway lines and (worst of all) the pylons with their electric power cables. Add to this the constant stream of heavy traffic on the main road, with its noise and its fumes.

The Pennine Way crosses the dam of the Torside Reservoir (405398) and ascends across the main road (where I am afraid we must leave it). The road from Glossop goes along the south side of the reservoir, and the deep valley of the Crowden Great Brook can be seen, opening up on the other side of Longdendale. (At Crowden, on the east side of the brook, is a youth hostel with a mountain rescue post.) Our road crosses the dam of the Woodhead Reservoir (408399) to reach the Manchester-Sheffield road, which skirts the north side of the reservoir. We then cross a short arm of the reservoir at the foot of the Heyden Brook, up whose valley a fine road climbs to the BBC television station at Holme Moss, the mast of which is a prominent landmark.

The railway keeps to the southern shore of the reservoir and beyond its head enters the Woodhead Tunnel (411399), which cuts right through the watershed of the Pennines. The first tunnel here, constructed in 1838-45 for the Sheffield, Ashton-under-Lyne and Manchester Railway, is 3 miles 66 yards long and was the longest railway tunnel in the world when it was built. The railway was designed mainly to take Yorkshire coal to Lancashire factories and mills. The first engineer of the tunnel was C.B. Vignoles, but he fell out of favour and was superseded by Joseph Locke. A second tunnel (for 'down' trains) was constructed in 1847-52; both tunnels carried single-line tracks and by the mid-twentieth century they were hopelessly inadequate. A new, third, tunnel for electric trains was built in 1949-54 by Balfour, Beatty and Company. The last steam train passed through the original tunnel in 1954, after which it was adapted by the Central Electricity Generating Board to take electricity cables carrying 400,000 volts through the Pennines.

The Sheffield road continues towards the upper reaches of the Etherow, passing into the West Riding at the Salter's Brook Bridge. The road climbs to a height of nearly 1500 feet on the watershed of the Woodhead Pass (415400), not named on the Ordnance Survey map. It then descends at an easy gradient to the Flouch Inn, at the junction of the roads from Penistone and Huddersfield.

A considerable area of moorland to the north of Longdendale, including Black Hill and Holme Moss, is inside the boundary of the Peak District National Park. The character of this region, however, has much more in common with the Pennine moorlands of the Yorkshire-Lancashire borderland and in consequence must be left for another exploration.

One of the impressions that will have emerged from this book, I hope, is of the immense variety of interest in the Peak District, not only in its landscape (the limestone dales, the gritstone moors with their rock-bound edges) but also in its human associations: its prehistoric remains, its villages and old manor houses, its great houses like Haddon Hall, Chatsworth and Lyme Park, its old customs such as well dressing and the Shrovetide football at Ashbourne, and its memories of people like the redoubtable Bess of Hardwick and events like the devastating plague at Eyam.

In the seventeenth century, Thomas Hobbes the philosopher

and Charles Cotton both wrote poems extolling the 'Seven Wonders of the Peak'. These were all concentrated in the northern part of the Peak, but even allowing for this, few people today would agree wholeheartedly with their choice. So by way of conclusion, and at the risk of offending all my friends, I would like to suggest not seven, but *Ten* Wonders of the Peak for your consideration: Dovedale and the limestone ravine of The Winnats, one of the Castleton caverns (say Treak Cliff), the moorland edges of Kinder Scout, the prehistoric stone circle at Arbor Low, Peveril Castle and Tideswell Church, Haddon Hall and Chatsworth House, Church Street with the church at Ashbourne, the Crescent and neighbouring buildings at Buxton, and a well dressing festival, say that of Tissington or Youlgreave. What do you think?

Index of Places

Abbey Bank, 209, 211
Abbot's Chair, 156
Abney, 185
Abney Moor, 186
Aldery Cliff, 62
Allgreave, 67
Alport, 110, 138
Alport Castles, 214
Alport Dale, 214-15
Alport Height, 33, 81, 102
Alport Low, 216
Alsop-en-le-Dale, 71, 76
Alstonfield, 60
Amber, river, 32-3
Ambergate, 86, 90, 95-6
Apes Tor, 22, 55
Aquae Arnemetiae, 143
Arbor Low, 114-15
Ardotalia, 157
Ashbourne, 15, 34-41
Ashford-in-the-Water, 81, 135-6
Ashop, river, 32, 207
Ashop Clough and Head, 207
Ashopton, 208, 211
Ashop Valley, 214-15
Ashwood Dale, 142
Aston, 192
Axe Edge, 28, 65

Back Tor, 198, 202
Bagshaw Cavern, 191
Bailey Hill, 210
Bakewell, 16, 86, 127-34, 194
Ball Cross, 127
Ballidon, 79
Bamford, 208
Barber Booth, 201, 205
Bar Dyke, 210
Barmoor Clough, 151
Baslow, 183
Baslow Edge, 184
Batham Gate, 143, 191
Beeley, 174
Beeston Tor, 52
Belper, 86-7, 105
Bennetston Hall, 151
Bentley Brook, 50, 72
Beresford Dale, 61-2

Biggin, 77
Biggin Dale, 61
Big Moor, 20, 187
Birchover, 107
Black Brook, 66
Blackden Moor, 207
Black Edge, 150, 153
Black Hill, 16, 218
Black Hole Mine, 169
Black Rocks, 29, 97, 102-3
Bleaklow, 14, 27, 203, 212, 214-16
Blore, 50
Blue John Caverns, 24, 26, 197-8
Bolehill Farm, 118
Bollin, river, 47, 67, 69
Bollington, 69
Bonsall, 105-6
Bonsall Moor, 106
Booth Farm, 155
Bosley, 46-7
Bostern Grange, 59, 76
Bottom House, 43
Bow Stones, 162
Bradbourne, 76, 79
Bradfield, 210
Bradfield Dale, 209
Bradford, river, 110-11, 114
Bradford Dale, 111, 113
Bradshaw Hall, 152
Bradwell, 191
Bradwell Dale, 191-2, 170, 172, 186
Bradwell Edge, 186, 191
Bradwell Moor, 191
Brassington, 79-80
Brindley Mill, 46
Broadleebank Knoll, 203
Brook Bottom, 163
Brookfield Hall, 189
Brookhouses, 156
Broomhead Hall, 210
Brough, 81, 190-1
Bubnell Hall, 184
Bull Ring, 150
Bunster, 20, 51, 56
Burbage, 149
Burbage Brook, 186-7
Burbage Edge, 100, 149
Butterton, 54

221

Buxton, 15, 25, 54, 99, 136, 143-50, 199
Buxworth, 151, 154

Cakes of Bread, 209
Cales Dale, 114, 117
Calton, 43
Calton Hill, 22, 142
Calver, 166, 185
Calver Mill, 184
Camp Hill, 169
Carl Wark, 187
Carsington, 80
Carter's Mill, 117
Castern Hall, 52
Castle Hill, 210
Castle Naze, 153
Castle Ring, 110
Castleton, 14, 26, 193-4, 196, 199
Castle Top, 87
Cat and Fiddle Inn, 68
Cats Tor, 69
Cauldon Low, 43
Cave Dale, 23, 194
Chamber Farm, 173
Chapel-en-le-Frith, 150-2
Charlesworth, 164
Chatsworth, 132, 165, 174-84, 199
Cheedale, 14, 23, 140
Chee Tor, 140
Chelmorton, 141
Chevin, the, 86
Chinley, 154
Chinley Churn, 154
Chrome Hill, 20, 64
Churnet, river, 43-4, 46
Cleulow Cross, 67
Cliff College, 184
Clifton Mill, 40
Cloud, The, 33, 45-6
Clough Brook, 67-8
Clough Edge, 216
Coldeaton, 60, 77
Coldwall Bridge, 56
Combs, 153
Combs Edge, 153
Combs Moss, 28, 149-50, 153
Combs Reservoir, 153
Conksbury Bridge, 116
Corbar Hill, 149
Cowburn Tunnel, 152
Cown Edge, 156, 163
Cratcliffe Rocks, 109
Cressbrook Dale, 170
Cressbrook Mill, 138
Crich Chase and Stand, 86
Cromford, 87-91, 94, 96, 101, 103, 105
Cromford and High Peak Railway, 69, 71-2, 77, 87, 94-102, 131, 154

Cromford Canal, 86, 89, 94-5, 100
Cromford Moor, 97, 102
Cromford Sough, 88, 94
Cromford Wharf, 95-6
Crooked Clough, 216
Crook Hill, 214
Crow Chin, 208
Crowdecote, 63
Crowden, 217
Crowden Brook, 204
Crowden Great Brook, 217
Crowden Head, 206-7
Curbar, 184
Curbar Edge, 185
Cut Gate, 212

Dale End Farm, 113
Dane, river, 15, 65-8
Danebridge, 67
Dane Valley, 65-7
Darley Dale, 93
Dean, river, 69
Deep Dale (near Monsal Dale), 119, 137
Deep Dale (near Wye Dale), 142
Deep Ecton, 55
Derbyshire Bridge, 68
Derwent Dale, 211
Derwent Edge, 209
Derwent Estate, 212
Derwent Reservoir, 209, 211, 214
Derwent valley, 14, 28-9, 32, 86-8, 91, 93-4, 96, 108, 120, 165, 174, 183, 191, 208, 211-12, 215
Derwent village, 188, 209, 211-12
Devil's Dyke, 216
Dieulacres Abbey, 44, 46
Dinting Railway Centre, 156
Dinting Vale, 156-7, 164, 216
Dirtlow Rake, 119
Disley, 158
Doctor's Gate, 215
Doll Tor, 109
Dove, river, 15, 20, 34, 42, 50, 56-65
Dovedale, 14, 19-20, 23-4, 51, 56-61
Dove Head, 65
Dove Holes (Dovedale), 24, 59
Dove Holes (near Buxton), 150
Dowel Dale, 64
Dowlow, 100
Drabber Tor, 61
Duffield Frith, 36

Eagle Stone, 184
Earl Sterndale, 62
Ebbing and Flowing Well, 151
Ecclesbourne Valley, 81, 102
Eccles Pike, 152
Ecton Hill, 22, 54-5
Edale, Vale of, 192, 201-2, 205

Index of Places

Edale Cross, 205, 207
Edale Rocks, 205
Edale village, 202-3
Edensor, 176, 180, 182-3
Eldon Hill, 173, 199
Eldon Hole, 173
Elton, 107
End Low, 116
Errwood Reservoir, 68-9, 100, 153
Etherow, river, 15, 157, 163, 172, 212, 217-18
Ewden Beck, 210
Eyam, 75, 166
Eyam Edge, 166-7
Eyam Moor, 169

Fairbrook Naze, 207, 215
Fairfield, 150
Far Slack Farm, 163
Featherbed Moss, 206, 215
Fenny Bentley, 72
Fernilee Reservoir, 69, 100
Fin Cop, 137
Five Wells, 141
Flash, 65
Flouch Inn, 211-12, 218
Foolow, 169
Ford, 43
Ford Hall, 152
Forest of the Peak, Royal, 76, 143, 151, 169-70, 172-3, 193, 195
Fox House Inn, 187
Friden, 99
Froggatt Edge, 185
Fullwood Stile, 201

Gardom's Edge, 184
Giant's Hole, 199
Gib Hill, 115
Glead Hill, 206
Glossop, 150, 152, 156, 216
Glossop Brook, 156-7
Glutton Grange, 64
Goyt, river, 15, 65, 68, 100, 152-4, 158, 163, 172
Goyt Moss, 20
Goytsclough Quarry, 68
Gradbach, 66
Grains in the Water, 214
Grangemill, 81, 104
Gratton Dale, 113
Great Hucklow, 169
Great Longstone, 137
Great Masson Cavern, 91
Great Rocks Dale, 24, 140, 151
Great Shacklow Wood, 137
Green Hall, 78
Green Low, 104
Grey Ditch, 186
Griffe Grange Valley, 104

Grindleford, 185-6
Grindon, 53
Grindsbrook, 31
Grindsbrook Booth, 201-2
Grindsbrook Clough, 202-3, 207
Grindslow Knoll, 202-4
Grin Low, 149
Gurnett, 47

Haddon Grove, 117
Haddon Hall, 116, 120-6, 165, 195
Hagg Farm, 214
Hallam Moors, 190, 209
Hall Dale, 59
Hamps, river, 43, 52
Hand Dale, 77
Hanging Bridge, 42
Hanson Grange, 59, 76
Harborough Rocks, 22, 80-1, 98
Harpur Hill, 100
Harthill Hall and Moor, 110
Hartington, 62, 71, 76-7
Hassop, 165
Hathersage, 188-9
Hayfield, 150, 155
Hazelford Hall, 185
Hazlebadge Hall, 192
Hen Cloud, 66
Henmore Brook, 34, 38-9, 80-1
Hereward Street, 34, 78, 80, 90, 102
Hern Clough, 216
Heyden Brook, 217
Higger Tor, 187
Highlow Hall, 185
High Neb, 190
High Peak, 14, 19, 27, 194, 204
High Peak Junction, 96
High Peak Rose Gardens, 191
'High Peak' Trail, 72, 77, 80, 94
High Rake, 138
High Tor, 21-2, 32, 91-2
High Wheeldon, 62
Hindlow, 95, 99
Hitter Hill, 64
Hollinsclough, 65
Hollins Cross, 198, 202
Hollins Hill, 64
Holme Bridge and Hall, 133
Holme Moss, 217-18
Hope, 191-2
Hope Cross, 201
Hopedale, 59
Hope Valley, 19, 21, 27, 191, 193, 196
Hope Woodlands, 214-15
Hopton, 80
Hoptonwood Quarries, 20, 104
Howden Reservoir, 211, 214
Hulme End, 52-3, 55
Hurdlow, 99

Ilam, 23, 51
Ilam Rock, 59
Iron Tors, 23, 60

Jacob's Ladder, 205
Jaggers Clough, 201
Jenkin Chapel, 69

Kerridge, 69
Kettleshulme, 69
Kinder Downfall, 206
Kinder Low, 205
Kinder Reservoir, 155, 207
Kinder River, 204, 206-7
Kinder Scout, 14, 27, 29, 31, 155-6, 192, 202-4, 207, 214-15
Kinder Upper House, 155, 205
Kirk Dale, 136
Kniveton, 78

Ladmanlow, 100
Ladybower Reservoir, 188, 208-9, 211
Lady Clough, 207, 215
Ladywash Mine, 169
Langley Hall, 47
Langsett, 211
Langsett Reservoir, 211-12
Lantern Pike, 156
Lathkill, river, 23, 110, 112
Lathkill Dale, 14, 23, 110, 116-18
Lea, 91, 94, 95
Lea Hall, 79
Leam Hall, 185
Lean Low, 116
Lee House, 205
Leek, 15, 43-46
Leek and Manifold Valley Railway, 52-5
Lindale, 57
Little Don River, 210, 212
Little Longstone, 137
Litton, 170
Litton Mill, 138-9
Lode Mill, 59
Lombersdale Hall, 113
Long Causeway, 190
Longcliffe, 98
Longdendale, 15-16, 172, 212, 216-18
Long Hill, 153
Long Lee, 163
Long Low, 53
Longnor, 64
Long Rake, 113
Longshaw Estate, 186
Longstone Edge, 138, 165-6
Lord's Seat, 200
Lose Hill, 32, 192-3, 198, 201-2
Low Bradfield, 209
Low Peak, 14, 19, 25
Loxley Valley, 209
Ludchurch, 66

Lumford House and Mill, 133
Lutudarum, 78, 82, 99, 102-3
Lyme Park, 158-62

Macclesfield, 15, 47-9
Macclesfield Canal, 47, 69
Macclesfield Forest, 67-8, 158
Magpie Mine, 118-19, 137
Magpie Sough, 137
Mam Nick, 198, 200
Mam Tor, 31, 197, 202
Mandale Mine, 116
Mandale Rake, 117
Mandale Sough, 116
Manifold, river, 15, 23
Manifold Valley, 51-5, 57, 65
Mapleton, 50, 72
Margery Hill, 212
Marple, 163
Marple Bridge, 163
Masson, 32, 105
Matlock, 14-15, 91-2
Matlock Bath, 90-1
Mayfield, 42
Meerbrook Sough, 94
Melandra, 157
Mellor, 163
Mermaid Inn, 43
Mickleden, 212
Middle Peak Quarry, 103
Middleton-by-Wirksworth, 103
Middleton-by-Youlgreave, 113
Middleton Dale, 23, 166
Middleton Top, 96-7
Midhopestones, 210
Mill Close Mine, 93
Milford, 86-7
Milldale, 59
Millers Dale, 14, 21, 23, 139-40
Mill Hill, 206
Millstone Edge, 28, 188
Minning Low, 98
Mompesson's Well, 167, 169
Monk's Road, 156, 164
Monsal Dale and Head, 137
Monyash, 118
Moorlands district, 28
Moor Lane, 113
Moorseats, 189
Morridge, 43
Moscar Cross, 189, 209
Moscar Lodge, 190, 209
Moss Castle, 206
Mountain Cottage, 103

Nab, The, 202, 207
Nabs Dale, 59
Navio, 81, 191
Nether Booth, 201-2

Index of Places

Nether Haddon, 116
Netherton, 79
Nether Tor, 207
New Engine Mine, 169
Newhaven House Inn, 77
New Mills, 162
Newton Grange, 75-6
Nine Ladies, 108
Nine Stones, 110
Noe, river, 32, 191-2, 202, 205
North Lees Hall, 189

Oaker Hill, 92
Odin Mine, 197
Offerton Hall, 185
Okeover Hall, 50
Old Ecton, 55
Old Glossop, 215, 217
Ollerbrook Booth, 201-2
One Ash Grange, 76, 114
Onecote, 43
Over Haddon, 116
Over Wood Moss, 214
Owler Bar, 187

Padley Gorge, 187
Padley Hall, 186
Park Hall, 155
Parkhouse Hill, 20, 64
Parsley Hay, 71, 77, 99
Parwich, 76
Peak Castle, 194-5
Peak Cavern, 24, 196
Peak Dale, 151
Peak Forest, 172
Peak Forest Canal, 94-5, 100, 151, 153-4, 158, 163
Peakshole Water, 192, 196
Peak Tor, 120
Pennine Way, 202-7, 215-17
Peter's Stone, 170
Peveril Castle, 172, 193-6
Pickering Tor, 58
Pikehall, 99
Pike Pool, 61
Pilsbury, 62
Pilsley, 183
Poole's Cavern, 24, 149
Porter, river, 210
Portway, 81, 102, 110
Pott Shrigley, 69

Rainow, 70
Rainster Rocks, 79
Ramshaw Rocks, 66
Ravenstor, 140
Raven's Tor, 59
Reaps Farm, 216-7
Redmires Reservoirs, 190
Reynard's Arch and Cave, 24, 58

Riber Castle, 92
Riley Graves, 168
Ringing Roger, 202, 207
Rivelin Mill and Rocks, 209
Rivelin Valley, 190, 209
Roaches, The, 28-9, 66
Robin Hood's Picking Rods, 164
Robin Hood's Stride, 29, 81, 109
Rowarth, 163
Rowland Cote, 201
Rowsley, 32, 90, 93
Rowtor Rocks, 107
Royal Cottage Inn, 66
Rudyard Lake, 46
Rushton Spencer, 46
Rushup Edge, 152, 199-200
Rutland Cavern, 91

Salt Cellar, 209
Salter's Brook Bridge, 218
Saltersford Hall, 69
Sandybrook Hall, 72
Seal Stones, 207, 214
Sett valley, 155, 205
Shallcross, 100
Sharplow Point, 58
Shatton, 191
Shatton Edge, 186
Sheen, 55
Sheldon, 119
Sheldon Moor, 136
Shelf Brook, 215
Shining Cliff Woods, 86
Shining Tor, 68
Shutlingslow, 67
Sir William Hill, 169
Slippery Stones, 211-12
Smalldale Hall, 191
Smerrill Grange, 113
Snake Inn, 215
Snake Pass, 206, 215
Snitterton, 92
Solomon's Temple, 149
South Head, 155
Sparrowpit, 173
Speedwell Mine, 196
Sponds Hill, 162
Starkholmes, 90
Stanage Edge, 28, 189
Stanage Pole, 190
Stancliffe Hall, 93
Stanton-in-Peak, 109
Stanton Moor, 29, 93, 107-8
Stocksbridge, 188, 210
Stoke Hall, 169, 185
Stoney Middleton, 26, 166
Strines Inn, 209
Sturston Mill, 40
'Surprise View', 188
Sutton Common, 46

Swains Head, 212
Swainsley, 53-4
Swamp, The, 215
Swine's Back, 205
Swinscoe, 42
Swythamley Park, 66
Sycamore Farm, 81

Taddington, 140
Taddington Dale, 137
Taddington Moor, 141
Thorpe, 56, 71-2
Thorpe Cloud, 20, 56
Thor's Cave, 53
Three Shire Heads, 66-7
Throwley Hall, 52
Tideswell, 75, 170-2
Tideswell Dale, 22, 139
Tissington, 71-5
Tissington Spires, 58
Tissington Trail, 71-2, 75-7
Toad Rock, 187
Topley Pike, 142
Torside Castle and Clough, 216
Torside Reservoir, 217
Totley Moor, 20
Totley Tunnel, 186
Traveller's Rest Inn, 65
Treak Cliff, 21, 24, 26, 196-7
Tunstead, 140

Upper Booth, 201, 204-5
Upper Greenfield Farm, 110
Upper Hulme, 66
Upper Midhope, 210-11

Via Gellia, 88, 104
Viator's Bridge, 59

Wain Stones, 216

Waterfall, 43
Waterhouses, 43, 52-3
Weag's Bridge, 53
Weaver Hills, 19, 43
Westend, river, 211, 214
Wetton, 53
Wetton Mill, 23, 54
Wet Withens, 169
Whaley Bridge, 95, 100, 150, 153-4
Whatstandwell, 87
Wheel Stones, 209, 211
Wheston, 172
White Hall, 153
Whitehough, 154
White House, 156
Wildboarclough, 67
Willersley Castle, 90
William Clough, 207
Wincle, 67
Wincle Grange, 67
Windgather Rocks, 69
Windy Knoll, 199
Win Hill, 192, 201, 214
Winnats, The, 24, 196
Winster, 106-7,
Wirksworth, 15, 26, 75, 81-5, 102
Wolfscote Dale, 23, 61
Wolfscote Hill, 61
Woodhead Pass, 212, 218
Woodhead Reservoir and Tunnel, 217
Woodlands Valley, 201, 208, 214
Wormhill, 140
Wybersley Hall, 158
Wye, river, 14, 32, 65, 100, 146, 149, 153
Wye Dale, 140, 142
Wye valley, 14, 23, 120, 126-7, 135-6, 138, 143

Yorkshire Bridge, 208
Youlgreave, 75, 111